In remembrance of my mother Eva.
And to all those brave souls who dare to dream.

ALEA IACTA EST.

(THE DIE HAS BEEN CAST)

Shod in mortal armour,
No warrior ever claimed death's defeat,
Or chained
Those blind vicissitudes of Fortuna's great divine.

No star to siege,
No sun to capture,
No breaking wave can cease—
For time and the past alone endure.

Aran Guest: Rome, 2011

< v >

FROM RAGS TO COUTURE

A Tale of Passion and Fashion
by Celebrity Hair and Make-up Artist

Aran Guest

www.fromragstocouture@yahoo.com

ISBN: 1477698531

ISBN 13: 9781477698532

Library of Congress Control Number: 2012911228
Independant Publishing Platform
CreateSpace, North Charleston, SC

ACKNOWLEDGEMENTS

With special thanks to Doris and Glen, Shaky, Annie and Val Russell, June and Dennis Dawkins, Ed Riley, Francine Chevalier, Gail Standen, Gary James, Karen and Julie, Beverley, Michelle, Cat, Lisa, Barry, Annie and Harrison, and all my other dear friends and family.

< vii >

PART 1

CHAPTER 1

I t was a cold, miserable night. As I trudged through the rain, I thought of how much I hated this walk; it seemed to go on forever. My icy hands tightly gripped the handles of the heavy plastic carrier bags. Rain poured from the growling grey sky, and tiny rivulets of water ran down the smooth nylon surface of my parka jacket. No one seemed to walk by. "You'll grow into your jacket," I'd been told, but I couldn't see much chance of that; my jacket was at least three sizes too big and hung like a tent on my small, skinny frame. I loathed the green nylon jacket almost as much as I hated the eternal rain.

Why couldn't I have a cloth one like everybody else? I cried in my anguished mind, because as soon as I'd been spotted in this hideous nylon creation that my father insisted I wear, I'd become the centre of attention for those "trendy" boys who would laugh and stare and provoke. "Hey John, can I borrow your nylon tent?" they'd shout. Sometimes I felt like a joke.

As lightening illuminated the dark heavens above and thunder roared through the crying skies, a bright spark called awareness ignited my fourteen-year-old brain, and my love affair with fashion began. In that moment of epiphany, when I became aware of the demeaning consequences of my appearance, I realized how important it was to embrace fashion. Entrenched in my thoughts, I

< 3 >

started to explore the possibility that all form—even non-form—is judged by the court of man, and that none of us can escape its mortal verdict. I realized that what lies shallow on the surface—what is regarded as superficial—has its own timeless, esteemed "high place," and its own sad, degrading disgrace. For we all cherish what we believe to be beautiful, and we run after happiness, choosing not to make friends with sorrow.

Walking through the stormy night, my poor dandy sensibilities drenched, I vowed never to let this dreadful state of affairs happen again. However, I spent most of my youth being ridiculed because of the sad clothes that I wore. I was a "second-hand rose" who everyone knows (cue the Barbra Streisand song), and looking back, I think that's why clothes and the world of fashion became so important to me. Through this kaleidoscopic world, I searched high and low for acceptance and recognition. I prized expensive labels and monograms that reinforced my low self-esteem and momentarily vanquished the inner demons of inferiority that haunted me. Like the sea, I was shallow and deep—I was Vlad the Impaler, I was Little Bo Peep. I was born a poor, handsome visionary, who had few prospects but exceptional taste. This valuable discernment could not be taught or bought; it was my precious jewel, for the rain was not the only gift the gods had showered upon me.

The further I walked, the heavier the plastic carrier bags seemed to get. They were filled to the brim with empty brown Guinness bottles that I had to return to the off-licence. The chilly night air smelt of fresh rain and stale beer, and I listened to cars driving past in the rain; their bright lights cast colourful reflections on the dark puddles on the road.

I always felt self-conscious and humiliated about returning the empty beer bottles. I hoped no one would see my struggle as I walked in shame in the rain, hood up, head down, trying to juggle the carrier bags so they didn't cut into my hands too much. I tried not to hurry, even though my hands were beginning to sting. You see, the key to my bottle-carrying success was walking at just the right pace so the bags didn't touch me and balancing

< 4 >

them so the plastic stretched as little as possible under the heavy weight of their load. If a bag broke and a bottle got smashed, I'd be in trouble, as there wouldn't be enough bottle returns to get the fresh Guinness and cigarettes that my mother wanted. Luckily, this never happened to me. I was an expert beer-bottle carrier, but I never took this skill for granted, and I always felt extremely relieved when I arrived at the off-licence counter with my bags and bottles intact.

• • •

Spring is in the air, Aran thought as he arrived at Berkeley Square in Mayfair, London. The branches of the trees swayed in the clear blue skies, and their tremulous leaves rustled with expectation. Cool shadows fell dark upon the grass beneath them. The square seemed unusually quiet as Aran walked towards the black shiny door and pressed the brass doorbell. A maid dressed in a black Armani trouser suit answered. Her hair was tied back, revealing a fresh face and a welcoming smile. With sweet French tones, she invited Aran in and directed him towards a large sitting room.

"Madame will be with you shortly, sir. Can I get you anything to drink?"

"No, thank you, Michelle. I'm fine. But how is your mother? I do hope she's feeling a bit better."

"Oh, thank you, monsieur, she is in much better health. In fact, she has made a full recovery and hopes to be home within the next few weeks."

"Oh, I'm so pleased. Do send her my love, won't you?"

A few minutes later, Aran was affectionately greeted by Valentina, an uber-wealthy Russian heiress. The pair chatted briefly for a few moments, and then Valentina quickly ushered

< 5 >

Aran through a vast marble lobby, towards the low-rise steps of a grand staircase.

"I'm so exhausted, darling, you can't imagine. It's so nice to see you—my hair is such a mess!" Valentina exclaimed as they walked upstairs.

Aran observed the alert but discreet bodyguards who looked in his direction as he walked down the art-encrusted corridor towards the inner sanctum of Valentina's boudoir. Upon entering the large en-suite sitting room, Aran's attention was drawn as usual to the magnificent antique chandelier that hung from the centre of the high ceiling; the transparent cut glass arranged in cascading circular tiers looked like giant crystal snowflakes. Fine Japanese calligraphy decorated the white walls of the en-suite's interior, whilst huge vases of white roses lay scattered on oriental antiques. Two luxurious white couches, embellished with white satin cushions of various shapes and sizes, welcomed them as they made themselves comfortable. After a quick look through some fashion magazines, they debated for a while about whether Valentina should have more highlights or maybe completely change her hair colour. The animated couple talked about the weather, the pros and cons of using waterproof versus non-waterproof mascara, and finally came to conclusions about the season's latest fashion trends as they walked into the main bedroom.

Valentina seemed agitated as she leant against the cream damask curtains and looked out of the window. Suddenly, she turned towards Aran, a look of dismay upon her lovely face.

"Oh, you've got to help me, Aran. I just don't know what I'm going to do! I've got this very important dinner party tonight, and I don't know what I'm going to wear. Will you be a darling and help me choose something? You know how good you are at that sort of thing. I just can't decide, and you always get it so right."

Moments later, Valentina walked out of her walk-in wardrobe and threw an array of garments onto her luxurious Louis XVI bed. One by one, Valentina showed Aran each dress she was considering. Valentino, Chanel, Dior, Yves Saint Laurent, and Gucci—Valentina

< 6 >

just couldn't decide. Aran made various suggestions as he held the beautiful dresses up against her. Valentina listened, but she didn't seem convinced.

"Well, you always look good in Chanel. What about that little number over there?" Aran asked, looking at a black-and-white dress that still lay on the bed.

"Oh, I can't wear that old thing, darling, I've already worn it. It's so last season," Valentina confirmed, with a slight tone of distain.

"Well, in that case, I think it's got to be a toss-up between the red Valentino and that other black Chanel number."

Valentina held the black chiffon cocktail dress against her body.

"I adore it, darling; you always get it so right. I know it's safe, but I can dress it up a bit with some jewellery. Thank you, sweetie."

"It's a beautiful dress, and I'm sure you'll look stunning. You can't beat a bit of Coco couture," Aran assured her.

"I bought this yesterday at Asprey's. What do you think?"

Valentina held a sparkling brooch up against her dress. The centre stone was a canary-yellow diamond, very substantial in size but not too big or garish, since vulgarity was something Valentina abhorred.

"What do you think of these?" Valentina asked, holding up a pair of yellow-and-white diamond earrings. "I just think they add a splash of colour, don't you?"

"Oh, Valentina, stop it. You're making me so jealous. You know how much I love yellow diamonds; they're my favourite. I just love the way they catch the light, the way they sparkle. I think they're an excellent choice. How was the skiing in Aspen, by the way? Not that I'm changing the subject or anything."

"Oh, I can't believe we haven't seen each other for so long. Oh, you know, darling—the usual. I didn't do that much skiing. I'm much better at the après-ski these days, but I do love all those handsome ski instructors and the snow and the mountains, don't you?"

< 7 >

After trying on numerous pairs of shoes and searching through an assortment of very expensive handbags, Valentina and Aran finally felt satisfied with the accessories they had chosen to go with her "little black dress." Valentina sighed with relief and sprayed herself with perfume, then sat at her dressing table and looked at her reflection.

"Now, what are you going to do with this mess?" she asked, running her hands through her beautiful blonde hair.

"Don't worry. When I've finished with it, you're going to look like a million dollars."

"Could you make that a billion dollars, darling? And could you sort out this tired old face? Nobody does my make-up like you; they always put too much on and make me look a hundred."

At the age of fifty-two, Valentina looked far from old and tired. She was in great shape, and her skin still glowed with health and vitality. All the private health spas, plastic surgery, Botox, and Restylane treatments had certainly ensured that she appeared more youthful than her years.

"Don't you worry about a thing. We'll soon have you looking shipshape. You just leave it to me."

"You know, darling, I don't know what I'd do without you. Now, next month, I've got to go to a very important party in Monaco, plus a wonderful luncheon at the yacht club the next day. Do you think you could come and work your magic? All of your flights and expenses will be taken care of. Oh, do say you'll come; it will be so much fun, and we'll have such a wonderful time."

"Of course I will, Valentina."

"Oh, thank you so much, sweetie. Now, where's Mimi gone?"

Valentina looked intently around the bedroom for her very sweet, but very spoilt, miniature poodle.

"Mimi! Mimi, where are you?" Valentina called earnestly.

"Mimi! Mimi, Mummy's going to be very angry with you. Oh, Aran, that damn dog will be the death of me!"

< 8 >

CHAPTER 2

Three Thomas Sharp Street, is the first home that I can vaguely remember. The prosaic terraced council house had three bedrooms and was situated at the end of a narrow road. Its red-brick exterior overlooked a small front garden and an overgrown hedge; a narrow pathway of paving slabs led to the empty milk bottles sitting on the step by the front door. In the large back garden lay a small, chaotic shed; nearby, a rusty lawnmower lay abandoned amongst an abundance of weeds in the wild, unruly lawn that served as the jungle home and hunting ground of Tiddles, the next door neighbour's cat.

It was from here in Canley, Coventry, that our family escaped the Midlands to enjoy the wonderful seaside resorts of Skegness, Weymouth, and Clacton-on-Sea. These happy sojourns were filled with sunshine and Knickerbocker Glory ice creams that seemed to last forever. With our buckets and spades in hand, my sister and I would run down the beach and build castles of sand and shell. Later, covered head to toe in calamine lotion to soothe our sunburnt skin, we'd watch the sunlight slowly fade as the tide swept our castles and dreams away. Like Dolly Parton, most of my happiest childhood memories are short and very sweet.

My father, Glen, was from Pontypool in South Wales, so we would often go there during our summer holidays. These carefree

< 9 >

days were spent visiting relatives, picking bilberries, and rolling down the hills of the lush Welsh valleys. On Sundays, we would listen to the choirs in the small local chapels and visit the old abandoned coal mines where my grandfather had worked from the age of ten years old.

My grandfather was called Granville. He was a lovely old gentleman who always showed me great affection. He was very tolerant and very open-minded; nothing seemed to shock him, and I always found great solace in his acquiescent attitude towards life. During his youth, he had known real starvation and hardship, working down the coal pits in the most horrendous conditions for very little money. One Christmas day, he was so desperate for food that he stole a chicken from a local farm because his family had nothing to eat. He always felt very ashamed of stealing that chicken. He believed very strongly that a man should work and provide for his family, and he never forgot this humiliation. My grandfather was a very proud and noble man.

My first clear recollection was an omen of things to come. I was about four years old when my mother asked me to carry some fairy cakes from the kitchen into the dining room. Treading carefully, I carried my precious cargo. As I approached the table, I suddenly lost my balance, tripped over my own feet, and catapulted the fairy cakes into the stratosphere. They landed everywhere—on the floor, on the window sills, on the table, under the table—everything was showered with fairy cakes! I stood rooted to the spot—red-faced, shocked, and horrified. I wasn't quite sure what I should do. As a child, I was always trying to run before I could walk. I was never very clever on my feet.

Things didn't improve much as I got older. In their youth, my parents had been wonderful ballroom dancers; they excelled at this pastime and had glided around the dance floor like Fred Astaire and Ginger Rogers. And so it seemed perfectly natural to them for their children to follow in their golden, fox-trotting footsteps.

Once dressed in the appropriate ballroom apparel, I felt very ill at ease, to say the least. In fact, I could hardly breathe because my

< 10 >

black elastic dickey bow clung round my neck, threatening to strangle me. However, apart from my red face and neck, I looked quite presentable in my white shirt, black trousers, and polished shoes. My sister looked beautiful in her white meringue dress sprinkled with tiny blue-printed roses. However, her hairpins, which were embellished with white paper daisies, proved to be problematic. They kept falling out of Abi's short curly hair, no matter how hard my mother tried to secure them. Oh well, what's a girl to do?

When we arrived at our class, the hours seemed to fly by as I put my "best foot forward." I did my best to follow the steps I was shown, but eventually it all became too much for my teacher. Angry, distraught, and frustrated beyond belief, Mr. Taylor just broke down and sat with his head between his knees. After regaining his composure, he came over to where we were practicing our steps.

"You don't know your left foot from your right, you have no coordination, no sense of rhythm, and absolutely no chance of ever becoming a dancer!" he informed me.

That was my teacher's final verdict on my limited dancing abilities. Needless to say, my ballroom dancing lessons came to an abrupt end. However, Abi found her feet and a more agile dancing partner, and she went on to win bronze, silver, and gold medals. I was just relieved to get that damn dickey bow off.

• • •

It was a windy afternoon when Aran stepped out of the car and onto the tarmac of the airport runway. *I'd better hold onto my seat belt. It's going to be a bumpy ride*, he thought as he approached the private plane bound for Nice airport.

After walking up the small flight of stairs leading onto the plane, he packed his carry-on luggage safely away and ordered a

< 11 >

drink. Sitting comfortably in his soft cream leather seat, he fastened his seat belt and opened up his new book, *Perdita: The Life of Mary Robinson*. Reading through the prologue, he felt intrigued by this famous Drury Lane actress whose immense beauty and intellect had inspired so many poets, writers, and artists. Aran had seen her portraits by Sir Joshua Reynolds, Thomas Gainsborough, and George Romney at the Wallace Collection museum in Manchester Square, London, and he'd decided he wanted to know more about this celebrated writer, poet, muse, and eighteenth-century fashion icon.

After arriving in the south of France, Aran found the journey from Nice to Monte Carlo exhilarating and exceptionally beautiful. The sky was clear and blue, and the sun was shining as the silver Mercedes convertible made its way through the winding roads, slowly climbing higher in the hills along the coastline. Aran asked his driver to open the roof of the car. Seconds later, he could feel the warmth of the sun and the wind on his skin. He looked down at the spectacular views. A multitude of luxurious villas with grand swimming pools populated the hillside; their terraces were covered with colourful bougainvillea and wisteria. Aran marvelled at the trees and the flowers. Everything seemed so alive, so vibrant. He looked down at the huge yachts peppering the coastline; they looked like children's toys from the high, steep hillside.

After checking into the Hotel de Paris, Aran quickly made his way to his room. He unpacked his case and decided to take a quick shower. Suddenly, the phone rang. He grabbed a towel and blindly stumbled and fumbled his way towards the repetitive ring tone. It was Valentina.

"Hello, darling. Sergei told me you had just arrived. I hope you enjoyed your flight. Do you like your room?"

"It's fantastic. Thank you so much—you shouldn't have."

"Of course I should," Valentina insisted. "I can't wait to see you. I've got so much to tell you. Speak later. Bye, darling," she said, and then hung up.

< 12 >

CHAPTER 3

My father was a working-class snob who dictated what was right and what was wrong. We were never given an opportunity to debate his bigoted views; what he said was "the law." If we challenged his authoritarian behaviour, he would fly into a frenzy of rage, furious that anyone had dared to question him. In order to avoid his violent mood swings and his verbal abuse and intimidation, my sister and I learnt very quickly not to oppose his opinions. Abi and I were told that if we didn't like what he said, we should "fuck off and find somewhere else to live." As young children this was a hard thing to do, there was little chance of that.

Glen called himself a Socialist, although he hated and despised almost everybody, including the "fucking Tories," "bastard Liberals," "wogs," "Pakis," and "queers." He also hated the middle classes, the aristocracy, the Irish, the Scottish, and the English. Glen was also anti-Semitic, which I always found quite surprising, because he had served in World War II and was well aware of the brutal persecution of the Jews and the indescribable horrors of the Holocaust.

Although my father wasn't a very tall man, he was well built and had the strength and constitution of an ox. In his youth, he had been a handsome devil and had proudly served in World War II

< 13 >

with the Royal Welsh Fusiliers after signing up for the army at the age of eighteen. He was very proud of his regiment, and he showed me a photograph of their triumphant march down the Champs-Élysées in Paris, celebrating the liberation of France. Many years later, when my father had become an old man, we would sit in his garden and he would tell me about his comrades in the army, the antics and practical jokes they had shared, and the women they had dated. He told me that they always tried to have fun, regardless of the terrible things that were going on around them. Even when he was in his seventies, my father still walked like he was on army parade. As a child, I was always told to put my shoulders back, my head up, and to look straight ahead as I was walking. Any deviation from this posture in his company meant a sharp clip around the ear.

After the war, my father moved from Wales to Coventry in search of work in the developing car industry. He eventually found employment in a factory owned by Massey Ferguson and spent the next thirty-two years of his life fitting the engines for their huge tractors. My father worked extremely hard all of his life, and I can never remember him taking a day off work apart from his annual holidays. Things changed after he had his first heart attack, which was shortly followed by a second. He then wisely decided to retire from work.

My mother, Eva, was a Lancashire lass from Dukinfield in Manchester. She came from a large family of ten children. Her mother, Annie, reminded me of the legendary Lancastrian singer Gracie Fields. She was funny, kind, and very tough. As a child, I can remember her taking me to the local corner shop to buy some homemade meat and potato pies. Her daughters, Martha and Lilli, were my favourite aunties, because they always used to tickle me and make me laugh. My grandfather was called Harold. He loved to breed pigeons and play cards when he wasn't working as rag-and-bone man on his horse and cart. Harold (no relation to Mr. Steptoe) was small, strong, and very direct in his manner, and although his life was hard, he always found away to support his large family.

< 14 >

Petite in stature, my mother was a natural beauty with lovely golden-auburn hair. She possessed a vivid sense of humour, and people said that she had the most pleasant disposition that anyone could have wished for. Eva worked at the biscuit counter in Woolworth's, and on the weekends she would always bring home bags of broken biscuits, which Abi and I eagerly devoured. She was a very caring and loving mother; she'd hold me in her arms and tell me how much she loved me and tell me of her dreams for my future.

"How's my big, fine son today? You wait and see—one day you'll be so clever and handsome," she'd tell me.

Eva made me feel special and secure, and she constantly showered me with love and affection.

"Nobody loves you more than me," she'd say. Then she'd hug me and the world would seem to drift away.

My mother adored her children; however, she was unable to conceive naturally. Eva and Glen adopted Abi and me when we were very young, and I had no recollection of my biological parents. However, my mother always saw us as her own children—the children she had so desperately wanted—and she loved us with a passion. I was born on September 9, 1960, and was given the name John, which my adoptive parents kept. In that same year, JFK won the US presidential election and Sirimavo Bandaranaike became the first female prime minister in the world, having been elected by the people of Ceylon (now called Sri Lanka). *Lady Chatterley's Lover* went on sale after it had been banned for thirty-two years in the United Kingdom, Roy Orbison released a single called "Only the Lonely," and *Coronation Street* premiered for the first time on ITV in the UK.

Even today, after all these years, I find it hard to transcribe the memories I have of my mother. The mind, it seems, is a strange thing. I don't remember much of certain periods of my childhood; maybe on some subconscious level I don't want to remember the dreadful pain, sorrow, and despair.

< 15 >

As young children, we realized our mother was ill, but we didn't realize that she had cervical cancer that was slowly killing her. We always thought our Mother would get better when she went into hospital and that things would resume back to normal, happier times when she returned. Abi and I would anxiously count the days and pray that she would get well quickly; we missed her terribly. My mother would return home all right, but slowly, as the hospital visits increased, she became a beautiful, frail shadow of her former self. We witnessed her battle and torment, her vomit and pain, and we watched as the thing we loved most in this world slowly, painfully, died. I learnt at a very early age that life wasn't just or fair.

One day, my father told us we were going to visit our mother in the hospital. We were so excited that we could hardly wait. I can still remember the ward's antiseptic smell that made my stomach feel strange, as I searched with eager eyes for her bed. My mother was so happy to see us; she immediately hugged us and told us how much she loved us both. As she gave us some of her sweets, we noticed and were shocked by her frail appearance. However, we made sure she didn't notice this. We told her about school and what we had been up to. When it was time to go, we kissed and said goodbye, but as we started to walk away, Eva called us back. From her bedside cabinet she took out her purse, which contained two pennies.

"I've been saving these for you. I nearly forgot!" Eva told us as she gave us a penny each. She hugged and kissed us once more.

As we left the ward, we turned back to wave goodbye. Tears were running down my mother's face as she blew us kisses and waved. Looking back, I realize now that deep within her heart, she must have realized this was truly goodbye. It was the last time we ever saw her.

I will never forget my mother's courage and bravery as she fought this terrible disease. It's strange, but forty-three years later, I still occasionally grieve over my mother's death. The pain of my bereavement still feels raw in those private moments when I miss her most. Even death, it seems, cannot conquer love.

< 16 >

A few days after visiting my mother, I was playing in the garden at my grandfather's house when my cousin Mathew ran up to me and spitefully said, "It's a shame about your mother. She's dead!"

I thought he was playing a cruel joke, so I ignored his spiteful outburst and carried on playing.

Although my father's step-mother was a lovely woman, Abi and I felt despised by other relatives from her side of the family. Though we gratefully received our cousins' "hand-me-downs," Abi and I were well aware that these relatives saw us as poor orphans who had invaded their family. That night, my father came to the house and took us upstairs to a quiet bedroom. Amidst his tears, he explained to us that our mother had died. Eva had only been thirty-eight years old.

At the age of eight, I couldn't really comprehend mortality or accept the finality of death. It wasn't until many years later, when I was in my late twenties, that I finally came to terms with my mother's death and the devastating effect it had upon me. After my mother's passing, I felt as if I had reached the nadir of my short life. I felt as if I was entrenched in darkness. I got used to the dark, and eventually, I learnt to live within the sorrowful confines of the bereaved. I didn't look back; I didn't look forward. Inside, I felt dead too, although physically I lived on. I prayed to God on a regular basis to let me die, so that I could be reunited with my mother once more, although I knew within my broken heart that this wasn't what my mother would have wanted. Luckily, my prayers went unanswered.

< 17 >

CHAPTER 4

I n Monte Carlo, the Hotel de Paris was extremely busy.
Distinguished guests were arriving at a party held in honour
of one the world's most eligible and handsome playboys. In
the lobby of the hotel, enormous crystal chandeliers twinkled and
glistened as jazz music drifted through the air, playing at just the
right tempo. The rich, the famous, and the beautiful were out in
abundance tonight, as were the monumental flower displays poised
on the chic, antique furniture. A heavenly fresco of carved exotic
fish looked down from the ceiling, observing the scene below.
Open- mouthed and mute, the fish watched in silence as beautiful
women mingled in the lobby, showing off their stunning figures,
their couture gowns, and their priceless jewels.

These well-groomed ladies had taken weeks to prepare themselves for this auspicious occasion. It had been tedious work,
searching through the endless rails of designer clothes in pursuit of the perfect dress, which then had to be coordinated with
the perfect bag and shoes. Some ladies had found their dress at
the couture shows they frequented in London, Paris, New York,
and Milan. It was important to these ladies to look their very
best, and they strove hard to fit perfectly into their chosen dress.
They had trained for hours with their personal fitness instructors
in private health clubs and spas, and they followed regimented

< 19 >

eating programmes prescribed by their dieticians. They flocked in droves to exclusive beauty parlours in search of the perfect tan, the smoothest wax, and the cleanest brow line. Dentist appointments, Botox treatments, facials, manicures, and pedicures were carefully scheduled into their busy social schedules. Their favourite hair and make-up artists were booked months in advance. Yes, it was hard work being glamorous, and yet this evening, it all seemed so effortless.

Guests sat around little tables in the hotel bar, sipping their drinks as they nibbled on olives and nuts. Aran picked up his glass of champagne and tried to relax. He couldn't decide whether to stay here and enjoy the music or go next door to the casino; he loved the casino's private gambling rooms with their sense of excitement and danger. Once he had decided to visit the casino, he took a few minutes to consider whether he should exchange the dark grey tones of his Christian Dior suit and vintage Hardy Amies tie for something a little more formal. Thirty minutes later he reappeared, dressed in a black Valentino evening suit, shirt, and bow tie; his hair was slicked back off his well-groomed face. Aran walked through the lobby and out of the hotel to the gardens by the side of the casino. He could smell the scent of jasmine in the warm evening air as he looked out into the darkness of the night. He could see black waves as they crashed against the shore and feel the salty breeze of the sea against his face.

• • •

On the stove in the small kitchen, the pig's head gently simmered; its snout poked out from under the saucepan lid as hot steam evaporated into the air. Next to the head, in a smaller saucepan, lay the

< 20 >

pig's trotters and tripe, cooking slowly and methodically. Chopped onions lay raw on the kitchen top, next to the empty milk bottles.

After our father had finished preparing the food, he put his supper on a tray and carried it into the sitting room. He turned on the television and flicked through the channels, watching the grainy black-and-white images on the screen. As he watched the box, we watched him scoff his food; he eagerly devoured the tripe and onions drenched in vinegar and white pepper. Carefully balancing our plates on our laps and feeling an enormous amount of dread, we slowly started to cut into our tripe, anticipating its thick, rubbery texture.

"Go on, get it down ya. Or isn't it good enough for you, Little Lord Fauntleroy?" my father sarcastically asked me.

"Fucking little nancy boy," he expounded.

I felt a deep sense of humiliation start to rise within me, and my face turned red. Frightened of upsetting our father any further, Abi and I tried to eat the tripe. Its rubbery texture caused us to retch and gag, making it impossible to swallow.

"You don't know what's good for ya; that's your problem. Go on, give it e'ya!" our father ordered, his mouth full of chewed tripe.

In fear and silence, we watched our father as he scoffed the remaining food.

"He looks just like a porky pig," Abi whispered, turning away and endeavouring to control the laughter that threatened to erupt.

After our father finished his food, he put his tray on the floor and walked over to Abi.

"It's your fault she's dead. You killed her!" my father screamed in Abi's face, his heart full of hatred and anger.

"You killed her, you little bitch!"

He stared viciously into Abi's face as he slapped her; his face was contorted and ugly. Abi stood in silence, shocked as the horrible reality sunk home.

I knew what she must have been thinking: *Yes, it was my fault. I did it. I must have—my father told me so. I killed my mother, not the cancer. Oh, what an evil little girl I am.*

< 21 >

"Hey you, you little bastard," he said, turning to me next. "Come here! I said come here, you little bastard! What are you? I said, *what are you?*"

He punched me hard in the stomach. "Answer me, you little bastard. I can't hear you!"

Winded by his punch, I struggled to reply. Eventually, I managed to repeat,

"I'm a little bastard, I'm a little bastard."

He made me repeat the affirmation over and over again.

My face stung from his slaps. I felt pain in my stomach and humiliation in my heart as warm tears ran down my face. Shocked and wounded, I starred numbly ahead.

After my mother's death, Abi and I became my father's emotional punch bags. There was nothing we could do to prevent it. There was nowhere to run, nowhere to hide. All the anger, sadness, and pain that he felt was taken out upon us. He abused us physically, mentally, and emotionally. We lived in constant fear of this new monster who had emerged from the dark depths of grief.

On several occasions, the next-door neighbour came around and threatened to call the police. She could hear our father's torrent of abuse and our pleas for mercy. My father's relentless rage and brutality didn't stop, but our screams and pleas for mercy decreased because of his threats and the fear he instilled in our lonely hearts. We learnt quickly that the slightest thing could trigger his violent mood swings.

One evening, I lay on my bed reminiscing about my mother. I missed her so much that I decided to quietly sneak into her old bedroom. There, I could still smell her familiar presence, which made me feel as if she were still alive. After I quietly opened the bedroom door, I stood for a few moments and looked at her bed. I didn't hear my father's footsteps as he crept up behind me, so when I heard his booming voice it made me jump.

"What you doin'? I'll teach you to come here!" he yelled.

His first punch took me by surprise. Its force knocked me off my feet, and I found myself flying through the air. When I landed,

< 22 >

I hit my head on the sharp corner of a chest of drawers, missing my eye by only centimetres. Blood started to flow out of the wound and run down my face. My father came over to where I lay; a look of disbelief animated his face. I started to cry.

"I'm sorry. I didn't mean it," he said, wiping the blood off my face with his jumper.

A few moments later I was in the bathroom, holding a cold towel to the cut. It wouldn't stop bleeding. My father's face was riddled with panic.

"If anybody asks, you tell them you fell over, all right? Don't tell them that I hit you, OK?" he commanded me.

For a few weeks after this incident, he left Abi and me alone, but it didn't take long before things resumed back to normal.

Most of my mother's family lived in Manchester, but after mother's death some of her sisters would come and visit us. We never told them about the abuse we were enduring—we were too frightened of the consequences once they had left. The idea seemed totally futile, as our father would have denied our allegations anyway. We were always so relieved to see them, and so sad when they left. When my Auntie Martha came to visit, she would always bring us chocolate and sweets, and she always gave us a shilling each before she left.

We were always so excited when we received our shiny silver shilling. Both of us would spend hours deliberating about how we were going to spend it. I decided that I was going to buy some marbles from a friend. Ecstatic, I ran up the street to his house, the shilling tightly grasped in my hand. Breathless, my heart pounding, I knocked on the door. Minutes later, after counting my precious marbles, I walked away feeling the happiest I had felt in a long time. After I had rushed home to show Abi my marbles, I went to my bedroom and emptied my new acquisitions on the floor. In my excitement, I decided it would be a good idea stay in my room and have a pretend game of marbles with myself. Then I heard the key in the front door, proclaiming the imminent arrival my father.

< 23 >

My heart sank. I quickly gathered the marbles together and hid them under my bed. As I made my way downstairs, I tried to act as normal as possible. It wasn't long before my father asked us for the shillings that our auntie had given us. Red-faced and anxious, I told him I had bought some marbles with mine.

"Well, you'll just 'ave to take 'em back, won't you, you little sissy. And don't come back without the shilling!" he ordered.

I ran to my room and collected the marbles, then made my way to my friend's house. As I knocked on the front door, I could feel waves of embarrassment wash over me. I anxiously clenched my fists in my pockets and waited for somebody to answer.

What if there's nobody at home? I thought.

Luckily, my friend's mother answered.

"I'm sorry, but I've got to return the marbles. I've got to have the shilling back or I can't go home," I desperately informed her.

I hoped with all my heart she would agree. *God only knows what my father will do to me if she doesn't,* I thought. After a few minutes, she came back with the shilling. She leant down, took the marbles off me, and gave me a kiss on the cheek.

"Don't worry, love, everything will be all right," she said, comforting me.

I was relieved, but hot coals of humiliation started to fuel my anger as I turned and started my journey home. The thing I hated most was that people always felt sorry for me. As I walked away, I swore that one day, things would be different.

• • •

On the top deck of the huge yacht, Aran laid back and relaxed in the cool, refreshing waters of the Jacuzzi. The erupting bubbles tickled his senses and his humour, as he laughed and joked with

< 24 >

two gorgeous models. The intimate crew splashed and played as they sipped their chilled champagne and looked out across the sea. In the bright sunshine, the cool, penetrating waters of the Côte Azur looked a mixture of aqua and deep blue. Aran felt as if he were floating on a sea of liquid lapis lazuli and turquoise. The yacht's huge reflection shimmered impressionistically on the surface of the sea below. As Aran basked in the sunshine, he decided that Antibes was definitely one of his favourite places. The luxurious yacht was too large to be moored in "millionaires' bay," so it was stationed a few miles offshore. The views from here were spectacular, and Aran felt like a billion dollars. His only concern was to figure out where to take these two gorgeous young ladies for dinner.

• • •

At the age of nine, I was finally given my first pair of long trousers. They were grey and far too long, but I didn't care; at least I wouldn't be the only boy at school still wearing short trousers. I doubt very much that this propitious event would have occurred at all, had it not been for some very special news; my father was about to be remarried. His new fiancée, Doris, was an attractive, well-spoken lady in her early fifties. Doris had met my father whilst "pulling him a pint" behind the bar of The Dilke Arms pub and restaurant in Ryton-on-Dunsmore near Coventry. However, how my father had ever managed to "pull" Doris still remains a mystery. When Abi and I were told the good news, we could hardly believe it. Feeling nervous, excited, and a little apprehensive, we hoped we would like our new mother.

One evening, my father told us that we could stay up late. He was going to bring Doris home so we could meet her. The climactic evening progressed, the night grew dark, and finally we heard

< 25 >

the familiar soft purr of his car engine as it pulled up outside the house. When the front door opened and Doris appeared, we were almost rendered speechless by this slim, elegant, glamorous lady who introduced herself. I could feel my face burning as I struggled to say a few words. I was conscious of my lisping voice, but I felt the kindness in hers. Abi and I liked Doris immediately. She was funny, charming, and very stylish; we couldn't believe our luck. Over the next couple of months, we would eagerly anticipate her arrival after she had finished work. Following our father's rigid instructions, we would prepare a small table in the living room, upon which we placed two glasses, two bottles of Guinness, ten "Craven A" cigarettes, and an ashtray. Doris always wore her lovely blonde hair in a classic French pleat that emphasized her beautiful facial structure and her dark brown eyes. She smelt of Chanel No. 5 perfume and was always impeccably dressed in a lovely cocktail dress which she accessorised with elegant costume jewellery.

Preparations for the big day began. The happy couple decided that they wanted to "keep things simple," so they booked their marriage ceremony at the local registry office and made a reservation for an informal wedding reception at The Dilke Arms. In a panic, my grandmother quickly knitted a mustard-coloured tank top to go with my new trousers and my father made a hair appointment for Abi at the local hairdressers.

Unfortunately, on the day of the wedding, Abi's hair didn't quite turn out the way she had planned. Her coiffure resembled one of those hairy helmets worn by the Queen's Scottish guards. Her poor hair had been set with rollers and was heavily backcombed. Then to finish the "look," it had been sprayed with lots of cheap hair lacquer until it was as stiff as a board. The result was quite astounding, and I have to say that although Abi may have only been nine years old, with her new hairstyle she didn't look a day under ninety. However, once her tears had subsided, she decided to ignore her hairy hat and make the most of the special day. Abi and I didn't go the registry office, but we did go to the reception afterwards.

< 26 >

The happy bride looked resplendent in her colourful silk cocktail dress; its rich floral design complimented her pale-green orchid corsage. No trace of white or ivory could be found in her elegant attire, which she accessorized with long black gloves, a wide-brimmed black hat, and a pair of peep-toe high heels. Looking very dapper in his navy-blue "made to measure" suit from Burton's, the groom made a small speech after he had welcomed his guests, and after a few drinks and a lot of encouragement from his friends, he decided to sing a few songs for Doris. My father had sung for years on the social-club circuit, and people said he had a very good voice. He was also very good at telling jokes and was an excellent entertainer. Even when he was in his late sixties, my father continued to go to nursing homes and charity shows, performing wherever he was invited, and every year without fail he would sing to raise money for the Royal British Legion Poppy Appeal. Glen especially loved the male-voice choirs from the Welsh valleys of his homeland. However, his favourite vocalists, apart from Tom Jones, Harry Secombe, and Perry Como, were of a more operatic nature. He would sit for hours listening to Mario Lanza, Luciano Pavarotti, Enrico Caruso, Franco Corelli, and Placido Domingo—he knew most of the songs that they had recorded. After the big day, Abi and I went to stay with my grandparents for week, while the happy newlyweds went off on their honeymoon to Newquay in Cornwall.

Upon their return, things at home started to change. Our new mother would get up every morning and make us breakfast, and after school there would always be a hot meal waiting for us. All our clothes were regularly washed and ironed, and our home was constantly cleaned until my mother thought it was "spick and span." In many ways, Doris was our saving grace. She didn't tolerate any form of physical abuse towards her new stepchildren. However, on many occasions our father told us we would "get it" as soon as our new mother wasn't around to protect us, and we were threatened with even worse punishment if we dared to inform her about it. Fortunately, these threats went unfounded. With the arrival of our

< 27 >

new mother, my emotional well-being improved and so did our standard of living. After a few months my parents decided to move home and make a fresh start, so we relocated to another council house in a different part of town.

< 28 >

CHAPTER 5

Our home at 5 Whittle Close was part of a large grey council estate in Binley. The characterless, austere building had three bedrooms and a small back garden that was surrounded by a high brick wall. The colourless hue of its bricks and mortar overlooked other properties that had a similar drab design. In front of the house, a long, barren lawn stretched towards the main road and a large recreational area. Each "close" had a deserted concrete playing area where children had discarded rusty bicycle frames, old tyres, and other paraphernalia. A small wood stood nearby.

Abi and I enrolled at the local school, and for the next couple of years things went quite smoothly as we settled down with our new mother in our new home. I have only one clear memory of Binley Park Junior School...

I stared out of the window, though my studies lay open on the table before me. The large classroom in which I sat felt still and peaceful in its newly acquired silence, but I wasn't alone. Cheryl Runton, the poorest girl in the school, sat next to me. We ignored each other, pretending to study our schoolwork. A dreadful sense of shame passed silently between us. Neither of us wanted to acknowledge what had happened in the empty classroom. The

< 29 >

sunlight illuminated my sorrow, and the tears that rolled down my face landed on my textbook. The teacher offered me a tissue in quiet condolence. Outside, I could hear the other children laughing and joking as they boarded the waiting coach. Their squeals of excitement echoed across the playground and floated into the silence of the classroom. The annual school trip had only cost one pound fifty, but it was one pound fifty that our parents had failed to submit; subsequently, we had been left behind. This year, the head teacher had decided to take the class on an excursion to see the Treasures of Tutankhamun at the British Museum, since this rare exhibition was touring the world. I was inconsolable, and I never did forget the sadness and injustice I felt in missing the school trip. None of my classmates had the slightest interest in Egyptology, and yet here they all were going to visit my hero. The first book that I owned was about the life of the Egyptian pharaoh. I had saved long and hard for my treasured book. I knew everything there was to know about the young pharaoh, and yet here I was, sitting in the classroom unable to go and visit his exhibition.

Maybe one day I'll take my revenge and go and visit the pharaoh in Egypt, I told myself, but in my sad heart I knew this could never be, and my tears, like the sacred waters of the Nile, seemed to flow for what seemed like an eternity.

• • •

Aran preferred Venice during the winter. There were fewer tourists, and only a slight aroma emanated from the canals. As he walked through the maze of narrow streets to St. Mark's Square, he noticed men staring at his beautiful companion. Wearing no make-up, a short trench coat, and a simple T-shirt with jeans, Kelly the super-model certainly made an impact without making any effort.

< 30 >

As they took their seats outside the Caffè Florian, a favourite meeting place of artists and writers for centuries, waiters quietly fought over who should serve their table. Eventually, a very handsome waiter arrived to take their order; his face was flushed and his smile bright. After he took their order, he hesitated for a moment before leaving their table, making eye contact with the gorgeous Kelly. Aran noticed the admiring glances of other men sitting at the surrounding tables, as they too discovered his gorgeous companion.

"Don't you ever get sick of men staring at you all the time?" Aran asked.

"Men just look at me like a piece of meat…and I love it!" Kelly joked. "Really, I don't take too much notice of it; I just ignore it. You kind of get used to it after awhile. I'll start to worry when they stop looking.

You know what they say about these handsome, Italian lover boys, don't you? What do they call them? Stallions? I wish!" Kelly giggled.

As the classical orchestra played, they sipped their tea and gossiped about the various shoots they had recently worked on. They talked about who was hot and who was not. They talked handbags, shoes, lip gloss, and hot sex. When they had finished their refreshments, Kelly asked for the bill and had a brief conversation with the handsome waiter in fluent Italian.

"They say Italian men make great lovers. Maybe it's time to find out," Kelly whispered to Aran as she winked at the waiter and wrote down her mobile phone number.

After some brief shopping in Prada and Gucci, they had a few drinks in Harry's Bar and then slowly made their way back to the hotel.

Later that evening, when most people were in bed, Aran roamed the deserted streets of Venice. They seemed to have a timeless, haunted quality about them. He thought about the history and romance of this incredible place, and he thought about Kelly and the famous Italian lover Casanova, one of the lucky few who escaped from the city's notorious prison.

< 31 >

• • •

My new mother seemed to be full of surprises. I soon discovered that she had been previously married, and that she had a son called Alex who lived in Australia. My newly acquired stepbrother had two children of his own, which meant that Doris was also a grandmother and I was an uncle. Alex, in search of a new life with fresh opportunities, had decided to emigrate to Australia in the early 1960s. Doris hoped to visit Alex and his family "down under" with the money she had recently acquired from the sale of her small maisonette. With the remaining money, she decided to refurbish our new home in Binley.

As soon as we moved into our new abode, Doris had the whole house painted and decorated professionally, and new carpets were laid throughout. (Who could forget that bright orange stairs carpet that I had to vacuum every week?) On the longest wall in the "lounge," a vinyl mural of a mountain range, complete with lakes, woods, and flowers, was pasted along its entire length; its vista repeated several times. A round smoked-glass coffee table took centre stage in the middle of the room, and a shell-shaped, silver-plated fruit bowl reflected off its dark surface. Two plastic chandeliers hung from the freshly painted beige ceiling above. On top of the brightly patterned Axminster carpet stood a black leather three-piece suite adorned with gold and red velvet cushions from Grattan's catalogue. A fibre-optic lamp sitting on top of the television, which my mother told me was "all the rage," changed colour every minute. On the 1950s G-plan sideboard stood an expensive cut-glass decanter with six sparkling glasses on a silver-plated tray.

Orange translucent lampshades hung from the ceiling in the kitchen-dining area; a wooden shelving unit separated the two spaces. Various pieces of ornamental china and selected items from a large dinner service cluttered its busy surface. Alternating red and blue plastic tiles covered the floor. In the centre of the dining

< 32 >

room wall hung a very annoying plastic cuckoo clock. Nearby lived Joey the blue budgie. He died of sunstroke when Doris left him out in the garden on a very hot day. She thought he would enjoy the sunshine, but sadly she was mistaken. We found him dead, claws up, at the bottom of his cage—not a cat in sight! For the kitchen, my mother chose a wallpaper design that featured various bowls of fruit. Their repetitive shapes and sizes changed across the walls. At least it was different from the hideous "wood effect" design she had chosen for the dining area.

Our beds were covered with pink bri-nylon sheets, also recent, trendy acquisitions from the catalogue. Flicking through the pages of those glossy catalogues, I would fantasize about what I would buy if I could have anything that I wanted. Top of my list was a barathea blazer—the latest must have in school blazers. Doris eventually bought me one, bless her heart. She was a very generous woman, and she bought Abi and me lots of new clothes.

Our new home was a very colourful place. It was the early 1970s, after all. We had the smartest house in our close, and my mother was always inviting her new neighbours over to proudly show off her little palace.

Although my mother still worked at The Dilke Arms on the weekends, she also took on a part-time cleaning job during the week at a company called the G.E.C. I became her little helper, emptying bins, cleaning ashtrays, and polishing the desks and floors. The floor polisher was almost as tall as me, and it seemed to have a mind of its own. I struggled in vain to control it. By the end of the night, my arms ached from all the polishing and cleaning.

Over the years, Abi and I had grown to loath and despise our father, and as we grew up, we realized that we didn't feel very close to him emotionally. I don't remember him showing us any affection or playing with us as children, and as adolescence approached, he spent little or no time in our company. My new mother slowly but surely realized what she had married—most evenings she was left at home to watch television while my father went down the pub and got drunk. On Sundays, he would go out for an extra hard

< 33 >

"session" with his mates at the local rugby club. After awhile, Doris got sick of his behaviour, and she found herself unable to share the same marital bed. Unfortunately for me, my father moved into my bedroom, which had two single beds. After his arrival, the room always stank of cigarette smoke, farts, and stale beer. Abi and I were often awoken late at night by the sounds of his drunken arrival and by the sound of my mother's protests as he forced himself upon her.

Looking back, I now realize how hard and disappointing it must have been for this macho Welshman, who was a fully paid-up member of the local rugby club, to have a son with such fragile propensities. Through gritted, rotten teeth, he'd call me a little fairy, a fucking sissy, or a little pansy. The paradoxical love-hate relationship I shared with my father only made me crave his approval more, but the more he renounced his love and affection, the more I hated myself, because I knew I wasn't the kind of son that he had wanted. It took me many years to stop looking for his approval, and when I finally did, I realized that I wasn't such a bad person after all, and I started to like myself.

When my father asked me what I wanted to do when I left school, I told him that I wanted to become a ballet dancer. After much ridicule, he told me there was a place for me at the factory where he worked. He reasoned that if it was good enough for him, it was good enough for me. Further education was never mentioned in our household. Sadly, since there were no dance teachers around like Julie Walters from the film *Billy Elliot* to help my dreams come true, there was very little chance of me fulfilling my ambition. My life was to take a different direction. However, like Billy, I did become a big T. Rex fan, collecting all of Marc Bolan's records. As soon as I heard Marc's magical lyrics, I realized that a poet lay hidden within my heart. I fell in love with his enchanting words, his glamorous clothes, and his funky corkscrew hair. I tried to emulate him by sprinkling glitter under my eyes, and I dreamt of buying a bright yellow satin jacket from C & A so I would look like my glam-rock idol.

< 34 >

Another glam-rock star who really inspired me was David Bowie. Abi gave me his iconic album, *The Rise and Fall of Ziggy Stardust and the Spiders from Mars*, as a birthday present. It was the first album I owned. I played it so many times that I knew all the lyrics from every song and nearly wore out the record grooves. I loved David Bowie's wonderful, creative character Ziggy Stardust, and I also loved his brilliant guitarist Mick Ronson, who thrashed out tunes on his beloved 1968 Gibson Les Paul guitar. Mr. Ronson later co-produced Lou Reed's album *Transformer* with Bowie, playing lead guitar and piano on the superb song "Perfect Day." I spent hours fantasizing about what colour to dye my hair. Should I dye it carrot orange like Ziggy's or platinum blonde like Mick's? David Bowie's character Ziggy Stardust was the first man that I saw wearing theatrical make-up. Of course, years later I wouldn't even leave the house without applying a full face of slap. Mr. Stardust's make-up really influenced me creatively, so I guess I have to thank his brilliant make-up artist Pierre La Roche for this inspiration. The elaborate make-up that La Roche chose for Ziggy was heavily influenced by the Japanese Kabuki theatre, and it was beautifully and effectively applied.

Born in Algiers, Pierre La Roche first moved to France and then to England, where he worked for the Elizabeth Arden cosmetics company. After five years, he decided to become a freelance make-up artist, working with the Rolling Stones and countless other rock stars and celebrities. Apart from creating the wonderful make-up for Ziggy Stardust, he also did the amazing make-up displayed on David Bowie's album covers *Aladdin Sane* and *Pin Ups*, the latter featuring the model Twiggy. Pierre also worked on two stunning album covers for Roxy Music. In 1975, he was asked to become the official make-up design creator for *The Rocky Horror Picture Show*, a role that he fulfilled with panache.

I suppose that indirectly, the first photographer who influenced me was photographic genius Brian Duffy. It was Duffy who drew the iconic lightning bolt across David Bowie's face for the *Aladdin Sane* album cover. After using red lipstick to fill the motif in, Duffy

< 35 >

and La Roche finished off this masterful piece of art together, taking their inspiration from a National Panasonic rice cooker that lay nearby. The creative brilliance of Pierre La Roche and Brian Duffy really opened my eyes; they made me realize that make-up could be an art form.

Influenced by music and the fashion it dictated, I was slowly growing up, discovering myself and the world around me. My parents never discussed sex or sexuality, and up to the age of fourteen, I thought the "facts of life" meant that you tried to pay your gas and electricity bills on time. My first sexual encounter was with a girl called Ginger Buggins—she had buck teeth, glasses, and dark, lank hair that drooped over her enormous breasts. We met by the local woods and decided to go for a walk. Ginger was more experienced than me, so I followed her amorous advances and soon learnt a few lessons about sex. Although I was unsure about my sexuality, I was determined to prove to myself that I was a normal heterosexual lad, even though my fantasies and nature included other ideas.

When I got older, I moved to Binley Park Comprehensive School. It wasn't long before I realized that this deplorable establishment was no better than its junior school. This ugly concrete mess has since been demolished, which I personally think is the best thing that ever happened to it.

Throughout my entire school life, I never owned a PE kit. When that class came, I always had to wear what I could find from the school sports bin—shorts that came down past my knees and odd football socks that I wore with my school shoes. I was always one of the last pupils to be picked for the sports teams because I was a small, skinny lad who looked like he needed to eat a few steak and kidney pies. Think of the character Billy Casper from the book *A Kestrel for a Knave* by Barry Hines, and you'll get the general picture.

I was quite a clever pupil. My favourite subjects at school were art and English literature. My first serious writing project was about the movie star Marilyn Monroe; it was called "Fatherless Child." I loved Marilyn—her glamour, her beauty, and her vulnerability.

< 36 >

She'd been an orphan like me, and I understood her loneliness, her feelings of rejection, and her desire to be loved. I also understood her passion to make something of herself, in spite of the world around her telling her she was worthless. I'd lie awake at night dreaming about her along with a host of other Hollywood stars, including Jean Harlow, Rudolph Valentino, Greta Garbo, Claudette Colbert, Cyd Charisse, Fred Astaire, Ginger Rogers, Marlene Dietrich, Lana Turner, Jayne Mansfield, James Dean, and Marlon Brando. In my loneliness, these stars illuminated my dark nights. They shone in my mind, and I dreamt of one day going to Hollywood where I would live an impossibly glamorous life and walk in the footsteps of my idols. Hollywood gave me a dream and something to believe in.

In reality, my life was totally different. I was bullied at school. I was spat on, beaten, and verbally abused. I lived in fear on a daily basis. I dreaded going to school; every single day was an ordeal with trials and tribulations. I was too ashamed and embarrassed to tell my teachers or my parents. Some days, like Marilyn, I wanted to escape permanently from this world.

• • •

As Aran's car pulled up outside one of the most exclusive florists in Beverly Hills, he felt a surge of excitement. Stepping out of the car into the cool morning air, he felt that he'd discovered his own little "Garden of Eden." He walked through the entrance and browsed through the incredible flower displays until he found the champagne-coloured roses that he'd been searching for—their stems long and elegant, their petals slightly open. *Yes, these were the roses he wanted*, he assured himself. As the shop assistant wrapped the wonderful flowers up, she smiled.

"These flowers must be for a very special lady, sir!"

< 37 >

"Yes, you could say that," Aran replied.

Thirty minutes later, Aran arrived at his destination. Everything appeared to be bright and peaceful as he walked up a little pathway towards a wall with a plaque marked "Marilyn Monroe." For a moment, he stood in silence in front of the mortal grave that contained the body of a goddess—a legend. He cut some of the long roses and put them in a little flower holder under the plaque; he placed the rest in a vase beneath the grave. As Aran made his small offering, he thought of the brave warrior who lay before him, and he prayed that her spirit had received his small token of gratitude.

Walking back down the pathway towards his car, the sun was definitely shining. Aran could feel its warmth as he said goodbye to that gentle soul who lay not so far away.

• • •

The 1970s exploded around me. Feather-cuts, Rupert trousers, flares with high waistbands, tank tops, and butterfly-collar shirts were in fashion. Mungo Jerry got a pushbike, Cat Stevens sang that morning had broken—although, sadly, my voice hadn't—and Marc Bolan rode his white swan straight to the top of the music charts. Elton John led us down a yellow brick road, Ziggy Stardust played his guitar, Pink Floyd took a trip to the dark side of the moon, and Mike Oldfield found some tubular bells. Roxy Music, Brian Eno, Cream, and Led Zeppelin rocked. Diana Ross couldn't find a mountain high enough, Michael Jackson had a pet mouse called Ben, and the Rolling Stones went on another tour. Girls screamed at Donny Osmond, and David Cassidy became the heart-throb of a television sitcom called *The Partridge Family*. An unknown pop group called Abba won the Eurovision song contest with a song called "Waterloo". Mrs Mills played the piano, and a dance troupe

< 38 >

called Pan's People appeared every week on a music chart show called *Top of the Pops*. My sister fell in love with a musician called Eric who played with a band called the Bay City Rollers; she cried inconsolably for weeks after he kissed her hand during a concert. Musical artists such as Slade, Suzi Quatro, the Sweet, and Mud became more outrageous and camp with every single they released. My father and Mr. Philips, my math's teacher, called these glam-rock stars "heathens." Needless to say, I put their pictures on my bedroom wall and wore platform shoes on my feet. Descending the stairs of the bus in these shoes, especially when the driver turned sharply, was as an art unto itself; the shoes should have carried a government health warning. My favourite pair of shoes had beige and brown horizontal stripes on their six-inch platforms and large beige stars on their dark brown toes. I bought them from a shop called Clog Hoppers, and I loved them to distraction.

My life really started to feel better when my best friend and I discovered a new musical phenomenon—the sound of disco. Every week, we would queue for hours outside the Coventry Locarno, a large venue in the city centre, in order to strut our stuff on the dance floor. I remember a song with the lyrics "last night a DJ saved my life," and in many ways, that's what the DJ did for me. He gave me something to look forward to every week; he gave me a reason to dance and be happy. His name was Pete Waterman, and I lost myself in the music that he played. It inspired me, and for those few hours, I escaped into a different world. Many years later, Mr. Waterman became a well-known music producer who worked with Kylie Minogue, Jason Donovan, and a host of other singers. I will never forget the first time I heard him play Donna Summer's "I Feel Love" and Sylvester James's disco anthem "You Make Me Feel." I felt an energy that I had never heard or felt before. The sound was revolutionary. As I danced away to George McCrae, Barry White, and the Bee Gees, I felt like the luckiest guy alive.

Off the disco dance floor, my life didn't taste so sweet. I hated going to school, and I despised my oppressors with a vengeance. I told myself every day that it wouldn't be forever. And I was right,

< 39 >

for even the darkest night must eventually grow lighter. After five long years, a new day dawned when my school days came to an end.

The education that I received at comprehensive school could only be described as basic; however, I did manage to discover the beautiful poetry of W. H. Auden, Dylan Thomas, Wilfred Owen, and W. B. Yeats. I left school with one English O-level (ordinary level) and GCSE (general certificate of secondary education) qualifications in both French and European studies. When I walked out of those school gates for the last time, it was the happiest moment of my life. I left home a week later. I was sixteen.

< 40 >

PART 2

CHAPTER 6

I had worked as a part-time wine waiter for almost a year when the manager of The Dilke Arms offered me a full-time job. I accepted Maude's kind offer immediately, as it seemed a far more prudent option than going to work on the factory floor, which my father had suggested. I also accepted her proposal that I should live-in as there were accommodations available on the premises.

Struggling with my suitcases, I climbed the endless stairs to the attic. I could almost taste a new sense of independence and freedom. As I walked across the threshold of my new home, the old floorboards under the tired carpet creaked. In the corner of the large room was a single bed—its crisp, white sheets lay proudly starched and pressed beneath a folded blue blanket. On the walls, beneath the sloping roof, pretty yellow roses danced upon the ageing wall-paper—their blooms full, their impressions faded. I felt like Mary Poppins as I unpacked my clothes and delved into the large ward-robe that dominated one end of the room. After I had unpacked my suitcases, I washed my face in my very own wash-hand basin and laid my toiletries out on the dressing table. As I peered out my bed-room window, I saw determined, noisy drivers speeding towards their destinations along the busy motorway nearby. Downstairs on the second floor was a cold, smelly, communal bathroom, which I shared with the other members of staff.

< 43 >

During my first week at work, the proprietor, Mr. Bill James, asked his Savile Row tailor to come from London to measure me up for part of my uniform. Within days, I received two pairs of beautifully tailored trousers made of navy-blue mohair. Mr. James was of medium height and build. He was a charming man, wrapped in an amicable but slightly roguish persona. In his early fifties, his hair had begun to thin out and recede slightly; its carefully combed side-part was styled with precision and pomade. Although years of serious hard drinking had taken its toll on his looks, Mr. James still retained the stature of a once-handsome man. He gave me three beautiful silk ties. Two were designed by Hardy Amies, and the other tie was designed by Christian Dior. He was a very generous employer who had a penchant for fine women, cigars, brandy, racehorses, and Rolls-Royce cars. I'd never met anyone like him, and although at times his presence terrified me, his casual self-confidence fascinated me.

Maude and Mr. James lived happily together "in sin," to the horror of the local village community. Their unmarried status was regarded as scandalous. Like an immaculately groomed vampire, Mr. James only seemed to materialize at night. When he appeared, he always wore a white shirt with a tie that complimented one of his impeccably tailored suits, and a crisp white handkerchief was always visible in the top left-hand pocket of his jacket. His hand-made shoes were polished to perfection, and his elegant cigarette lighter was made of eighteen-carat gold. He possessed a dark, dry sense of humour. I still treasure the ties that he gave me, and I only wear them on very special occasions.

One of our regular customers was nicknamed "Mr. Champagne." No prizes for guessing why—he had very expensive taste. Mr. Champagne would always sit alone at his reserved table and order the finest bottles of his favourite drink. Chatting away as I carefully opened and poured his champagne, he would always insist on giving me a glass of the chilled bubbly to taste. I soon found myself able to discuss the subtle differences between fine vintage champagnes, and by the end of the year, Mr. Champagne had transformed me into quite a connoisseur.

< 44 >

My musical taste buds also changed, and I started to listen to a lot of reggae music by Bob Marley, Junior Mervin, and Burning Spear. On my days off, I'd sit and play my new records or I'd go into town and look around the shops. It was during one of these shopping excursions that I bumped into a friend of mine and found my vocation in life.

Lorraine was a Debbie Harry "lookalike"—she loved to emulate the lead singer of the pop-punk band called Blondie. The truth was, she didn't look anything like Debbie, but that didn't seem to bother Lorraine or anyone else. All of her closest friends called her "Debbie" and told her she was the spitting image of her idol. Lorraine knew all the lyrics to Blondie's songs, and she regularly imitated her idol's singing performances in front of her full-length bedroom mirror. She dyed her hair and applied her make-up just like Debbie's. Even in the middle of winter, Lorraine insisted on looking like her idol. Wearing her black-and-white striped swimming costume with high black stilettos and fishnet tights, she braved the chilly elements. She waited in the rain at the bus stop, clutching her umbrella, determined not to let the freezing weather conditions and a force nine gale stop her from dressing like her gorgeous idol.

After a brief discussion about Blondie's latest record, "Debbie" asked me if I had ever considered becoming a hairdresser, as there was an apprenticeship vacancy available at the hair salon where she worked. I knew the salon she was talking about. I had passed its huge smoked-glass windows many times; it appeared to be very hip and trendy. After much deliberation and a lot of encouragement from "Debbie," I decided to make an appointment for an interview. To my complete astonishment, my interview was successful, and I was offered the position as trainee apprentice. Although I felt very excited to start a career in a creative industry, I felt a little daunted by the prospect of finding somewhere else to live. However, I'd heard that my old school friend Tom Rock and his fiancée were looking for a tenant for their spare room. I rang and told them about my predicament, and a week later, I moved into

< 45 >

a block of flats in Willenhall, Coventry. It was one of those rare times in life when everything seemed to fall into place without too much effort. Within two weeks, I'd found a new home and a new career. However, I kept my wine-waiting job on the weekends so I could supplement my meagre hairdressing wages of twelve pounds a week.

I was seventeen years old when I signed my hairdressing "indenture" papers with Barbarella's hairdressing salon. Almelo Casco, the Italian barber who owned the salon, suggested that it might be a good idea for me to attend hairdressing college once a week, as was the usual practice for a trainee apprentice. Due to my previous experiences in educational establishments, I felt very discouraged by this suggestion, and I decided not to go. However, after a little gentle persuasion from my work colleagues, my tenacious decision was overruled, and I reluctantly enrolled. Overwhelmed by fear and boredom I left after my first day, and I never went back.

Almelo Casco also owned a gentlemen's barbershop situated near Coventry train station. Here, Almelo would often raise money for charity by shaving people blindfolded with a cut-throat razor. Needless to say, I never volunteered to be a guinea pig—although, in all fairness to Almelo, I can honestly say that I never saw him cut anybody with his razor. He was highly volatile, however, and his Sicilian temper could erupt at any time and get the better of him. You never quite knew what kind of mood Almelo would be in—sometimes he was incredibly funny, tolerant, and kind, and at other times, he was incredibly mean.

One day when Almelo was out of the shop, I saved all the used teabags and hung them out on the washing line where we normally hung the towels to dry. The washing line was at the back of the shop, right next to Almelo's parking space and in full view of all the other motorists who parked nearby. When he returned, he came rushing into the salon.

"What's going on? Who's hung the blimmin' teabags on the washing line?" Almelo asked, infuriated.

< 46 >

"Oh, don't worry about the teabags. I just thought if we hung them out to dry, we might be able to use them for a third time and really economize," I replied.

Almelo was not amused, and he made me dispose of the tired teabags immediately. I was quite lucky I wasn't disposed of myself— after all, Almelo had been born in Sicily and was very handy with a cut-throat razor!

• • •

Aran felt relieved as he walked out of the airport in Palermo, Sicily. The seven-hour flight delay at Rome airport had stretched his tired nerves to their limit. He felt happy to be back at work on this beautiful island with its eclectic mix of Sicilian, Norman, and Arabic architecture. He loved the island's raw rustic charm and its wild, rugged landscape scattered with mountains and volcanoes.

After a short drive to the pretty seaside town of Mondello, Aran arrived at his hotel. He quickly checked in, picked up his work schedule for the next day, and ordered some food from room service. It was 10:35 p.m., and Aran's first model was due to arrive at his room at six o'clock the next morning.

Esmeralda, a gorgeous Spanish supermodel, arrived on time. *Thank God*, Aran thought. He led Esmeralda towards a chair on the veranda where the daylight wouldn't throw any nasty shadows on his beautiful canvas. Aran started to go to work on Esmeralda's hair and after careful consideration; he decided it might be a good idea to warn the lovely Esmeralda about the photographer's temperamental disposition.

"I think there's something you should know about Gino. He's a lovely guy, but he can be a bit rude and bad tempered. Take no notice of him. He doesn't mean any harm; it's just the way he is. He

< 47 >

can be the life and soul of the party—it just depends on what side of the bed he gets out of, if you know what I mean."

"Oh, don't worry about me, darling. I'll cut his fucking dick off if he upsets me."

"How very Sicilian of you, and you've only been here for one evening," Aran quipped.

After preparing Esmeralda's hair and make-up, the hungry duo quickly made their way to the breakfast room in an attempt to grab something to eat before their speedy departure. On their way in, they bumped into a grumpy Gino. *Here we go*, Aran thought.

"Morning, Gino. This is Esmeralda."

"Yes, I know who the fucking model is, I fucking booked her. And you'd better take some of that slap off her face. She looks like a bloody drag queen with all that powder and foundation. Go back up stairs and do it again," Gino ordered.

Clutching a couple of boiled eggs and a few tired bananas, Esmeralda and Aran found themselves in the elevator on the way back to his room. Upon their arrival, Aran rang room service and ordered some coffee.

"I can't believe that, the way he spoke to you—and I wouldn't mind, but you didn't use any foundation when you did my make-up. You only used a bit of powder and concealer. What's he talking about?"

"Oh, take no notice of him. He's like a bear with a sore arse in the morning. He probably drank too many glasses of wine last night. Gino can be such a dickhead sometimes, but he is a brilliant photographer."

For the next twenty minutes, Esmeralda and Aran ate their boiled eggs and tired bananas as they laughed and joked about Gino's outrageous behaviour.

"Well, I suppose we should make a move," Aran suggested, finishing his coffee.

"You wait and see. I can guarantee you he won't notice that I haven't changed your make-up. Don't worry about it—I always do it. It's like a ritual. Gino tells me to change the make-up, so I

< 48 >

take the model back to my room, sit and have a coffee, and then go back downstairs twenty minutes later without changing anything. Well, I suppose it gives him a bit more time to wake-up and have another coffee."

Outside the hotel, they were warmly greeted by the rest of the fashion crew. As Aran packed his "tool bag" in the waiting location van, he noticed Esmeralda talking to Gino. Taking a cold bottle of water out of the freezer box in the back of the van, Aran laughed and joked with the clothes stylist as she carefully checked her garments for the forthcoming shoot. A couple of minutes later, he decided it was time to face the music, so he casually walked over to the animated couple.

"What did I tell you? She looks gorgeous! You've done an excellent job with her hair and make-up. I love her new look," Gino declared dramatically, waving his hands animatedly into the air.

Aran smiled, quickly winked at Esmeralda, and thanked Gino for his gracious compliment.

. . .

I worked hard at Barbarella's hairdressing salon, shampooing hair and neutralizing perms until the skin on my hands cracked and bled from constant exposure to the chemicals and detergents. In order to protect my raw hands, I constantly applied barrier cream and wore thin latex gloves whenever I possibly could. I also made sure that I dried my hands well in between every shampoo and perm application. I swept floors, cleaned mirrors, and made numerous cups of tea and coffee. I washed brushes, tore endless books of perm papers, and collected lunches and dry-cleaning. It was hard work, but I loved my new vocation. Surrounded by these highly creative people, I felt like I was in my element. Although I struggled to

< 49 >

survive on my paltry wages, it was one of the happiest periods of my hairdressing career. These happy days were during the late 1970s, when every woman wanted to look like Farrah Fawcett-Majors, and every man wanted a perm so they looked like the famous football player Kevin Keegan. Shaggy perms, wedges, and Purdey haircuts were terribly fashionable.

I became Chloe's "junior," which meant that I worked with her 24/7. If anybody else required my assistance, they had to ask for her permission. Chloe took me under her wing and showed me the ropes.

Chloe was very beautiful, unique, and kind. With her dark, cropped hair, brown eyes, and olive skin, she looked Mediterranean, although she'd been born and bred in England. She was funny, talented, and very understanding. I adored her, and in my mind I put her on an imaginary pedestal, where I felt she belonged. Chloe became my idol, and I worshipped her. She wasn't bigoted or ignorant, and her refreshing outlook on life gave me hope and inspiration. Her best friend was a fellow stylist named Toby Carson. He was handsome, gay, and very talented. Chloe smoked Café Crème cigars and wore baggy shirts with tight jeans that she tucked into her riding boots. Occasionally, after a visit to the ladies' toilet, she would wear her skirt tucked into her knickers. There was never a dull moment working with Chloe.

Every week, whilst I listened to the *Court and Spark* album by Joni Mitchell or the *Transformer* album by Lou Reed, Toby or Chloe would change my hair colour and style. In fact, I worked my way through the entire colour chart. As my hair colour turned numerous shades of burgundy, blonde, copper, and red, I felt like a human butterfly that had just immersed from its chrysalis. I was a rebel with a cause. The sedition in my heart grew, and I started to oppose my father's oppression.

Toby was an amazing hairdresser, and he was always very busy. Most hairstylists have one column of appointments per day; Toby had two. He had a great sense of personal style, and he was always very generous, giving me carrier bags full of designer clothes and

< 50 >

aftershave that he no longer wanted. I learnt an awful lot from Toby, not only from his incredible hairdressing skills but also through the way that he lived his life. Toby never looked to others for approval. He liked who he was, and he celebrated his life and his sexuality. His behaviour was considered outrageous at times—he could be quite a diva when he got a bee in his bonnet. If he was cutting hair and a client dared to light a cigarette, he would casually snip it with his scissors. When the lit cigarette fell, the client would scream in horror and jump up. This happened so frequently that in the end, nobody took any notice of the screaming clients. Everyone just thought, *Oh well. There goes another one!*

On the rare occasions that I ventured home, my father would become so exasperated and disturbed by my appearance that he'd ring up Barbarella's hair salon to find out what these "bloody hairdressers" were doing to his son. But it was too late—my spirit had already escaped the manacles of suppression, and it roamed in fenceless gardens, picking the sweet fruits of freedom and expression. Like Dame Shirley Bassey sings, I had become "my own special creation." There was no turning back.

One quiet Sunday morning, I was busy cleaning the tables and chairs at The Dilke Arms when one of my work colleagues, "Randy Andy," started to jump up and down and sing,

"I am an anti-Christ, I am an anarchist. Don't want to be rich, but I wanna be famous."

For a few uncertain moments, I thought he'd lost his mind.

"You've got to listen to this new band. They're called the Sex Pistols, and they're amazing," Randy Andy informed me.

It was then that the punk movement started for me. Before you could say "God save the Queen," I was covered head to toe in safety pins. I quickly expanded my new punk wardrobe with bondage trousers and punk T-shirts that I bought from Vivienne Westwood's shop called Seditionaries, which was situated on the Kings Road in Chelsea, London. I disguised my bright orange hair by covering it with a brown hairspray, and I styled it in a more conventional manner when I was working in the restaurant on weekends. By the

< 51 >

end of a busy Saturday night, the heat and perspiration would cause the brown hairspray to fade and run down my face and neck. I'm not quite sure how to describe the way I looked, but my restaurant manager didn't seem to be too impressed.

Meanwhile, back in the salon, Toby encouraged all the juniors to enter as many hairdressing competitions as possible. He believed this would build our confidence and give us the valuable experience of working under pressure and with limited time. Of course, if we won any major competitions, this would also give the salon some good publicity, as our pictures and a small report would appear in the *Hairdressers Journal*, the biggest industry magazine of the day. Toby was a master hair colourist and stylist, and more often than not, if he entered a competition, he won. His favourite model was a tall, glamorous blonde called Karen Sing. Her mother owned a very exclusive boutique, which meant that Karen had access to the most wonderful clothes. Karen always looked stunning on the competition floor, and with Toby's imagination and skill, his work always outshone his competitor's.

By now, my sister Abi had grown into a very beautiful girl. If she had been just a few inches taller, she would have been a professional fashion model walking down the catwalks of Paris and Milan, but as fate and genetics would have it, she became my first hair model instead.

We worked hard. Week after week, I'd cut, colour, and style her hair with difficult finger waves to achieve the "look" that I craved. I'd practice until her head was sore and I could do no more. Abi was a very patient model. After I had completed Abi's hairstyle, Toby would scrutinize it like a competition judge, circling around my masterpiece and showing me its strengths and weaknesses. Toby would also direct Abi with her modelling poses, showing her the positions that he felt would highlight her hairstyle to its maximum effect. I couldn't help but laugh as he sat in position, sucked in his cheeks, and struck his finest poses.

Finally, after months of preparation, the big day dawned, and Abi and I found ourselves on the competition floor. As the

< 52 >

competition started, I could feel my hands shaking. I realized that if I didn't pull myself together, all my months of preparation and hard work would be wasted. From somewhere deep within me, I managed to calm my nerves and summon my self-control. Abi stayed relaxed and tried to encourage me, and as my confidence returned, Abi's hair took shape. When I left the competition floor, I felt that I'd done my very best, and after what seemed like an eternity, the judges finally finished allocating their marks, and Abi was freed from the confines of her rigid pose.

The other competitors were desperately flocking to the bar for a drink, and we decided to join them. In this surge of sparkling body glitter, we were surrounded by some hair creations that were truly out of this world. You had to see them to believe them. After several hours and a lot of drinks, everyone was asked to return back to the stage area to hear the competition results. Trying to look as relaxed and confident as possible, Abi and I waited for the judges' announcement.

"And the winner of the first-year apprentice section is…number seventy-two!" Abi and I just looked at each other. We couldn't believe it—we'd won!

Shocked and excited, we stood up and walked through the maze of surrounding tables towards the stage. As we received our prizes and were photographed by the staff of the *Hairdressers Journal*, I tried in vain to grasp this proud moment of triumph. I felt elated and slightly embarrassed by the deafening sound of applause from the audience. Minutes later, Abi and I made our way back to our table and waited for the other results.

"…And finally, the overall winner of the apprentice section is…number seventy-two!" Abi and I jumped up and made our way back to the stage.

I felt so proud of my beautiful sister. We had done it again; we had won for the second time—it was unbelievable. I'd never won anything before in my life. Basking in the glory of our victory, we felt that our assiduous labours had paid off. We laughed and danced all evening; however, at the end of the magical night, when

< 53 >

everything had calmed down, I felt a little melancholy. I wished that my mother and father had witnessed our victory, but they were nowhere to be seen. Embarrassed by my hair colour and my chosen profession, they had decided not to go.

For a brief time I became Barbarella's golden boy, until my success was forgotten and things resumed back to normal. Then one day, Mrs. McAlpine came in. She was a regular client of Toby's and had been a loyal customer for years. Eliza, Toby's busty and blonde apprentice, mixed up some bleach as usual and applied it to the roots of Mrs. McAlpine's hair. When her hair was light enough, Eliza lightly shampooed the bleach off, dried Mrs. McAlpine's hair, and applied a toner. Toners generally kill the yellow tones in bleached hair and give the hair a more natural look, which is what most clients want. There are exceptions, of course—Jayne Mansfield preferred to use a champagne pink toner for her blonde hair, as did the infamous "pools" winner Viv Nicholson, who vowed to "spend, spend, spend!" But generally speaking, most ladies prefer something a little more discreet. Everything seemed to be going smoothly until Eliza rinsed off Mrs. McAlpine's toner. Suddenly, the colour drained from Eliza's face, and she wrapped a towel around Mrs. McAlpine's hair and showed her to her seat.

And so it was with shock and horror that Mrs. McAlpine greeted her unexpected new hair colour. It was a wonderful shade of khaki green. Eliza had put the wrong toner on! When Toby first heard the screams coming from Mrs. McAlpine's direction, he thought she had seen a mouse, when in fact she had seen her new hair colour for the first time. Eliza grabbed her bag and ran out of the salon; Toby followed in pursuit. Upon his return, he did his best to console the distraught, green-haired Mrs. McAlpine, and he promised to restore her hair back to its former blonde glory. When Mrs. McAlpine finally left the salon, you would never have believed that five hours earlier she had looked like the Jolly Green Giant. Yes, her hair was short, very short, but it was a glorious colour. Needless to say, Eliza was never allowed near Mrs. McAlpine's hair again.

< 54 >

A few months earlier, I dyed my own hair a wonderful shade of forest green. It did nothing for my complexion and made me look rather sick, but I didn't care, I just loved the colour. Whilst catching the bus one day, a horrified old lady called me "a freak of nature" because she thought my forest-green hair colour was natural. I wasn't quite sure whether to take her assumption as a compliment.

As the punk scene became more notorious, it also became more popular. The Sex Pistols "bad boy" appearance on the television, coupled with their music being banned from the radio, only seemed to fuel the fires of rebellion. The band was the voice of a disillusioned generation. Lots of new punk bands formed, and they played their music at any venue that dared to hire them. With my bleached-blonde hair sprayed with a mixture of hairspray, soap, sugar, and water, I looked like I'd had an electric shock. In bondage clothes covered with safety pins, I was proudly refused entry to a number of clubs and pubs in Coventry's city centre. Of course, this was exactly the reaction I had been hoping for, because it confirmed that I looked like a "real" punk.

My favourite new wave band was called the Jam, so I went to see them perform during their In the City tour. I wore a 1960s mod suit with a shirt and tie, emulating their charismatic lead singer Paul Weller. After that, I went to see lots of other bands such as Sham 69, the Buzzcocks, the Clash, the Stranglers, Blondie, Poly Styrene and X-Ray Spex, Iggy Pop, and Generation X. There was also new band in Coventry that was causing quite a stir—the Coventry Automatics. They played a mixture of punk and ska-inspired music that had a strong political and social awareness. I'd seen their enigmatic lead singer, Terry Hall, around town, and I found his unique style and mysterious persona intriguing. Terry was a star before he became famous—he always seemed to shine out amongst the crowd. He was never frightened of being provocative or controversial with his attire or with the lyrics that he chose to sing. I became a bit of a Coventry Automatics groupie, regularly

< 55 >

meeting up with other local supporters as we followed the band from venue to venue around Coventry.

Somewhere in all this madness, I met a punk rocker named Stacy who was a big David Bowie fan like me. She was kind and thoughtful, and she made me feel at ease with my ambiguous sexuality. Within a short period of time, we had become friends and lovers. Stacy was an attractive, fun-loving girl who constantly changed the colour of her spiky blonde hair. One minute, it was a shocking pink; the next, it was blue, vermillion orange, or canary yellow. In fact, her hair colour changed almost as frequently as my own. Stacy loved to shock people, and she always made a point of looking as outrageous as she possibly could. What a pair of "punk peacocks" we made. On our way to music venues, people would shout abuses at us, or even worse, laugh at us, but we were young and didn't care. The more attention we got, the more we loved it.

· · ·

Nikita shook her mane of chestnut-coloured hair after she emerged from the depths of the hotel swimming pool. Smoothing it away from her beautiful face, she turned towards Aran. For a moment, he lost himself as he looked into her lovely green eyes. Her beautiful breasts were firm and tanned beneath the surface of the cool, blue water. When she slowly pulled herself out of the pool, Aran noticed the small ripples of sparkling water that ran down her back towards her white Gucci thong. Nikita grabbed a towel and started drying her face and gorgeous body. Then, turning towards Aran, she slowly walked to the side of the pool where he was relaxing. As he looked up at Nikita, his eyes followed the sleek contours of her incredibly long, million-dollar legs. The beautiful Brazilian model smiled

< 56 >

and held her arm slightly out towards him. Curling her finger, she beckoned him to come closer.

"Come with me," she purred. "I've got something I want to show you."

< 57 >

CHAPTER 7

As my hairdressing career crawled into its third and final year, disaster struck. Toby Carson decided to leave Coventry so that he could open his own hair salon in Leamington Spa. I was devastated. This blow was compounded when I learnt that Chloe had decided to join him in his new venture. What was I going to do? I knew my position at Barbarella's wasn't secure without Chloe and Toby's protection. Almelo Casco would make my life hell; he hated my appearance almost as much as my father. I decided to jump ship, and a couple of months later, I found myself working in a new hair salon called Billy's, also located in Coventry's busy city centre.

I became an assistant to a hairstylist named Julian. He was fabulous, but at times he could be a little crazy and dangerous to know. He once chased me around the hair salon brandishing a pair of scissors, threatening to kill me. What can I say? That was Julian. However, most of the time Julian was great fun to work with, as long as you didn't upset him. Julian was popular and highly creative, and he was also very courageous—he was always willing to try out any new hairdressing techniques. Julian dared to tread where other stylists feared to walk.

One of Julian's regular clients was nicknamed "the Green Goddess." This lovely lady shaved her eyebrows off; however, with

< 59 >

diligence she endeavoured to recreate them using thick strokes of brown eyebrow pencil, which she speedily applied about half an inch above her original brow line. In addition to this, she always applied a vibrant lime-green eyeshadow, from her eyelids to the top of her "new" eyebrows. When the Green Goddess arrived, all the juniors disappeared—except for me. Nobody wanted to shampoo her hair because she had really big cysts on her head. As I shampooed her hair, my fingers would go up and down all over the huge cysts. Although my face retained its composure, I found it hysterically funny, and so did all the other juniors who were hiding in the staff room. After I had shampooed the Green Goddess Julian would then set her hair in rollers, but because her cysts were so huge, the rollers would sit unevenly on her head, some inches higher than the others. After her rollers had been put in, I would apply her hair-net and escort her to the hood dryer, then give her a magazine and a nice cup of tea. Later, whilst dressing her hair out, Julian would always use lots of backcombing to disguise her little problem. By the time he had finished her hair, there wasn't an egg-sized cyst in sight. The Green Goddess would then make her way to the ladies' room. Here, she would redefine her eyebrows and apply more of her favourite lime-green eyeshadow. Happy with her hair and make-up, she would reappear at the reception, book her next appointment, and disappear in a cloud of Tweed perfume.

Sometimes I wished that I could disappear too. Unfortunately for me, the winds of change continued to blow me off course in a direction that I'd fought hard to avoid. I felt as if I had taken one step forward but two steps back—back to a place and a person that I despised.

I must admit that I was a little surprised when I learnt that my rented room was about to be taken over by a new arrival. I think Tom Rock was also a little surprised when he learnt that his wife was expecting their second child. Of course I felt happy for Tom and his wife, but I also felt a little sad to say goodbye to my friends and the home where I had spent so many happy days. Alone, with

< 60 >

nowhere to go that I could afford, there was only one option. I would have to move back home.

Stacy and I immediately went to the local council and made an application for a council property. As we put our names on the housing register, we were informed that there was a very long waiting list. I walked out of the council housing office in despair, realizing there was little I could do.

Nothing had really changed at home. My father was still the same insufferable tyrant he had always been. I calmed down my appearance, kept a low profile, and did my best to stay out of his way. None of my efforts to please him ever met with his approval or made the slightest bit of difference in his attitude towards me. He saw me as a threat who should be kept in his place.

"You'll never be as smart or as handsome as I was, and you'll never be too big for me to give you a good hiding. You remember that, sonny Jim," he informed me.

However, one thing he hadn't informed Abi and me about was our natural parents. We would often make up stories and have wild fantasies about who our real parents might be. After much deliberation, we decided to ask our father for more information. I think every adopted person wonders who his or her natural parents are and why they chose adoption. So, after years of waiting, Abi and I finally plucked up enough courage to ask.

"Who were ya natural parents? Why were you adopted?" Glen screwed up his face in disgust. "I'll tell you who they were. Your father was a jailbird and your mother was a whore, that's who— they were a right pair of bastards, they were."

We sat shocked and amazed, feeling vulnerable and hurt by his callous prevarication.

The days drifted into weeks, and the weeks drifted into months. I rang the council on a daily basis to enquire about my housing application; I was desperate to escape from this awful environment. My father would open my mail and stand behind the living room door, listening to my phone calls. Whilst rummaging through my personal belongings, he came across my telephone book and found

< 61 >

Stacy's telephone number. He promptly rang her parents, informing them that I was staying over at their house and sleeping with
their daughter. Stacy's parents surprised my father by saying they
were well aware of this, and that we were both legally entitled to
have a sexual relationship. They told me that my father started
shouting and swearing because he was so enraged; however, he was
eventually rendered speechless when they hung up.

Four long months passed, and finally, Stacy and I moved into
our own home. Our small maisonette had two bedrooms and was
situated in a moody-looking block of council flats in Wood End,
Coventry. We didn't want to move into this depressing area, but
we had little choice. The alternative was to wait for another two
years on the housing list until we became eligible for a place in
Hillfields, Coventry's notorious red-light district. At this time,
Wood End was a dilapidated array of boarded-up blocks of council flats and houses; other homes were burnt out or inhabited by
squatters.

The first time that I ventured to the shops, I came across what
seemed to be a derelict shopping precinct—the buildings' windows
and doors were boarded up and covered with graffiti. It wasn't until
I actually saw somebody coming out of one of the doors with their
shopping bags that I realized the shops were open and trading.
When I entered this new neon world of fluorescent shopping, it felt
like night-time, and it always felt very strange walking out of these
shrouded shops into the bright daylight.

Stacy and I scrubbed our new maisonette clean. We painted and
decorated the entire interior to make our new home comfortable.
Stacy's parents gave us a washing machine and a double bed, and I
managed to scrape enough money together to buy a second-hand
cooker and fridge. It took time, effort, and all our money, but as the
months passed by our new home took shape, and we were happy in
our own little way.

We had a coal fire, so when the coal lorry came around, I'd wait
for the coalman to make his delivery and then I'd make a dash for
the back of his lorry. I'd fill up my carrier bags with any loose bits

< 62 >

of coal that had escaped from the coal sacks, and then I'd hurry home, undetected, with my precious booty.

We decided to add a new member to our family: a beautiful Afghan hound that we called Blondie because of her light colouring. It wasn't long before she came to the attention of a local group of Hell's Angels, who decided to give us a call. They asked us if we would consider selling Blondie since they liked the look of her; however, I nervously declined their offer, telling them that she had been given to me as a birthday present. They had their own ideas for Blondie. They thought her fur would make a very nice lining for one of their leather jackets. From that moment on, I always kept Blondie on the lead when I took her for a walk. I was taking no chances.

Time passed by, and Stacy and I enjoyed a normal sex life together; we were happy and in love. After about a year, Stacy received the joyful news that her sister was pregnant. A few months later, Stacy's best friend also became pregnant. Stacy became broody and suggested we have a child. I told her I wasn't ready for a family, and that we too young to have children. However, this didn't seem to change her feelings, and I soon discovered that she had stopped taking her contraceptive pill. Heated arguments followed, and I realized it was only a matter of time before Stacy also became pregnant. I decided to put a stop on our sex life, and slowly, our relationship broke down.

One day, a friend of mine called Mickie popped around to see me. His girlfriend was at work, and Stacy had gone to visit her mother. He was a very handsome guy, and after we had chatted for a while, he told me he was bisexual and he started to flirt with me. Although nothing physical happened, I felt guilty because I realized that I also felt attracted to him. I knew that I wasn't being fair or honest with Stacy or myself, and I could no longer keep up the pretence of my hidden sexuality. One thing I certainly didn't want to do was complicate the situation further by involving an innocent new life. I decided to leave Stacy and tell her the truth. I had tried to end our relationship on several previous occasions, but Stacy had

< 63 >

always managed to persuade me to stay, telling me she would kill herself if I left her. This time, I didn't want any big scenes. I didn't want to hurt her any more than I had to.

Desperate, I rang Chloe in Leamington Spa and explained my situation. I asked her if I could stay with her until I had sorted myself out. Chloe agreed to my suggestion and told me to come at once. On the day I left Stacy I felt guilty and very sad, because I knew I was going to break her heart. I packed my bags and wrote her a letter explaining the reasons why I had to leave. I gave Blondie a big kiss, and I locked the front door—and my past—behind me. As I walked down the garden path, I turned and looked at our little home. I thought of Stacy and the love we had shared, knowing deep within my heart that I would never see her again. I swore I would never hurt anyone like that again.

I arrived on Chloe's doorstep with my suitcases in hand. Her mother showed me to their spare room. The next day, Chloe gave me some happy news. Toby had offered me a job as a senior apprentice in his new, and very blue, hair salon called Bonkers. I got another lucky break when one of Chloe's clients told me she was in charge of some housing association flats that were about to be leased out. I immediately made an application for a flat, which was accepted. I was told that my flat would be available in a couple of months, and I was ecstatic. Things appeared to be looking up for me, until one night I got a bit drunk whilst celebrating at friend's birthday party. During the night, half asleep and a little disorientated, I mistook Claire's front doorstep for the toilet. When I awoke the next morning, Chloe's horrified mother asked me to leave.

Frantic, I rang a few friends in Coventry and begged them for a place to stay. I spent the next two months sofa surfing and counting the days until my own flat would be available, since I commuted to Leamington Spa for work. On the nights that I had nowhere to stay, I'd go to nightclubs that closed really late. Then I'd walk the streets as if I were going home, until I found somewhere I could hide away for a few hours. Exhausted, I would attempt to get some

< 64 >

sleep until the cold became unbearable; then, I'd wait for a cafe to open so I could get a hot drink and something to eat.

. . .

Aran met "Dirty Desdemona" whilst doing a catalogue shoot in the Caribbean. She was a top lingerie model who appeared pretty until you got to know her personality and sexy if you didn't look at the abundance of spots on her bottom.

Upon Desdemona's arrival, she was asked to share a beautiful chalet with her client for one evening. The next day, after the current model had departed, the client asked Desdemona to move into a chalet with Aran instead. It hadn't been long before the client realized what a "generous" disposition Desdemona possessed—she was always leaving little "presents" here and there. Within hours of moving into the luxurious chalet, Desdemona had deposited her first gift. She left it by the side of the wash-hand basin in their shared bathroom; needless to say, her client wasn't too impressed with her used tampon.

The next morning, on the first day of the shoot, Desdemona did her best to make life as difficult as possible for Aran as he did her hair and make-up. Aran disregarded Desdemona's ignorant, arrogant attitude; after all, he had to work with this princess for the next five days, and he didn't want to cause any bad feelings that might upset his client. Of course, Desdemona knew this, and she revelled in pushing Aran's patience as far as she possibly could.

After a short drive in the warm sunshine, the small crew arrived at their exclusive location—a huge colonial house surrounded by beautiful gardens. Luxurious white sun loungers covered with soft, white towels lay scattered around a magnificent turquoise pool.

< 65 >

This stunning location oozed taste and charm. Small pathways led towards a wrought iron gate that opened onto a white sandy beach and the ocean.

After Desdemona had taken a brief tour of her new surroundings, she asked Aran for a razor and a pair of tweezers. Aran happily obliged. *Maybe Desdemona wanted to tidy-up her eyebrows*, he thought. But Dirty Desdemona had other ideas. Moments later, Aran watched Desdemona as she lay on one of the luxurious sun loungers, placing his tweezers by her side. With his razor in her hand and her legs spread wide apart, she proceeded to shave any stray pubic hairs that she could find around her bikini line, oblivious to the open-mouthed photographer and his assistants watching close by. In a state of shock, the client approached Aran.

"Can you believe that? And you're not going to believe what that dirty little madam left by my wash-hand basin last night," she added.

Aran started to laugh.

Satisfied with her handiwork, Desdemona casually walked over to Aran and gave him his razor and tweezers. She looked him up and down and smiled at him sarcastically. If looks could kill, Aran would have been certified as dead.

"Thanks," he said sarcastically with a slight mocking tone.

"It's my pleasure," Desdemona replied, puffing on her cigarette.

Aran carefully wrapped the razor and tweezers in a wet wipe, put them in the bin, and washed his hands. Later that evening, the walking, talking nightmare that was called Desdemona moved into Aran's chalet. The next five days seemed like the longest in his life. Things went from bad to worse; her tantrums and unhygienic personality were on unrelenting display.

Up bright and breezy at five fifteen every morning, Aran needed all the beauty sleep he could get during this challenging sixteen-day shoot. However, he was woken up every night at two or three in the morning by the persistent ring of the telephone. Eventually, when Aran couldn't stand the persistent sound of the ring tone any longer, he would answer the telephone. It was always the same

< 66 >

person calling—Desdemona's boyfriend. When Aran walked to Desdemona's bedroom to tell her that her boyfriend was calling, he would find her wide awake—yet for some bizarre reason she never bothered to answer the phone. She was a strange girl.

Through ringing telephones, tantrums, tears, and tinted moisturizer, Aran decided to "carry on regardless," his humour and strength inspired by the old "Carry On" films that he loved so much. He thought about some of the actors who appeared in the hilarious films, such as Joan Sims, Hattie Jacques, Barbara Windsor, and Kenneth Williams. He wondered what some of these illustrious stars would have done in his tricky situation. After a lot of thought, he concluded that it was best to keep his job, so he decided not to take any action. And so every morning, Aran did his best to get Desdemona's hair and make-up finished on time so that the crew stayed on schedule.

When the location van arrived on the high cliff that overlooked the endless blue ocean, an elderly grounds man warmly greeted the crew. He opened a large gate that led to a private estate, and then cheerfully directed them down a narrow road immersed in a dense, arboreal landscape. After the small photographic crew unloaded their equipment, they took a few moments to explore the grounds of the sprawling bucolic villa. Sun-drenched terraces, cool fountains, and tropical gardens surrounded the magnificent abode. Searching through the labyrinth of endless terraces and gardens, Aran eventually found the swimming pool a little distance from the main villa. Cut out of the edge of the cliff, the natural pool was fed by streams of crystal-clear water. Trees, flowers, and palms flourished with abundance in this hidden domain overlooking the ocean. Aran imagined what it would be like to swim in this magical pool at night with the stars and the moon gazing down upon him.

After the morning's hard work, the crew sat down for a wonderful lunch, which was prepared for them by a renowned chef and his assistants. On the grounds of this hot, idyllic setting, they were served cool, refreshing drinks and dishes of fresh fish with organic

< 67 >

vegetables and salad. A selection of mouth-watering desserts followed. After the delightful food, the crew relaxed in the sunshine for a few moments before they returned to work.

At the end of the shoot, the whole team agreed that they had experienced a truly wonderful day in an amazing environment. However, not everyone felt so enthusiastic. Desdemona thought the swimming pool was too small, and its crystal-clear waters were too cold. She hated the hot weather almost as much as the tea that the waiters patiently served. Lunch was OK, but it nothing special, she concluded. However, there was one thing that Desdemona did like, and that was herself. She took endless delight in admiring her reflection whenever she possibly could. She wasn't that interested in anything else, really, apart from the possibility of finding a boyfriend who was richer, more affluent, and more powerful than her present one. It's funny how attitudes and opinions change. Before Dirty Desdemona's arrival, Aran had noticed all the young, hot-blooded photographer's assistants admiring Desdemona's composite card. They had felt very excited about spending some time with this sexy babe with her natural, "stupendous bust," but after just two days in her company, they were all counting the days and hours before she would leave.

With only two nights to go before Desdemona's departure, Aran started to see the light at the end of the tunnel. In anticipation of her imminent departure, Desdemona rang the reception and asked for a preview of her telephone bill. There seemed to be some sort of discrepancy, because Desdemona's voice became louder and louder until she was screaming down the phone at the hotel receptionist. Aran sat in silence, amazed. Ten minutes later, the hotel manager knocked on their chalet door, and Aran invited her in. After talking to the receptionist, the manager had come to see what all the fuss was about. She didn't have long to wait. Aran called Desdemona. The hotel manager patiently explained where the misunderstanding had taken place—"we all make mistakes," she reasoned—but within seconds Desdemona started screaming and shouting. The manager called on her mobile phone for assistance, and a few

< 68 >

minutes later, two female staff members arrived. Desdemona continued screaming and shouting, refusing to pay her telephone bill. The manager became very distressed and asked Desdemona to pack her things and leave the hotel premises at once. When Desdemona refused, the manager threatened to call the police. All the reasoning in the world fell on deaf ears, because Desdemona continued her querulous onslaught. She ranted and raved like a child who couldn't have her own way. Five minutes later, the distraught client arrived. Aran breathed a sigh of relief. Desdemona calmed down as the client pleaded with the manager not to call the police or have her evicted. Reluctantly, the manager agreed, on the condition that Desdemona would pay the entire telephone bill.

The finale of the Desdemona experience made Aran smile, as he'd waited patiently for his moment of retribution. After carefully preparing themselves to go out for dinner, Desdemona and Aran found themselves in their shared kitchen. They both poured a glass of white wine from their separate bottles in the fridge, and then sipped their cool refreshments in silence until the clock struck eight twenty-five, reminding them it was time to leave. Upon locking their chalet door, they were greeted by the sound of crickets. Their voices croaked in the warm darkness of the night, and the local frogs and toads peered out from their hiding spots amongst the shrubs and giant ferns. As Aran watched Desdemona walk down the small pathway towards the chalet gate, he noticed the word "Rich" written in diamanté and crystals on the butt of her John Richmond jeans.

"Oh, I love your sparkly jeans. They're fabulous. What does it say?" Aran enquired pretending he didn't know.

Desdemona flicked her hair back off her face in that "I think I'm so gorgeous" kind of way and looked at Aran as if he was illiterate.

"It says "Rich", darling. You know, after John Richmond."

"Oh, they're fantastic, but I think they've got the slogan wrong," Aran suggested.

"What do you mean?" Desdemona enquired, looking at Aran as if he was stupid.

< 69 >

"Well, I think 'bitch' would be more appropriate since you're wearing them, don't you?" Aran quipped, passing her by and making his way to the hotel bar.

It was only a short taxi ride to the famous fish restaurant that overlooked the ocean. As the crew sat at their reserved table and observed the magnificent panorama, huge waves crashed and bubbled up the deserted shore. On Desdemona's last night, a sense of relief permeated the evening air. After placing their orders, the motley crew drank and made merry, chatting and joking amongst themselves, they tried to ignore their pangs of hunger. A few minutes later, superb seafood was delivered to their table. Freshly caught that very morning, the seafood promised to be a feast to remember. Everything seemed hunky-dory until Desdemona decided to moan and throw a tantrum. Her plate was so hot she could have burnt her fingers, Desdemona whined, and she turned her back to the waitress and quietly called her "a stupid girl." Embarrassed and angry, the client looked at her other contented guests, then leant over and comfortably touched Desdemona's plate.

"Desdemona, what are you moaning about now? Your plate isn't hot enough to burn your fingers," she declared.

For the first time in the entire trip, Desdemona was at a loss for words.

< 70 >

CHAPTER 8

Two long months had passed by the time I finally moved into Flat 6, 10 Parkview Road, Leamington Spa, Warwickshire. My new home was located on the third floor of a large Victorian house that overlooked an ominous Victorian "pile" known as the old library. In 1852, the Great Western Railway had decided to open up the first through-line station in Leamington Spa. When I opened the window of my studio flat for the first time, I was greeted by the faint sound of trains as they sped through the nearby station.

Excited by the prospect of decorating the interior of my first "solo" home, I quickly gathered together an assortment of colour charts and paintbrushes. My imagination ran riot. I decided to keep my bathroom and toilet white, and I painted my small bedroom in tranquil, relaxing tones of pale blue. However, I decided to use a more vibrant colour scheme for the other living spaces. I painted the entire kitchen and sitting room bright red, including the floor and ceiling. I feel sure Mr. Sigmund Freud would have had something to say about that decision. And so, ensconced in the confines my safe, womb-like environment, I finished my handiwork by painting a series of narrow black cornices around the ceiling, using masking tape to stencil my design. I saved hard, and with the little

< 71 >

money that I earned from Bonkers, I bought some red and black furniture to complete my vision of the perfect home.

After walking through the beautiful gardens and parks of Royal Leamington Spa, I felt as if a new world had revealed itself to me. The new genteel surroundings in which I found myself felt very different from those of Wood End. For here, wealth and affluence had thrived after the discovery of the healing properties of the town's spring waters, popularized by a Dr. Kerr in 1784. The town boasted a very elegant high street known as "the Parade"; its fashionable boutiques and department stores were ensconced in an imposing Regency facade. It didn't resemble the shopping precinct that I had frequented in Wood End, that was for sure. Having recently emerged from the confines of my dusty "closet," this haven of retail therapy promised to be an ideal source of merchandise for my deficient wardrobe.

I started to socialize around town, and I soon made lots of new friends. It wasn't long before my flat had become a kind of open house—a place where my friends and I would meet before we went off to a party, a club, or a concert.

As the punk scene started to diminish, a new musical god emerged from the remnants of its ripped T-shirts and rusty safety pins. Its devotees were known as "the New Romantics." Vivienne Westwood reinvented her designs, swapping her punk-rock creations for swashbuckling pirate gear, and a new singer named Steve Strange painted his face with make-up and sang a haunting song called "Fade to Grey." The song quickly shot up the music charts, and the New Romantic scene took off in a flurry of frilled buccaneer-style shirts.

Luckily for me, one of my new friends was a make-up artist. Her skill proved invaluable when trying to recreate the current *visage de la mode*. Every Saturday night, Lillie would graciously come to my flat and do my make-up before we went out. As Lillie worked her magic, she told me all her little tricks of the trade and explained to me the basic principles of how to apply make-up. I guess you could say that most of my new friends lived for the night. For it was then

< 72 >

that we could transform ourselves and become our own inimitable creations. However, all my shocking efforts to express my individuality were soon to be overshadowed by some even stranger creatures of the night.

My life started to revolve around Saturday night excursions to the New Romantic clubs in Birmingham, which was only half an hour away from Leamington Spa by train. Every weekend, I would go to the clubs with a different image; my hair changed colour as frequently as a busy traffic light. After I applied my thick avant-garde make-up, I hardly recognized myself—I seemed to morph into the character I had created. It was always fun getting ready to go out, because my friends and I would encourage each other to look as outrageous as possible. However, since our shocking appearance could cause some serious repercussions, I would always plan our escape route to the nearby train station with precision, taking care to avoid as many dangerous confrontations as possible.

How wonderful we thought we looked when we boarded the train, shocking members of the public as we took our seats. Looking back, I realize that our enthralled audiences must have thought we were going to some kind of weird, fancy dress party. Upon our arrival at New Street station, we would make a mad dash to the Rum Runner club or whatever venue we were going to. Amidst our flight to safety, we ignored the verbal and physical assaults directed at us from the outraged public. "A man wearing lipstick? What is the world coming to?" Once inside the safe confines of the night-club, we entered into our own world—a world immersed in music such as "This Is Planet Earth" by Duran Duran, "Tainted Love" by Soft Cell, and "She's Lost Control" by Joy Division.

I would also go to Birmingham to buy my clothes. The trendy place to shop at the time was an alternative shopping complex known as "the Oasis." Whilst browsing through its many stores one day, I came across this wonderful crocheted dress knitted in ghoulish shades of red, green, and yellow. It was a kind of "Bob Marley meets the Addams family" creation. *Perfect*, I thought to myself, picking it off the rail and holding it up against me.

< 73 >

"Hi, my name's George. Can I help you?" a voice asked in a London accent.

As I turned around to answer, my jaw dropped and my voice evaporated, for in those few seconds, I realized that I was looking at someone totally unique and special. George looked like some kind of mad, exotic geisha. His face was a perfect white canvas, shaded and skilfully contoured in various shades of blue and purple. Vibrant pink rouge accentuated his well-defined cheekbones, and jet-black angular lines replaced his shaved eyebrows. His lips were golden, and his beautiful opalescent eyes were defined with thick strokes of black liquid eyeliner. His shocking pink-and-purple hair seemed to defy the laws of gravity, towering high above his head. George's image was magnificent and devastatingly powerful. His sexuality seemed ambiguous, and his presence felt surreal. *This is somebody you won't forget in a hurry*, I thought to myself. I knew immediately that this boy was going places.

I turned to my friend who was with me and told her, "George is going to be very famous one day."

"George? You've got to be joking!" my friend responded.

However, it seems that my prophetic instincts were correct. George eventually became a singer and performed with Malcolm McLaren's group called Bow Wow Wow. He later went on to form his own band called Culture Club, and the rest is music history.

A small group of fashion elitists led the New Romantic scene in Birmingham: Patrick Black, Patti Bell, Jane Kahn, Martin Degville, and George. They were like fertile trees trying to grow and express themselves in a concrete jungle. Martin eventually became the lead singer of a very successful electronic rock and roll band called Sigue Sigue Sputnik. He formed his outrageous band of wild rockers with Tony James, ex-bassist of the punk band Generation X. Martin Degville was a notorious, brave soul. With his feather boa, high stilettos, and extraordinary outfits, he really did risk life and limb as he walked through the streets of Birmingham, impervious to its dangers. He made Marilyn Manson look like Julie Andrews in *The Sound of Music*.

< 74 >

In London, the striking figures of Judy Blame and his friend Scarlett Cannon were causing quite a stir. Judy shaved his head and wore eccentric clothes with huge oversized jewellery, and Scarlett wore her fringe in the shape of a crucifix. However, something tells me that her choice of coiffure had no religious connotations. Judy later became a very successful style guru in the fashion industry. I wasn't surprised; this creative visionary possessed style by the bucketload. Humorous and inventive, he was a clever artist who was way ahead of his time when it came to interpreting what was going to happen next in the world of fashion and music. Judy was one of those rare individuals who could make the most amazing unique creations out of next to nothing.

Slowly, I started to feel trapped and frustrated by the social confines of small, conservative Leamington Spa. I was young and ambitious with a "lust for life," as Iggy Pop would say. I couldn't afford to move to London, but I'll admit that a part of me also felt frightened by the prospect of leaving the security of my home and moving to a city where I didn't know anybody. I had met people socially on the club scene in London, but I didn't really have any close friends there that I could stay with for any period of time. So my busy social life continued, and I escaped to London and Birmingham whenever I possibly could.

One fateful evening, I was sitting at home watching the television when the doorbell rang. When I answered, I was greeted by two of my friends from Coventry, Chad and Daisy, and a third person that I hadn't met before.

"Come on in. Fancy a beer?" I asked, my attention turning towards the handsome stranger.

"This is Jason," Chad announced, opening his beer and raising his eyebrow mischievously.

As I shook Jason's hand, I could feel my face burning, turning a wonderful shade of pillar-box red. *Well, at least I'm colour coordinated with the bright red interior of my surroundings,* I consoled myself.

It seems at times that we have no control over our feelings and emotions. It's funny how strangely we can act when Cupid fires

< 75 >

his sharp arrow into our hearts. One minute you're perfectly fine, and the next you're a bumbling idiot, falling over things, spilling drinks, and making all kinds of stupid comments that you don't really mean. You tell yourself to pull it together, but instead you walk into doors (ouch!), stutter, and trip up the stairs (not down them), making yourself look completely ridiculous. This is how I behaved on the cold, dark, and windy night that I met Jason.

He stood tall and poised in my sitting room. There was a slight arrogance in his manner and a cheeky grin on his devilishly handsome face. As I looked into his dark eyes, I told myself to stop being silly, but it was too late—I had already caught the love bug. The immediate intensity of my feelings towards him came as a surprise to me, but I soon realized that men and women were equally captivated by this deadly handsome friend—I was no exception. In my pounding heart, I sensed a feeling of victory and defeat that was both thrilling, passionate, and oh so sweet.

● ● ●

The ultra-modern design of the villa was cohesive, stylish, and slick. Shrouded in privacy, its magnificent swimming pool and terrace overlooked the hidden depths of the rolling blue ocean. The walls inside and out gleamed white and bright like the freshest snow in winter, and the clear skies above were as blue as Steve McQueen's eyes. Relaxing, ambient music breezed through the luxurious sun-kissed interior. Sipping a glass of chilled white wine, Aran walked onto the terrace and looked towards the ocean. The warmth of the sun brightened his mood and eased his jet lag. Once again, he'd found himself in Camps Bay, Cape Town, South Africa. How many times he had been to this enigmatic country? He couldn't remember. Here in this captivating city, extreme wealth and poverty lived

< 76 >

side by side, and "black and white" lifestyles appeared to be as different as day and night. Aran looked at the magnificent views around him, feeling the pulse and breath of nature. He had seen some of the most spectacular sunsets ever in the dusky skies of Africa. As the light quickly dropped, the sun kissed the sky goodnight, and the moon took over nature's night shift, slowly patrolling the jet black skies of Africa. Suddenly, Jenny, the clothes stylist, appeared.

"Hi, darling. How are you? I hope you had a good flight; we all arrived yesterday. I'd like to introduce you to Kendra. She's our model for the next eight days."

As Aran turned towards Kendra and kissed her on both cheeks, he felt overwhelmed by her natural beauty and sensuality. Intrigued by the appearance of this feline beauty, he asked her where she was from. When Kendra replied, Aran didn't quite understand what she said.

"By the way, darling, Kendra is a little deaf, so if you're going to chat you'd better get yourself a pen and paper," Jenny suggested.

Aran looked at Kendra, and they both started to laugh. Over the next couple of days, they constantly wrote each other notes, making sure to destroy the ones they wanted to remain private. Slowly, bit by bit, note by note, Aran started to hear Kendra's silent voice. During their lunch breaks, Aran tried to teach Kendra the phonetic sounds of words in English. She learnt fast, this silent beauty with so much expression in her eyes.

It wasn't long before Aran found out that Kendra had been scouted by a top American modelling agency in Rio de Janeiro, Brazil. Aran thought how hard it must have been for this courageous young girl to have moved to New York in search of her dreams, leaving her family and friends far away. Kendra could lipread Portuguese perfectly, but she wasn't as proficient in English. However, realizing that fate and a top modelling agency had given her an opportunity, Kendra had taken it with both hands, searching for a better life for herself and her family.

Her agency had supported Kendra one hundred percent. They had told her she had the potential to become a top model.

< 77 >

It seems their predictions were correct, because the next time our client tried to rebook Kendra, her career had taken off into the stratosphere and they were unable to secure a booking. Aran wasn't surprised, and although he was sad not to work with the lovely Kendra again, he was very happy that her career was doing so well.

One evening, Kendra and Aran decided to go out for a night on the town, so the production team who was looking after their shoot put them on the guest list of the trendiest nightclub in Cape Town. Excited by their little nocturnal excursion, they quickly dined with the rest of the crew and headed off into the night. As soon as they arrived at the nightclub, Aran noticed the admiring looks of the other "party people" who stared in their direction. It was quite extraordinary. Dressed in jeans and a T-shirt and wearing a minimum amount of make-up with her hair scraped back into a ponytail, Kendra's natural grace and beauty astounded others. Her presence had the strangest effect on men; it was very funny watching them as they walked into walls, pillars, and each other as they passed by, staring in her direction. They couldn't take their eyes off her. She had an intoxicating, hypnotic effect on them, something Aran had never witnessed before.

With drinks in hand, Kendra and Aran walked around the nightclub until they found themselves standing near the dance floor. As soon as Bob Marley's music started to play, they decided it was time to dance. Kendra explained to Aran that reggae music was the only kind of music that she could sense—she could feel the vibrations. Aran watched as this beautiful girl moved in time to music that she could feel but couldn't hear. It felt strange, as if he was being introduced to something new and unrecognizable. For a moment, they looked at each other, and Aran understood all he needed to know. He realized that Kendra had revealed her world of silence to him, and he felt very humbled and honoured by the experience. He knew he would never forget this gorgeous girl from Brazil.

< 78 >

Many moons later, a speech therapist who worked at the Portland Hospital in London, told a friend of Aran's about a beautiful model who was about to have an operation to, hopefully, restore some of her hearing abilities.

"She's from Brazil, and her name is Kendra. I don't suppose you've ever worked with her?" Aran's friend asked him.

Aran's face lit up. He couldn't believe it.

"Oh my God," Aran replied, delighted by the wonderful news.

• • •

It wasn't long before Jason was spending most of his spare time in Leamington Spa, staying over on weekends and occasionally during the week. I looked forward to our meetings. He would bring me little gifts, and we would stay up late into the night, laughing and joking as we listened to music. Jason was a shy, private man, uneasy with his sexual identity, and he avoided the subject whenever he possibly could. I carried on as if everything was fine and secretly hoped that things would work out. As the months flew by, my feelings grew, and I asked Jason if he would like to live with me. This seemed perfectly natural, because as far as I was concerned, I had found the love of my life. Jason wasn't so enthusiastic about the idea, and he decided to carry on living in Coventry, where he worked as a still-life photographer. Logically this made sense, but in the emotional language of love, I felt slightly rejected and resented his lack of commitment. *Maybe I was rushing things. Maybe in time, he might change his mind*, I thought. After a while, I decided it was best to ignore his rebuke, and so I swept my bruised emotions under the carpet. I was intoxicated by love, and I wanted to dream of our future together.

< 79 >

I'd made lots of new friends since moving to Leamington Spa, and one of my favourites was an Irish girl called Cathy. Bubbly and blonde, she was an attractive girl with a great sense of humour. We would go out drinking and partying together, and while I was busy dancing on the tables, she was busy drinking most men under them. Cathy always looked on the bright side of life; her humour and positive attitude made her a very popular girl. For several months of the year, she worked on the island of Jersey picking potatoes. Eventually, she moved there permanently, working as a housekeeper for many years for a family who adored her. Cathy had two sisters named Isabella and Alex, and it wasn't long before we were introduced to each other and became friends. Isabella was a brunette with beautiful porcelain skin, a wonderful smile, and a bosom that could make a man sin. Humorous and intelligent, she possessed an inquisitive mind and a compassionate nature. At times, she could be very outspoken if she felt an injustice of some kind had taken place. Isabella was never frightened to speak her mind or challenge someone's opinion if she didn't agree with it. Strong-willed, she stood by her convictions. Alex became my best friend. She was a natural blonde with beautiful bone structure and an athletic physique. She was articulate and very bright; her intellectual mind fascinated me. Alex's life revolved around stable yards and cross-country events. She possessed exceptional equestrian skills and a deep appreciation for all kinds of horses; my life revolved around "dressing up" and going to nightclubs. We were like chalk and cheese—we couldn't have been more different. Alex was also a brilliant writer and poet who introduced me to the world of words and classical literature. Reading soon became my *raison d'être*, and I pursued my lust for knowledge with a vengeance, until my eyes were sore and I could read no more. It wasn't long before I had read a lot of the Russian, French, Greek, and English classics; I hungrily devoured their pages until my intellectual appetite was satisfied. Reading inspired me, and I began writing poetry and lyrics.

< 80 >

Although Alex was from a working-class family, she had an unassuming aristocratic demeanour. Her parents, Moira and Charlie, were exceptional people who always made me feel welcome whenever I turned up at their house with one of their daughters. On Sundays, Moira would make the most wonderful lunch. After I had finished my meal, I would sit in front of the fire and watch television. Moira's lovely Dublin accent and laughter filled the busy living room. As I relaxed in the friendly atmosphere, surrounded by shelves and walls covered in a cornucopia of ornaments, vases, jugs, and plates, I felt secure and content.

The kettle always seemed to be on in Moira's house, and after several cups of strong tea, I would start to feel creative. I'd ask Moira to be my hair model, because she was always willing to try something new. I'd exuberantly suggest all sorts of wonderful, wacky, and creative hairstyles that I thought she might like. "Oh well. In for a penny, in for a pound," Moira would say, chuckling as she cautiously sat in front me. Covered by a plastic cape that I had nicknamed "Doreen," she would patiently sit for hours while I bleached and toned her hair. Once I had finished cutting and styling my masterpiece, Moira always seemed delighted with the results. If she wasn't, she never said anything to me. Nothing seemed to shock or ruffle Moira's feathers, not even the results of my early "experimental" hairstyles. When I visited her home with waist-length dreadlocks, a shaved Mohawk, or blue hair, she didn't bat an eyelid. Moira accepted me for who I was, and I listened carefully to her wise council—the result of an experienced life. Charlie was always there by her side, except when he went off to do his night shift at the local pub. Freshly groomed, his smooth skin splashed with cologne, he'd run downstairs, quickly put on his jacket, and pop his head around the door to offer a cheery farewell. After he closed the front door and walked out into the early winter night, the sound of his footsteps falling on the crisp, frozen ground slowly faded away.

As my dormant literary yearnings emerged from their deep slumbers, I started to write more poetry and lyrics, and I pondered the idea of singing and recording some of my own material. Some

< 81 >

friends of mine had their own recording studio in the basement of their house, and they offered to record and compose the music for a couple of my songs. Although I'd never had any vocal training or singing experience, for some reason I thought this was a great idea, and I went ahead and recorded three songs. To my surprise, they actually sounded quite good. Several weeks later, Jason took a photograph of me for the cover of my "demo tape." The recording stayed on my dusty bookshelf for months doing nothing. I wasn't sure what to do with it, since I had no band of my own and no way of recording any more material. However, just around the corner from where I lived, a record producer named Johnny Rivers was recording a song called "Ghost Town" by the Specials (aka the Coventry Automatics)—the same band that I had supported around the club scene in Coventry some years earlier. I felt envious, frustrated, and disillusioned, because I couldn't make any further progress with my musical ambitions. I knew many musicians, but they were already established in other bands that were busy rehearsing and recording their own material. And so it seemed for now that my quest to become a rock star had been put on hold.

I started to take more interest in photography, and I found myself standing in front of Jason's camera on a regular basis. Standing five feet eight, I was too short to be a professional model, but I was perfect practice material for Jason. I learnt and forgot the basic principles of photography and I soon got bored with being a photographer's muse. Jason decided to turn his camera lens towards my friends, and after several months of collaboration, we produced a portfolio of wild and wonderful hairstyles that were totally inappropriate for either man or beast. However, enthralled by the fruits of my creative endeavours, I decided to study photographic imagery in more detail. I soon discovered the brilliant photography of Norman Parkinson, David Bailey, Irving Penn, Helmut Newton, Guy Bourdin, and Bill Brandt. I also fell in love with the photographic images of Jeanloup Sieff, Paolo Roversi, Bruce Weber, William Klein, Henri Cartier-Bresson, and Robert Doisneau. The photographer who made the deepest impact on me was Richard

< 82 >

Avedon. I spent hours studiously observing his masterful work, and his sublime, potent imagery imprinted itself in my mind.

However, photographic reflections were not the only impressions floating around in my brain. I felt turbulent waves of insecurity and anxiety flooding my senses as I watched the one I loved slowly drift away. I had noticed Jason's behaviour changing towards me for months. He was friendly and pleasant enough, but he seemed to be more introverted and emotionally distant. I started to feel like Jason's secret weekend lover—quietly and conveniently hidden away. Jason seemed to be living a double life due to the mounting pressure from his family, who wanted him to settle down and find a nice girlfriend. It became increasingly obvious that at some point, Jason would have to make some big decisions. Jason's father started to question why his son was spending so much time in Leamington Spa. His mother had heard rumours of our affair, but she didn't seem to be too concerned. "He'll grow out of it," Jason had overheard her comment. Funny enough, her prediction was very accurate, because as soon as Jason's father withdrew his financial support from his son, Jason quickly lost interest in me. Our clandestine meetings became less frequent, and the hopes I had for our future together died. I knew it was only a matter of time before we said goodbye forever.

< 83 >

CHAPTER 9

rriving at the photographic studio a little early, Aran
said hello to the busy photographer assistants preparing
the first set, then walked over to the make-up area to set
out his cosmetics. Satisfied with the way he had arranged the huge
assortment of make-up, brushes, cleansers, moisturizers, and other
products, he quickly restyled his hair in the huge diagonal mirror
hanging above the make-up table and checked the time. A few
seconds later, he flicked through a copy of *Vogue Italia* in search of
inspiration for the forthcoming shoot. Checking his watch once
more, he decided that he had just enough time to spend a penny
before everyone arrived and the shoot kicked off.

Walking into the corridor outside of the studio, he bumped
into the stunning model called Kitty Kat.

"Hi, darling. I haven't seen you for ages," Aran warmly cooed,
hugging Kitty.

"Oh, it's so lovely to see you, but I've got to go. I won't be a
minute. I've just got to smarten myself up in the ladies' room. You
know me, darling—I always try to make a good impression," Kitty
purred.

A few minutes later, Kitty stooped over and held a rolled
twenty-pound note to her nose, through which she sniffed two lines
of white powder, one after the other, from neatly chopped lines.

< 85 >

After placing her tiny silver mirror back in her bag, Kitty walked out of the toilet cubicle. She washed her hands and stood for a few moments in front of the mirror, silently scrutinizing her beautiful face. Her meticulous inspection was focused on a microscopic spot and two stray hairs under her eyebrows, which she immediately plucked. Finally satisfied, she placed the tweezers in her oversized designer handbag and walked out into the corridor.

Kitty Kat—supermodel, cover girl, and international catwalk queen—was back in town and raring to go. As she walked into the photographer's studio, she was warmly greeted by the fashion team she had worked with on many previous occasions. Everyone in the crew was genuinely happy to see this fun-loving party girl. After laughing and joking with everyone for a short time, Kitty Kat sat in front of Aran on a stool next to the make-up table. She took off her powder-pink baseball cap emblazoned with the baby-blue initials KK (a present from her best friend, with whom she had recently stayed whilst in Ibiza) and checked that her long, dark hair was still tied firmly back in a ponytail.

"God, Kitty, you're looking fantastic. It's so good to see you. What's been happening? I've got so much to tell you, girlfriend, you won't believe it," Aran exclaimed, and the pair started to have a good gossip.

"Well, darling, before we go any further, I think I should tell you that I won't be using any powder on your face today."

Kitty looked puzzled.

"No, sweetheart. I think you've powdered your nose enough for one day," Aran said, passing Kitty a cotton bud.

"Oh, shit! You don't think anyone noticed, do you?" Kitty asked, taking the cotton bud and discreetly cleaning away the traces of the white powder around the brim of her nostrils.

"Well, I won't say anything if you don't. Mum's the word," Aran promised. They both started to giggle.

For the next hour and a half, Aran worked on Kitty's beautiful face, and the pair chatted non-stop. Happy with the look they had created, Kitty took her hair out of her ponytail and went to sit in

< 86 >

front of the hairstylist. An hour later, Kitty Kat's hair was ready, and she made her way over to the fashion stylist to get dressed for the shoot. It was a lengthy process, preparing this beautiful girl for the camera.

After Kitty tried on several dresses, she anxiously called Aran over to the dressing room.

"I've put on so much weight. I look like a big, fat, bloated pig in most of these dresses. Oh, Aran—what am I gonna do?" Kitty asked, looking at her stunning figure in the full-length mirror with disgust.

"A big, fat, bloated fucking pig—that's what I look like!" Kitty declared, grabbing the tight skin clinging to her skinny hips. "Fuck! I've got a fitting next week, and they're never going to book me for their show looking like this." *God, if only I could lose just a few more pounds*, Kitty thought, zipping up her dress.

"I've put on half an inch on my hips," Kitty confessed to the fashion stylist standing nearby. Distraught, she looked into the mirror again and asked, "Do you think I look fat in this dress, Aran?"

Aran looked at Kitty in disbelief. "No, you look fantastic. You always look gorgeous," he assured Kitty.

"Be a darling and pass me my green tea, would you?" Kitty asked Aran. *If I only eat fruit and cereal and drink lots of water for the next couple of days, I should be able to lose the weight*, she assured herself.

``Well, I guess I don't look too bad, and if I'm really good, I should be okay for the fitting—I've still got a couple of days to go. I've never put half an inch on my hips before, you know," Kitty told the stylist. Then she turned to Aran. "Oh, darling, would you be a sweetie and pass me my mobile? It's in my bag."

As Kitty tried on several pairs of sexy, glamorous shoes, she looked at them from different angles in the mirror.

"Oh, I think these shoes work really well with this dress. What do you think, Aran?" Before Aran had the chance to reply, the stylist interjected.

"I'm not sure. Try these," she suggested, passing Kitty a different pair.

< 87 >

Kitty tossed her thick brunette hair from side to side as she held her mobile phone in one hand and chatted away with her booker; her other hand busily worked on the straps of her mile-high stilettos. When Kitty put down the phone, she excitedly turned to the Aran.

"You're not going to believe it, darling. I've just been booked for a campaign. It's my second season in a row. I just love the clothes, and they always give me a few to keep," Kitty excitedly announced.

"Aran, would you be a darling and get me that lipstick we were using? I know you don't mind, but I've got a thing about my lips, and you know I'm not happy unless I've touched them up myself."

Walking over to the make-up table to collect the lipstick, Aran felt great affection for the lovely Kitty. He also felt a deep sense of sadness, because although Kitty appeared to be happy, Aran felt that under that shallow veneer of beauty and make-up lay a very vulnerable soul. He thought about that coveted guise called beauty, and he thought about the extremes to which women went as they tried to possess and keep it. He knew that beauty—like fame, recognition, wealth, and power—didn't guarantee a fulfilled happy life. He also felt that some individuals never appreciated their beauty, because for them it was a natural state until it slowly disappeared. Only then did they realize the true value of what they had possessed. Aran considered the curse that beauty imposes upon its recipients—the grief of knowing deep within your heart that some shallow people judged and only valued you because of your appearance or saw you merely as a saleable commodity. He realised the immense power that beauty yields is fleeting and the fear of losing that potent force could be destructive. Sadly, instead of loving the gift of beauty, certain individuals start to hate themselves because of it.

Lipstick in hand, Aran sashayed back into the dressing room's private domain and declared, "Here's your lipstick, darling. Well, dolly, it looks like you won't be having fish and chips for your tea tonight. Oh well—what's a girl to do? Now put that bloody phone down and give me a hug," Aran commanded, walking over to Kitty.

< 88 >

• • •

My first spiritual awakening took me by surprise, since the only spiritual awareness that I knew of before then came out of a vodka bottle and was usually enhanced with tonic water, ice, and lemon.

Petite, slim, and immaculately turned out, Pearl was a pretty lady in her early fifties. I met her in Toby's new hair salon, which had recently relocated to a more prestigious part of town. As we chatted away, I felt very at ease in her eloquent company, and I found out that we were almost neighbours. Whilst perming her fine grey hair, I talked the usual hairdresser's lingo—the weather forecast, her holiday arrangements, and Einstein's theory of special relativity (in my dreams)—when suddenly, out of the blue, she told me something very personal. After doing so, she apologized.

"I'm sorry, dear, but if I get a message, I just have to tell you. I hope you don't mind," Pearl told me.

Astonished and curious, I wondered how this lady who I had never met before could tell me this private information so accurately.

"I'm sorry, dear. They've been nagging me ever since I saw you. I just knew I had to tell you," she continued.

Shocked, I tried to regain my composure.

"It's not me, dear. It's just my little friend on the other side—my little spirit guide. He tells me things, and I just pass the information on," Pearl explained.

I wondered what on earth this nutcase was going on about. Maybe she was off her rocker, but I was intrigued by her perceptive words and agreed to meet her for a more in-depth conversation. After all, a walk across the road wasn't too far to travel.

As our rendezvous got closer, I became nervous and apprehensive. What if she told me something terrible that I didn't want to know? The hours passed by, my curiosity grew—as did my courage—and I soon found myself bravely knocking on her front door. When I entered Pearl's spotless home, she directed me towards her

< 89 >

sofa, where I gratefully accepted a cup of tea with one sugar. As I sipped my hot beverage, a sense of peace and serenity emanated from the warmth of her cosy surroundings. Pearl came and sat by my side on the sofa. Then, she took my hand in hers and looked into my eyes...

When I left Pearl's home, my mind was awash with spirits, guardian angels, and predictions of my future. Although I felt sceptical about the information, I didn't feel that Pearl was a money-grabbing charlatan like some so-called mediums I had heard about; after all, she had given me her energy and time freely. Pearl's words of wisdom echoed through my head, giving me food for thought. As I drifted off to sleep that evening, I reminisced over her prophecies. *Yes, and pigs can fly*, I thought. Little did I know how accurate her predictions would be.

Another interesting character I met around this time was called Jackie. When I think of her, I think of tattoos and luncheon vouchers. Jackie was a kind of hippy-chick. She smoked plenty of weed and had a deep interest in crystals, organic food, and astrology. Jackie had originally studied to become a graphic artist, but disillusioned by this profession, she had transferred her skills and had become a "body-design artist" instead. Jackie believed her body was her temple and canvas; consequently, she covered every inch of her body with her own permanent artwork (I guess you have to practice on someone), and any areas that she found inaccessible were eagerly tattooed by her body-artist friends. Jackie regarded herself as a living, breathing work of art, and she adorned her tattooed body with numerous body piercings and lots of patchouli oil.

As our friendship grew, we decided to trade our skills. I agreed to plait and bead her long red-hennaed hair in exchange for a tattoo of my choice. Jackie drew a few sketches of the tattoos she had in mind and brought them over to my flat. The first sketch that she showed me was of a peacock—the design would cover my entire back and the peacock's feathers would stretch wide over my shoulders. The second design was of the Egyptian goddess called Isis. It

< 90 >

was beautiful, and I fell in love with it immediately. A week later, a large image of the Egyptian goddess was tattooed on my left arm.

Jackie had another part-time job, working as a kind of "dinner lady." Or at least, the outrageous madam she worked for accepted luncheon vouchers in return for Jackie's "favours." Her name was Cynthia Payne, and the sex parties that she held at her home in Streatham, London, were her game. When police finally exposed the parties of "Madam Sin," she became an instant celebrity. The public was intrigued by this charming lady who refused to disclaim the social service she provided for her "friends." "After all," she explained, "I'm only giving the old boys a bit of company, a nice cup of tea, a slice of cake, and a bit of how's your father."

Jackie introduced me to Ryan, one of her work colleagues. He was tall, thin, and nineteen years old. He had a mischievous nature and a cheeky smile that was as radiant as his wonderful complexion. A pair of old spectacles with very thick lenses enhanced his dreadful eyesight. These visual accruements dominated his pretty face, which was engulfed by a mane of floppy blonde hair. One evening, Ryan came around to my flat and insisted on showing me his work "outfit." Before I could shout "Madam Sin," he had changed into his French maid's uniform. What a vision he must have made at Madam Sin's parties as he served the drinks. I can still see him now, pulling the seams of his stockings straight and tidying his hair, a nuance of Paco Rabanne aftershave floating in the air.

A few years later, I heard that Ryan had died during a severe asthma attack. I'll never forget him. Sweet, gentle Ryan, he always made me laugh and smile at this world.

Finally, I completed my hairdressing apprenticeship and was promoted to the rank of junior stylist. However, nothing really changed—I still did the same old quotidian chores I had done a thousand times before: applying tints, blow-drying, and winding other stylist's perms. On Saturday nights things were a little different. My girlfriends would come over to my flat for their weekly makeovers. Taking full advantage of the creative opportunities that

< 91 >

presented themselves, I let my artistic juices flow. I'd cut, colour, and style hair into outrageous hairstyles, finishing each creative endeavour off with a complimentary make-up lesson. To be honest, I didn't have a clue about how to apply make-up, but that didn't seem to matter to me at the time, and it didn't seem to deter my protégés either. After I had completed my makeover transformations, I'd tell my participants that they were the best thing since sliced bread and send them off into the night. My most patient muse was Alex—that's right, the girl who spent most of her time in horse stables, never wore make-up, and tied her hair back in a ponytail 24/7. Poor Alex would sit for hours as I experimented with her hair and make-up. Never once did she complain about the truly hideous hairstyles that I managed to create on her head or the mascara brush that I always seemed to smudge in her eye. We would talk late into the night about our ambitions while listening to music by the Simple Minds and the Smiths.

Life was fresh and full of possibilities, and I was young and hungry for adventure. I knew there was a massive world out there that I wanted to explore. Confined by my economic constraints, the seeds of my ennui started to grow. My frustration was compounded further by some of the vacuous, inescapable, and narrow-minded mentalities that I encountered in the small town called Leamington Spa.

It was around this time that I heard a voice on the radio—the voice of an angel soaring towards the heavens. Jimmy Somerville's falsetto tones made the hairs on my arms stand on end; his soulful song called "Smalltown Boy" seemed to touch a resounding chord within me. For the first time in my life, I felt like I had connected with somebody who really understood my anguish. Thousands of other people must have felt the same way, because his song climbed to the top of the music charts. I respected Mr. Somerville for many reasons, not only because of his obvious vocal abilities, but also because he was an openly gay man who was unashamed and unembarrassed by his sexuality (a celebrity attitude like that was very novel and honest at the time). I really wanted to meet him, but I

< 92 >

realized that the chances of that happening were zero. Many years later, I finally became acquainted with Mr. Somerville. I met him at gym called Centre Point next to Tottenham Court tube station in central London.

Motivated by my frustration and inspired by Mr. Somerville's beautiful voice, my rebellious nature went into overdrive. I walked up and down the Parade (the previously mentioned main high street in Leamington Spa) sporting full make-up and the most outrageous outfits that I could muster. It wasn't long before I was discovered by the local skinhead fraternity, who pursued my gender-bending persona like a pack of bloodthirsty wolves. Although I experienced a few close shaves with my foes, I always managed to escape their eager clutches.

After much deliberation, I decided that if I couldn't beat my oppressors, I would do my best to aggravate them. Within a month, I had transformed myself to look like a skinhead. I wore stay-pressed trousers, Ben Sherman shirts, red braces, and highly polished full-length Dr. Marten boots. My new image seemed to infuriate the skinhead fraternity even more than my previous incarnations. Gripped by a renewed vengeance, they threatened and pursued me. Every time I left home, I looked over my shoulder in apprehension, afraid that one of them would see me and discover where I lived. It took a while for the penny to drop— I wasn't the brightest shilling on the block—but eventually I decided for safety reasons that it was probably best to keep a low profile.

Although I wore a brave face, I wasn't happy. By now, I realized that my relationship with Jason was going nowhere; however, I also realized that was exactly where I was going, until one bright day when I ran into a ray of sunshine that I hadn't seen for a while.

Like a breath of fresh air, Cathy breathed new life and possibilities into me. Having just come back from her potato-picking season in Jersey, she suggested that it might be a good idea to go travelling, and so for the next few weeks we hatched our plan to escape from Leamington Spa.

< 93 >

We decided to take the Magic Bus to Greece, since it was the cheapest mode of transport available. Our getaway vehicle was to leave from the Victoria coach station in London and was due to arrive in Athens three days later. I saved every penny that I could, and I managed to pay my rent in advance for four months, thus ensuring that I had somewhere to return to. However, I wasn't so sure I'd have somebody waiting for me, since Jason was not amused by my forthcoming adventure.

I had decided to run away from my turbulent relationship. I hoped that in my absence, Jason would miss me madly and decide to make a commitment to me. Right or wrong, I knew I couldn't carry on in the same old scenario. Cathy and I booked our seats on the coach, packed our bags, and counted the days until departure.

I embarked upon my journey on the Magic Bus with a light wallet in my pocket and a one-way ticket in my hand. Unbeknown to me, my life would never be the same again.

< 94 >

PART 3

CHAPTER 10

After three long days, our tired coach finally arrived in Athens, the City of the Gods. Weary and hung-over, Cathy and I made our way to the nearest youth hostel. After we slept for a couple of hours, we headed out into the sunshine on a mission to discover this hot, busy city. During our first week in Athens, we went on numerous tourist excursions to the local bars, where we discovered the historic delights of ouzo (an anise-flavoured aperitif), traditional Greek music, and dancing. However, we did manage to squeeze in some rather more conventional sightseeing here and there by visiting the magnificent Acropolis and some truly incredible monuments. After several more days of merry making, we started to grow restless, and we decided it was time to look for further adventure. A few days later, we caught a ferry from Piraeus that was bound for a Greek island called Mykonos.

As the ferry pulled into the small harbour of Mykonos Town, an excited feeling of exhilaration fuelled our hasty preparations to disembark. With our sunglasses and backpacks on, we made our way onshore and quickly got lost in the maze of streets that furrowed through the busy, whitewashed town. In the blistering heat, we clutched our bottles of water and searched for accommodations. After several hours of investigation, we discovered that most of the pensions and small hotels were either too expensive or

< 97 >

already occupied. Our stomachs gripped with hunger and despair, we decided to get something to eat at a traditional Greek taverna. It didn't take long before we started chatting with some of the friendly local folk, who came up with an alternative solution to our problem.

An hour or so later we arrived in paradise—"the Paradise Beach Resort" to be precise. The campsite was situated on the other side of the island, only a few hundred metres from the seashore. After struggling to erect our tent for a few hot, frustrating hours, we made our way to the beach. When we felt the warmth of the sun on our bodies and played in the sand and the sea, in our hearts we both realized—this is where we wanted to be. The following weeks really were like a Greek version of the *Carry On Camping* film. Wrapped in my favourite sarong with a colourful flower placed strategically above my ear, I seemed to be the campiest thing on the site. With Cathy's gregarious, extroverted personality, we soon made numerous friends and shared lots of fun. I felt so happy; I didn't want my days in the sunshine to end.

After a couple of weeks of hard partying, our money started to run out. I took matters literally into my own hands, and I started to cut people's hair on the beach, earning enough money so we could both "carry on camping." However, this temporary existence wasn't enough for me. I didn't want to leave this beautiful island, and it wasn't long before I decided to explore it further.

I caught a bus into town and wandered through its sensuous winding streets. I looked in awe at the expensive jewellery shops, the exclusive boutiques, and the fine restaurants. In this sophisticated, international environment, where "the jet set" came to play, I felt like a fish out of water, although I also felt very excited by this new world—this new reality.

My trips into town became more frequent, since I was looking for work in the local restaurants and bars. No major hair salon existed in Mykonos, so I realized there was little chance of finding a job as a hairstylist. However, I did find one tiny Greek hair salon. It was full of old Greek ladies, dressed in black; their hair was set

< 98 >

in rollers, and they sat under dilapidated hood dryers. I enquired within asking if they needed any assistance with passing the hair rollers or other chores of this nature, but it seemed they weren't looking to take on any new staff. After several fruitless attempts to find work, I was beginning to feel a bit disheartened, and then one evening, Lady Luck decided to smile upon me.

Whilst meandering through the streets of Mykonos, I bumped into a local shopkeeper who informed me that a couple of girls called Jayne and Tamar were about to open up a trendy new hair salon. I could hardly believe this encouraging news. Over the next few days, I prayed a lot and tried to track them down. I was a determined hound and I vowed to sniff them out. I discovered that they usually hung out at a bar called Pierro's, and so every night, I'd go to the bar in search of their elusive scent. Sometimes, I didn't have the bus fare to travel into town, so I'd hitch and walk from one side of the island to the other. One evening, my faith and persistence paid off.

Jayne's broad smile and friendly manner made me feel at ease, and I soon found myself happily chatting away to this pretty girl from Nottingham. Jayne had fallen in love with the beautiful island of Mykonos whilst on holiday, and after several more trips to this sunny idyll, she had decided this was the place where she wanted to live. Having established a strong friendship with Tamar, the entrepreneurial duo had decided to open up the first hair and beauty salon in Mykonos. Tamar was married to a Greek national named Costa, which made it relatively easy to acquire a trading permit (Greece was not a member of the European Union at this time). Jayne told me they were planning to launch their new venture in a week's time. I hardly dared to ask the question, but finally, I plucked up the courage and asked Jayne if they were looking to employ any other hairstylists. Jayne told me she would speak with Tamar, and we arranged to meet the following evening. As I said goodbye, I felt hope in my heart and a spring in my step as I walked towards the bus stop and waited for my bus.

When I arrived at our rendezvous point the next evening, I crossed my fingers and took a deep breath. Happily, my feelings

< 99 >

of apprehension and fear were soon vanquished. Although Jayne and Tamar didn't resemble each other, they seemed to share some kind of invisible bond that made them appear like sisters. Tamar was a Maori from New Zealand. When we were introduced, I felt immediately attracted to her warm, strong, and vibrant personality. She was a handsome woman with long dark hair, and her beautiful face was proud. In her mid-thirties, this mysterious woman oozed sensuality; her gentle touch felt like nothing I had experienced. Tamar fascinated me, and I fell under her charismatic charms. After a few large vodka and tonics, I felt as if I was falling under a different kind of charm, as we excitedly discussed their new business venture. After a few more vodkas, Tamar and Jayne decided to offer me a position as a hairstylist. I felt over the moon—and definitely over the driving limit. Tamar and Jayne told me that my wages would be quite low to start with; however, they told me that given time, they would increase my earnings as their business became more established. I accepted their exciting offer immediately. They also suggested that I move into a vacant room situated in the back of their new hair and beauty salon.

Making my way back to the campsite, I could hardly believe my luck. I'd gotten a job, accommodations, and a wage that would grow in time. I felt apprehensive about breaking the news to Cathy, but when I finally told her about my plans, she reacted as I had hoped—she was happy and pleased for me. A week later, I waved goodbye to Cathy and the Paradise Beach Resort and caught the bus into town.

Upon my arrival at the newly christened "Le Salon," Tamar and Jayne showed me to my new living quarters. The cool back room was comprised of a small kitchenette and seating area; luckily, a bathroom with a shower lay close by. I unpacked my belongings and made myself at home. That night, as I lay on my new sofa bed, I looked out of the window to the sea of stars above. As I tried to count the stars, I fell asleep, wondering where this journey I had embarked on would lead me.

< 100 >

I awoke the next morning to the sounds of hearty laughter and the high-pitched whistle of a boiling kettle.

"Come on, princess, get up. We're going shopping," Jayne informed me, handing me a cup of coffee. Thirty minutes later, I found myself being marched to the local shops.

After much derision and changing of clothes, I acquired several pairs of cotton trousers and matching shirts. These lightweight items of clothing were ideally suited for the hot environment of a busy hair salon. I was ready, dressed, willing, and able—all we needed now were some clients.

Slowly but surely, customers started to arrive. At first they were mostly passing tourists, but as word quickly spread about the new hair and beauty salon, local women bearing gifts of homemade pies and cakes nervously entered Le Salon's open doors. After receiving a manicure or a relaxing facial, they were massaged, waxed, and plucked to perfection. With their fresh, modern hairstyles that were beautifully coloured and highlighted, it wasn't long before we became very busy.

Le Salon had been converted from a spacious house, with its high ceilings and large windows it appeared light and airy; the walls were painted in shades of white and soft pastels. The hairdressing units, which stood in front of large ornate mirrors, were made from the bases of old sewing machines that had been covered with marble tops.

Every afternoon we would close the salon for a siesta. During these breaks, Jayne and Tamar often invited me to join them at their friend's hotel situated high up in the Myconian hills overlooking Mykonos Town. Surrounded by a spectacular panorama, we would swim in the huge swimming pool and lay in the hot sun, listening to the relaxing music of Andreas Vollenweider. As I enjoyed the sunshine and a chilled glass of white wine, my new life felt almost surreal.

As the summer progressed my wages were increased, and I eventually saved enough money to rent my own room across the road from the salon. I spent so little time in my new abode that I

< 101 >

could hardly remember where it was. I went out every night and sometimes all night; my life seemed like one long party. Pierro's bar became my favourite haunt. An eccentric American lady called Margo managed this flamboyant establishment; she threw themed parties every night. Here, the rich and famous, festooned with opulent jewels, would gather to dance and have fun, their fine champagnes immersed in cool buckets of ice.

Every evening, Pierro's would feature a cabaret drag show. The shining star of these outrageous extravaganzas was a Puerto Rican drag queen called Carlos. Carlos possessed a wicked sense of humour and a big heart that had been broken many times. "Queen of Puerto Rico" and reigning queen of Mykonos, he was the darling of the jet set, and everyone who knew him, adored him. He performed every night to a packed audience, which flocked to see his hilarious show. He had eaten the fruits of a full life—the hardships of which could be traced upon his once-beautiful face. At times his speech could be slurred and incoherent, but when he got on the bar and performed his show, he was always brilliant, like a rare diamond. Carlos controlled his audience with the ease of a true professional.

Although he was very funny, there was also a very sad, tragic quality about Carlos that his audience could sense. When Carlos impersonated Judy Garland, he almost became her. It was extraordinary—you just couldn't take your eyes off him. On more than one occasion, I saw him impersonate a famous celebrity who watched his performance with bated breath in the audience. Carlos would smile sweetly and mischievously in the celebrity's direction, and then go on to do his impersonation with expert precision, timing, and skill. Afterward, he'd wink in the star's direction, bringing the whole house down with laughter. People laughed at his audacity and cheek; it was wise to have a sense of humour whilst in the company of Carlos.

For me, there was only one Carlos. I'd look into his big brown eyes and tell him he was beautiful, because in my eyes, he was. Carlos never wanted to look at the vulnerable side of his nature— he lived his life in the fast lane, his foot firmly on the accelerator.

< 102 >

He taught me a lot about life, love, and survival. I can still see him now, walking across the harbour in his sarong with his huge straw hat and "Jackie O" sunglasses, waving at his friends in the cafes and laughing at the friendly cat whistles he received from the local Greek boys. Many years later, when I heard that he had died, I cried for over a week. Dear, beautiful Carlos—if there was ever a person who lived life to the fullest, who grasped life and lived it, it was him.

Once Le Salon had become more established, our clientele diversified. One minute I'd be tinting a client's hair shocking pink, and the next, I'd be setting an old lady's hair with rollers. It certainly made my working environment an interesting place. I became very busy styling the hair of the fashionable elite who frequented the club and bar scene. My clientele also consisted of international fashion designers, the wives of Greek oil tycoons, famous writers, painters, and jewellery designers. Socially, I became a bit of a party animal. I felt alive in the hustle and bustle of the island's cosmopolitan social scene, and I received free admission and drinks at many of the bars and clubs that I frequented.

I'd learnt a lot from my experiences over the summer, and as the season drew to a close, I felt as if I had grown in many ways. But like that old cliché says, "All good things must come to an end." Sadly, I knew I had to return to Leamington Spa. Just when I was about to book my return ticket home, Jayne and Tamar told me they had a surprise for me. Later that afternoon, they handed me an envelope. Inside it was a flight ticket to Egypt and a return ticket to Leamington Spa.

"This is for all the hard work you did for us, when we really couldn't afford to pay you very much," the girls told me.

What could I say? I was finally going to Cairo to see Tutankhamun after all these years. Words failed me. I mentally visualized the little boy I had once been, left behind in the class-room because he couldn't afford the school day trip. I felt a few tears

< 103 >

roll down my face as I hugged my dear friends, but this time they were tears of joy.

Fortunately, during my summer season in Mykonos, I had made good friends with an English secretary called Susan who lived and worked in Cairo. I rang her immediately and asked if I could visit her. Delighted and excited, she told me that I could stay for as long as I wanted. We made arrangements and stayed in touch by phone. Time passed, until one day I found myself waving goodbye to my dear friends on the island's tiny airport strip. As I said my final farewells, I promised to return the following summer. An hour and a half later my plane touched down at Cairo airport where I was greeted by my friend Susan. As we drove towards her apartment, Susan told me she had arranged a special surprise for the following evening.

It was starting to get dark by the time we arrived at the horse stables; the first stars in the sky had begun to shine. With great trepidation, I attempted to mount my horse. I didn't have the heart to tell my friends that I didn't know how to ride—I didn't want to ruin Susan's wonderful surprise. The night felt surprisingly chilly as we cautiously rode into the desert. I'd asked for the slowest horse on the yard, and boy, was this horse slow. *I could have walked there quicker*, I thought, frustrated by trying to keep up with my friends. However, every ounce of effort that I had exerted seemed more than worthwhile when our small riding group arrived at our awe-inspiring location.

Here, under the starry skies of ancient Egypt, lay one of the Seven Wonders of the World. The ancient structures looked tall and immensely powerful in the desert sands of Giza. A huge sphinx lay like a guardian nearby. Partially buried in the sand, the gigantic cat seemed to watch our small group of riders as we approached. When we drew nearer to site of the Pyramids, we dismounted our horses and gathered together to observe the wonderful scene. In the silence of the desert, we shared this magical moment—a moment I would remember with almost as much joy as I had felt when I visited the Tutankhamun exhibition at the Museum of Ancient Antiquities.

< 104 >

When I arrived back in Leamington Spa, dark grey clouds coloured the sky above me. I felt as if I had moved back in time, because nothing seemed to have changed since I'd departed for Greece months ago. I hung my Egyptian mementos on the wall, played traditional Greek music, and with gusto and excitement I shared my travelling adventures with my friends. Alex thanked me for the perfume I had sent her, and she informed me that its box and wrapper had smelt wonderful amongst the bottle's broken glass. Jason was happy to see me, and for the first couple of months we got on really well, but it wasn't long before things started to revert back to our previous clandestine existence. Nothing had really changed within our relationship. In my despairing heart I knew it never would, but something inside me just couldn't tell him to go.

I was quite surprised when I received a telephone call from my parents, because it was the first time I had heard from them in almost two years. They told me they were going to retire to a mobile-home site just outside of Grantham in Lincolnshire, and they asked if they could come and see me before they left. I hadn't seen or heard from them since I had left Coventry, so it felt strange and a little sad that they were coming to visit me to say goodbye.

After a brief chat and a quick cup of tea, my parents gave me an array of unusual gifts, including some old mats, a pair of chalk dogs, and a rolled-up picture. Upon unrolling the plastic wall hanging, I was greeted with the image of a pair of Welsh ladies dressed in traditional costume, spinning yarn at a spinning wheel. However, their eyes looked suspiciously oriental to me. (The mats had been manufactured in Hong Kong, China.) I accepted my parents' gifts and waved them goodbye, but my heart was wounded by the fresh pain of rejection. I knew that they didn't really want to stay in touch with me; they had never bothered to phone or write, and I knew that it would be many more years before I'd see or speak to them again. All they really wanted was to ease their conscience before they left, but they weren't aware of this because they had never dared to question their motives. In a funny way, this is why I could forgive them. And although I found this scenario incredibly

< 105 >

sad, all the tears, pain, and sorrow that I felt in my life led me on an inner journey many years later, where I stopped looking for emotional support from people who were unable to give it.

I spent all winter and spring working, saving as much as possible so that I could return to my special island in the sun. For me, the summer couldn't arrive too soon, and when it finally did, I booked my fight to Mykonos and got my knickers in gear so fast that you couldn't see me for the dust.

< 106 >

CHAPTER 11

Walking off the plane into the hot sunshine, I was immediately greeted by the clear blue skies and the warm breeze of the Mediterranean. I was also welcomed by my friends Jayne and Tamar, who waved madly as I made my way through the tiny airport.

For the first few weeks, I stayed in the familiar bedroom and kitchenette at the back of the salon, but it wasn't long before I moved into a large whitewashed house a few streets away.

My new air-conditioned home consisted of a large bedroom with an en-suite bathroom. In the mornings, I'd wake-up to the cries of old Greek ladies proclaiming their wares as they led their donkeys laden with flowers, fresh bread, and cheese pies down the street. Lying in my bed, I'd hear the hollow sound of donkey hooves walking over the cobbled streets as they passed by. Around the corner lay a small Greek Orthodox chapel. A flight of stone steps led down into its cool interior. The walls were adorned with Greek icons, and old metal lamps hung from the low ceiling. The smell of burnt incense lingered in the air. Jayne and I would visit this tranquil chapel in the earth to light candles and send our thoughts out to our loved ones.

By now, the salon had become so popular that the girls decided to take on some new staff. Lisa was a Greek-Australian who spoke

< 107 >

fluent Greek. With her huge bosom and short skirts, she was a very popular stylist indeed. Lisa never seemed to have any problems when it came to communicating with her abundant male clientele or the handsome Greek boys who constantly followed her everywhere. In her early twenties, Lisa was pretty, petite, and brunette. She had a tough attitude, a deep sexy voice, and a bubbly, enthusiastic personality. Lisa's favourite pastimes were drinking vodka and having fun. Needless to say, we got on immediately. The new manicurist was called Eljanor. She hailed from New York City and spoke with a cute Brooklyn accent. Eljanor had a big personality and a figure to match. This larger-than-life lady had the face of a movie star. She had perfect teeth, flawless skin, and a mane of long dark hair. We soon became friends and started hanging out.

I'm not quite sure when Eljanor's transformation began. It was a slow, gradual process, but I think it started when she changed the colour of her hair. At first, she asked me to give her some very natural, sun-kissed highlights; the next week, she asked for some more—a little lighter. A week later, she went even blonder. As Eljanor's hair got lighter, her hemlines became shorter and her necklines plunged. Thankfully, her enormous breasts finally got the support they deserved when she decided to invest in some seriously upholstered bras. With these new amendments to her appearance, Eljanor's confidence and self-esteem soared.

One day, Eljanor turned to me, and in her cute Brooklyn drawl, she declared, "Honey, I wanna be a blonde."

"You are a blonde," I retorted.

"No, silly, I mean a real blonde, like Marilyn or Mae West. I wanna cut my hair, go shorter. I wanna look like an extra, extra-large Marilyn Monroe."

A week later, I cut Eljanor's hair much shorter. I dyed it platinum blonde and styled it like Marilyn's using rollers and curling tongs. Once her new hairstyle was completed, Eljanor plucked her eyebrows and did her make-up exactly like the famous movie star she wanted to emulate. She replaced her sensible shoes with high satin mules, and her extra-large cleavage was enhanced by

< 108 >

a skin-tight satin dress—its soft creamy tones highlighted the golden hues of her silky skin. With her white feather boa, some elegant diamante earrings, a sexy pout, and a touch of Chanel No. 5 perfume, she certainly got the response that she had been looking for. Eljanor was big, beautiful, and she certainly had the "X factor"; at least, those naughty Greek boys seemed to think so.

"This is the summer of my life. I'm having a ball! I can't believe it," Eljanor squealed with delight, tossing her platinum locks off her face.

Well, I thought, *if Eljanor can do it, so can I.* In my effort to transform myself, I grew my hair, bleached it, and styled it like the rock star Billy Idol. I wore black leather trousers, ripped T-shirts, and a leather eye patch that made me look like a punk pirate. When I got bored with being Billy Idol, I'd transform myself into Alex, a character from the film *A Clockwork Orange*. I'd wear a short black wig with a bowler hat and apply false eyelashes around one of my eyes. Night after night we would go out partying, returning from the yacht club or Remezzo nightclub as daylight broke. Eljanor and I would quickly go home, take a shower, get changed, and crawl into work. Upon our arrival, we would drink strong black coffee and endless amounts of water with vitamin C. As the day progressed and our energy waned, we would count the minutes until our siesta break.

It was during one of my quieter social periods, on a lazy, intensely hot afternoon, that a very strange occurrence took place. After making my way home for a siesta, I lay down in the coolness of my room and started to read. I must have been very tired, because I drifted off to sleep. I remember, very vividly, emerging out of my deep sleep, but realizing that I wasn't quite awake. During those fleeting seconds, I tried to move my arm, but I realized that I couldn't move. As this realization started to sink into my consciousness, I panicked, because I was also aware that I wasn't dreaming. The next thing that I knew, I was looking down at myself from the ceiling. I could see myself lying on the bed, motionless. It was an odd feeling, looking at myself from outside of my body. A moment later, I felt

< 109 >

my whole body physically jolt, and I awoke—almost like you do when you realize you have overslept and are late for work. Shaken and frightened, I quickly showered, dressed, and left the room; it was several days before I could be persuaded to return. Many years later, I read about a phenomenon known as astral projection, and I feel pretty sure that is what I experienced.

• • •

Aran felt tired as he walked through JFK airport. All the travelling he'd been doing lately was catching up with him. Tony, his driver, greeted him with a smile.

"How are you, sir? How was your flight?" he enquired, opening the door of the black town car.

As the car sped towards New York City, Aran smiled and thought how good it was to be back in "the city that never sleeps." He loved this gigantic metropolis, with its energy and style. Every time he came back here, it seemed like a different place; the city constantly evolved and reinvented itself. He thought back to the numerous times that he'd worked here before and remembered the adventures he'd had while exploring this vibrant city. As the car drew nearer to Fifth Avenue and east Fifty-Fifth Street, the traffic was congested, and Aran became a little agitated and anxious.

"Don't worry, sir, we'll soon be there. I know all the shortcuts," Tony assured him.

When the car pulled up outside the St. Regis hotel, Aran felt relieved. After the porter had taken his luggage, Aran thanked Tony, gave him a tip, and made his way to the hotel's reception desk.

"I hope you enjoy your stay with us, sir. If there's anything you require, please don't hesitate to ask. This is Lucy; she'll show you to

< 110 >

your room. Your luggage will be sent up shortly," the receptionist informed him.

Aran unpacked, ran a bath, and poured the contents of a Bijan bath gel into the hot, steamy waters. After a relaxing soak, he lay on the huge bed, wrapped in a luxurious white bathrobe. *God, I feel like Julia Roberts in the film "Pretty Woman." It's odd how you can step out of one world and into another,* he thought, looking around at his elegant, sumptuous surroundings. He loved the ambience of this fine hotel. It had been built in 1904 by Colonel John Jacob Astor IV, who later died on the Titanic in 1912. The St. Regis was the first hotel to install telephones in every room, have a fire alarm, and possess a central heating system. Salvador Dali and his wife Gala had chosen to live here, and Aran could completely understand why. Moments later, he fell asleep.

The next morning, seeking company, he decided not to take breakfast alone in his room. Instead, he made his way downstairs to the grand breakfast suite. Walking through the magnificent interior to his table, he smelt the flowers in the huge decorative displays and noted the huge crystal chandeliers above; their light sparkled on the silver cutlery laid out on the table. He sat down, ordering breakfast and a copy of the *Wall Street Journal*. Surrounding him sat the powerful and wealthy of American society, loudly discussing business deals, real estate, golf, and their vacations. Aran ate his breakfast, took a last sip of coffee, and requested his bill. He gave his room number, a tip, and slowly made his way to the hotel foyer.

• • •

On my days off from work at Le Salon, I would visit many of the beautiful Myconian beaches. One beach that took me by surprise

< 111 >

was called Super Paradise. This beach was strictly for the brave and daring—half its occupants were nudists.

I was happily lying on this beach one hot afternoon when I noticed twelve men dressed in blue Speedos and matching blue swimming hats walking in single file towards the sea. To my surprise, each swimmer was carrying a large piece of inflatable fruit. After a lot of shouting and splashing, the swimmers waved to their astounded audience on the beach and formed a perfect circle. Seconds later, they began a synchronized swimming routine. I watched, hot and speechless, as huge inflatable strawberries, bananas, and apples bobbed up and down in perfect synchronicity. After their hilarious performance, as they walked out of the sea clutching their pieces of inflatable fruit, the whole beach gave the synchronized swimmers a standing ovation. Mykonos seemed to be full of surprises; you never quite knew what was going to happen next.

One busy Saturday afternoon, Tamar walked into the salon and excitedly announced that her old friend Simon and his partner Bobby were planning to spend their summer in Mykonos. Tamar said that she'd become friends with Simon when she had first moved to the island many years ago. It had been a very different place then, because there were no direct flights to the island's tiny airport. It had been a quieter, more exclusive playground, where the rich and famous came to relax and mingle whilst cruising around the Greek islands on their yachts. The international jet set would always visit their entertaining friend and host Pierro Aversa at his charming bar, and this is how the island established itself as a glamorous destination.

Having worked herself up into a state of frenzy, Tamar decided to tell us more about her intriguing friend, Simon. Apparently, Simon's family were from America and were enormously wealthy, as they had founded one of the most powerful investment banks in the world. Simon resided in the famous Dakota building in New York, and he enjoyed the usual pursuits of a fun-loving playboy coupled with the intellectual stimulus derived from travel, theatre,

< 112 >

literature, and art. Unlike Mr. Getty, Simon didn't own an extensive private art collection. He left that task to his mother, who had procured one of the finest collections in the world. We held our breath and counted the days until Simon's arrival—I had never seen Tamar so excited.

Late one evening, just as we were finishing our last clients in the salon, Simon walked through the door. Tamar rushed to greet him. I felt a little nervous and apprehensive about meeting Simon after all the tales I had heard about him, but that was soon resolved when I shook his hand, shared a joke, and drank a large glass of white wine.

The first thing I noticed about Simon was his smile. It seemed to convey a certain mischievous, naughty schoolboy quality. This warm expression animated his handsome face, and his friendly manner lit up the faces of his company. I could sense immediately why Simon was so popular—he was highly entertaining and possessed a vivid sense of humour. In his early forties, Simon appeared to be confident, educated, sophisticated, and highly intelligent. In many ways, Simon reflected everything that I was not; we were like night and day. As the summer progressed, so did our friendship, and I realized that although Simon was extremely wealthy, he too had his own problems that were just as valid as mine, only different.

A professional socialite, Simon was always inundated with invitations of one kind or another. People wanted him around at their dinner parties or little soirées because he was so fascinating. His conversation was so fluid and informed that it seemed as if he could talk about almost anything, from fifteenth-century Bible manuscripts to Madonna's bra size. On countless occasions it was handbags at dawn, as people literally fought over his company. Occasionally, I would accompany Tamar and Jayne to Simon's small dinner parties. We never knew who our fellow dining guests would be—a famous film director, his decorator, a classical composer, or his cleaner—because Simon loved to invite people from all social spheres, which made his company very amusing. Simon was a gentle man, and he was never boring, arrogant, patronizing,

< 113 >

or conceited. Through his wise, caring, and educated eyes, I saw a different world—a world of extreme wealth, power, and affluence.

Another very interesting person who frequented Le Salon was a gentleman called Oliver. Nobody really knew too much about him, except that he was a very successful art dealer; at least, that's what he told everybody. Oliver spent most of his summer months leisurely cruising around the world on his gigantic yacht. I met him and his handsome young partner, Thomas, as they were about to make their way to the famous carnival of Rio de Janeiro in Brazil.

"Don't cut it too short at the back, darling. If you do, I'll get a white line at the back of my neck where it isn't tanned, and I don't want to look ridiculous for my party," Oliver directed me.

"Your nails look great. You'll be the belle of the ball," I enthused, changing the subject.

"Yes, your manicurist always gives me a good hand job," Oliver joked. "You are coming to my party on Saturday, aren't you?"

"Yeah, sure. I'm going to Mrs. Smith's to help her get ready first—then we'll be right over."

"I'll send Jimmy to pick you up at ten. You know where to meet, don't you?"

"Don't worry, we won't get lost. We couldn't miss your yacht, not with that great big helicopter."

"Believe me, darling, you don't want to skip my party. Everyone's going to be there. By the way, I've got a very special surprise that I think you and Mrs. Smith might appreciate."

"That sounds promising. Don't worry, we'll be there."

Mrs. Smith had made her money in pilchards. Her company packed and distributed tons of the silvery fishes around the globe every year. It was quite ironic, since Mrs. Smith wasn't very partial to *les fruits de mer*. In fact, she never ate seafood, and she detested the smell of fish. It had been her husband who had founded the business and built the factories. He had worked with a passion, and his pilchard-packing business went on to be worth a fortune. After his untimely death, Mrs. Smith had found herself extremely wealthy and almost sixty years old. The loneliness of widowhood

< 114 >

had darkened her days and given her sleepless nights, for she deeply missed the companionship she had once shared with her late husband. They had been married for almost forty years.

It was whilst on holiday in Portofino, Italy, that she had decided to visit the beautiful isle of Capri. While there, she met and fell madly in love with a handsome young Italian called Enrico. He was tall and dark, muscular, and thirty-five years old, and he dressed with elegant, expensive taste and displayed impeccable manners. Enrico spoke French, German, and English fluently. He was witty, proud, and had a penchant for fine living, fast cars, and model airplanes. Mrs. Smith was so happy she worshipped the ground that he walked on, for he made her an extremely satisfied woman.

Upon my arrival at the old whitewashed windmill, I was warmly greeted by Elena, Mrs. Smith's elderly Greek housekeeper. We talked briefly about the weather and her cats; then I walked up the staircase to Mrs. Smith's bedroom. After kissing each other on both cheeks and briefly congratulating each other on how wonderful we looked, Mrs. Smith took a seat in front of her dressing table. Twenty minutes later, she finally decided that she wanted to style her tinted blonde hair into a bouffant French pleat. After rearranging the front of Mrs. Smith's hair for what seemed like the millionth time, I breathed a sigh of relief—she finally turned towards me and told me how much she adored her jazzy new hairstyle. I sprayed her hair with an enormous amount of hairspray, so that with the help of a headscarf, it would be able to withstand any wind conditions on our journey across the sea. After a quick sip of wine and a little direction from Mrs. Smith, I located a velvet box lying on her bed. I removed a beautiful, sparkling diamond tiara from the box and placed it in the front of Mrs. Smith's hair, securing it firmly in place with some hairgrips. Leaving Mrs. Smith to change into her party clothes, I walked down the stairs to a small lounge area, where I was greeted by the handsome Enrico. A few minutes later, Mrs. Smith emerged in a flurry of leopard-skin chiffon. As she tossed her black feather boa over her kaftan and floated down the stairs towards us, she reminded me of the legendary torch singer known as Dorothy

< 115 >

Squires. Her tiara was accessorized with matching diamond ear-rings, bracelets, and a beautiful necklace. Mrs. Smith "rocked." After complimenting her on how wonderful she looked, we opened the windmill door and walked out into the night. Above our heads, the skies were dark and the stars were plentiful.

As the small motor boat powered its way towards the sound of music and laughter, we looked in awe at the enormous white yacht that lay still in the black waters ahead. As we grew closer, we could see people dancing under reels of coloured lanterns hanging high above the smooth wooden decks. Nearby, a helicopter sat bathed in electric-blue light; its silhouette resembled a giant mechanical insect.

Upon boarding the yacht, a fine-looking steward wearing white gloves, a cheeky smile, and a very smart white uniform welcomed us on board and directed us to a luxurious cocktail bar. We each accepted a glass of chilled champagne from a hunky waiter who wore nothing except a pair of skimpy red Speedo's with the word "lifeguard" written in white letters on his bottom.

"Looks like it's going to be an interesting party," Mrs. Smith giggled.

A few sips of champagne later, our excited host arrived. After a brief chat, Oliver suggested that we go and see his "surprise."

"Listen, guys, I know it's early, but I simply can't wait any lon-ger. I've got to show you my new baby. Follow me," Oliver ordered, ushering us down several flights of stairs. Once below deck, we made our way through his sumptuous living quarters and into his bedroom suite.

Above his huge bed, with its perfectly laundered cream-coloured silk sheets and gold damask cushions, was a cubist paint-ing by the Spanish painter Pablo Picasso.

"So what do you think? I bought it last month in New York. Isn't it beautiful?" Oliver declared, his eyes bright with enthusiasm.

"Oh, it's fabulous, Ollie!" Mrs. Smith exclaimed. "But what exactly is it?"

Oliver pretended he didn't hear Mrs. Smith's last remark.

< 116 >

"I just love it," he said. "The lines, the structure—every morning I wake up and just look at it. I love Picasso. The man was simply a genius."

"Let's just hope the ship doesn't go down, then," Mrs. Smith quipped, turning as she walked towards the bedroom door.

Weaving through the partying crowd, we made our way to a small table by the side of the swimming pool and ordered some champagne cocktails.

"Oh, I do love a good raspberry Bellini, but nobody makes them better than my Enrico," Mrs. Smith cooed, squeezing Enrico's hand. Then she turned to look in the direction of the swimming pool.

"Oh my God, I've seen it all!" Mrs. Smith exclaimed, seeing the naked, life-size, inflatable rubber dolls bobbing around in the water. "What will they think of next?" she asked, bursting into a fit of laughter.

All around us, people were dancing and throwing themselves and their friends into the swimming pool. Everyone seemed to be having a great time. A few glasses of bubbly later, an intoxicated guest came over to our table and asked us if we had any "charlie."

"Oh, I'm sorry, dear. I haven't worn that perfume for years," Mrs. Smith innocently replied, disappointing the guest.

< 117 >

CHAPTER 12

One monotonous evening when I was sitting at home doing nothing, I decided to visit one of my favourite haunts situated high above Pierro's bar. I loved the friendly atmosphere of this busy lounge bar, and its large open balcony overlooked the streets below. It was great fun to look down and watch the multitude of people walking by or socializing. It was whilst manoeuvring the steep, treacherous steps leading to this haven of fun that Cupid struck. When his arrow pierced my heart, I was stopped in my tracks on the stairs, much to the annoyance of the other guests climbing up behind me. As my eyes made contact with the gorgeous stranger in the bar above me, he walked towards the top of the stairs and waited for me to arrive.

During our brief introduction, I discovered my mysterious handsome beau was called Leon. He was half Moroccan and half Greek god. The local Myconian people said he was the most hand-some man in Piraeus, the Greek port from whence he originated. In my eyes, he was simply the most beautiful man I had ever seen. He was bisexual, and his devastating looks and strong sexual charisma attracted admiring glances from both men and women of all sexual orientations. Yet Leon wasn't arrogant or conceited; in fact, he was just the opposite. I'd never gone out with anyone who had the kind of sexual magnetism he possessed, and I found it fascinating to

< 119 >

watch those reactions that this powerful force evoked. Although Leon was from a very humble background like me, I noticed his attitude was much more sophisticated and cosmopolitan. He seemed highly educated in classical literature and music, especially opera, and he knew a lot about international cuisine, classical antiquity, film, and art. It wasn't long before our friendship grew, and we found ourselves spending more and more time together. However, our friendship was slightly overshadowed by the fact that Leon was living with a very wealthy older American gentleman who showered him with money, jewellery, and anything else that he wanted. His "friend" became aware of our relationship, and he hated and despised me because of it.

We both knew that our life together on the tiny island of Mykonos wouldn't last forever, so we made the most of the time we shared. We would visit remote beaches, dine together, and party like there was no tomorrow. Some evenings, we would lie under the night's starry blanket and laugh and joke at the cards life had dealt us. My life couldn't have been sweeter, for although I was well aware of my poverty, I felt like the richest man in the world.

One day as we were walking down the street, I overheard a few comments that were conveyed in our direction. I asked Leon to translate what our Greek voyeurs had said.

"They said you look like an angel—a beautiful angel," Leon assured me.

"You've got to be joking. I'm no angel, but you are a horny devil. Come on, this hot, thirsty angel needs a cold beer!"

• • •

Dining at The Cliff restaurant in Barbados was a relaxing yet sophisticated affair; Aran could completely understand why this

< 120 >

friendly place had become so popular with its famous clientele. He loved the quirky design of the unique restaurant with its open balconies, stunning views, and little bars that lay precariously situated on the edge of a cliff overlooking the ocean.

As the small fashion crew was shown to their table, Aran noticed the huge medieval torches illuminating the sides of the steep terraces; their golden flames gently danced, swayed by the breeze of the night. A handsome waiter gave each guest a menu and recommended some Caribbean cocktails that he thought they might like. Aran watched rolling waves as they swept towards the white sandy shore beneath them. A bright, crescent-shaped moon appeared as if suspended in the dark sky above, and below, beside the seashore, a lover's seat made from concrete, shells, and pebbles lay abandoned on a ledge looking out towards the sea.

. . .

Soft ambient music drifted into the atmosphere as the waves, soothing and gentle, lapped rhythmically against the side of the boat. After taking a sip of water from my bottle, I decided it was time to cool down. When I dived from the side of the boat into the depths of the clear turquoise waters, the extreme change in temperature momentary took my breath away. Surfacing from the water, I was greeted with cheers, laughter, and applause, and my new friends dived off the boat to join me. Refreshed and breathless, we returned on deck and lay back down on our towels. The hot, penetrating rays of the sun warmed our cold bodies. Lunch was simple and served on the boat: fresh fish, Greek salad, and chilled white wine.

My new friends, Jan and Ankie, were a very fit and athletic couple. They were real sports enthusiasts who positively glowed with health. Jan was a stunning and distinguished man in his

< 121 >

mid-forties; his hair was grey and his strong body was tanned and muscular. His pretty wife, Ankie, was funny and clever, and she always had a twinkle in her bright eyes. Her classical facial features were beautiful, as was her long, dark, shiny hair. Of Dutch heritage, this adventurous couple had decided to build their very own Greek fishing boat in the Netherlands. Upon completing this mammoth task, this courageous duo had decided to sail their boat around Europe. After stopping off in Mykonos to take a break and visit their old friend Tamar, they decided to stay for the rest of the summer.

After Tamar introduced Jayne and me to this talented duo, they kindly offered to take us out on their boat for day trips to the more remote beaches only accessible by water. Here in these beautiful secluded locations, we would relax and unwind. As daylight faded, we would sit on deck with a glass of wine and look out into the distance as the sky and the sea slowly melted into one soft blue hue.

Wearing a colourful sarong and a flower placed behind her ear, Tamar would join me for long strolls on the deserted beaches. As we walked, the sea breeze blew her long black hair.

"You know, John, most Maori people are born with flat feet. In our culture, they say it's so we can feel the pulse of the earth, its rhythm. I hope one day you will be able to go to New Zealand and hear my people sing and dance their ancient songs. If you do go, think of me, because my spirit and those of my ancestors will always be with you."

After this comment, she held my hand and turned her face away from me, towards the gentle wind that was coming from the sea. I noticed a tear fall onto her cheek before she had chance to wipe it away, and I felt her strength and love as she embraced me.

One bright, sunny afternoon, Jayne and Tamar briskly walked into the salon with some very mischievous smiles upon their faces.

They've got something up their sleeve. I can feel it in my water, I thought.

< 122 >

It wasn't long before they ``spilt the beans`` and Tamar told us about their idea.

- "Listen, guys, we've had an idea. We were out last night, and we met this video producer called Igor and his friend Andy, who's a body painter. They suggested we make a video to promote the salon. What do you think?"

Over the next couple of weeks, the staff of Le Salon put forward their ideas. After much discussion, we decided to shoot our creative venture on the remote beaches and in the busy nightclubs of Mykonos, incorporating stills and live performances into the promotional video.

Tamar asked Len, a well-known Swedish drag queen, if he would make a guest appearance in the video. Wig and mascara wand to the ready, he generously agreed to Tamar's proposal. Len also graciously offered to promote the Le Salon video by showing it on the huge video screens in the popular nightclub where he performed. Jayne decided not to appear in the video, being the sanest amongst us. She decided that it would be a good idea to hold fort at the salon and keep things ticking over there while filming was in progress.

After weeks of careful preparation, our merry little troupe of performers boarded a small boat bound for a secluded beach in Mykonos, where we hoped we wouldn't be disturbed. As the strong sea winds blew and our boat started to rock, Len, our resident drag queen, turned green. Dressed as Marilyn Monroe, he clasped tightly onto the side of the boat with one hand and held onto his platinum wig for dear life. Tamar looked resplendent as the Egyptian queen Cleopatra, but she had more than an asp to worry about—she struggled to retrieve the golden beads that had escaped from her plaited hair extensions. With my spiky blonde hair, I had decided to dress in my Billy Idol ensemble, complete with a pirate's eye patch. I didn't make much of a pirate, however, since I nearly fell overboard. Eljanor's hair had been backcombed and was reminiscent of those huge bouffant hair creations in the film *Hairspray*. However, her hairstyle took on a whole new direction when the strong sea winds

< 123 >

blew and large waves hit against the side of the boat, spraying her skyscraper hairstyle with water. Lisa hadn't risked the journey over the temperamental sea, for she'd realized that her multicoloured "bird of paradise" hair creation would not withstand the forces of nature. We arrived at our location dishevelled but not defeated, determined to carry on and give the performances of our lives.

With a little encouragement from our director, Igor, work soon got underway. He photographed and filmed our revitalised crew. Len looked a vision as he impersonated the seductive Marilyn. With his wig firmly secured, he brilliantly portrayed her. The odd nudist sun-worshipper looked shocked and bemused when Len stood high on the nearby rocks miming to "Diamonds Are a Girl's Best Friend." Cleopatra certainly wasn't to be found bathing in asses' milk—she was too busy swimming in the clear blue waters of the Mykonian sea. Her dark, mysterious, kohl-enhanced eyes seductively made contact with Igor, and he eagerly devoured the Egyptian queen's image with his camera. Once Eljanor's towering hairstyle had been restored to its former glory and direction, our talented body painter Andy then airbrushed the huge beehive with various outrageous designs. After a short lunch break, Len reappeared with his ghetto blaster, dressed as the punk-rock diva Nina Hagen. Wearing an outrageous pink-and-white wig, a ballet tutu, Dr. Marten boots, and ripped fishnet stockings, he performed one of her outrageous songs. After his remarkable performance, the few remaining nudists gave him a well-deserved round of applause.

After a few days of rest, filming resumed, and I became Andy's new muse and canvas. I sat for what seemed an eternity as he painstakingly airbrushed my entire upper body. When he was finished, I looked at my reflection in the mirror. I was quite shocked by the transformation. I had become a strange sort of creature vaguely resembling David Bowie's creation "Aladdin Sane." My face, which had been sprayed black, pink, and yellow, looked like a futuristic mask. On my torso, falling meteorites fell from a starry sky onto a desert landscape complete with palm trees, camels, and pyramids. The following day, Andy transformed me into an ethereal Pierrot.

< 124 >

My face and body were sprayed alabaster white and various shades of pink, and black diagonal lines ran across my body, face, and through my bleached hair. Andy was truly an exceptional artist, and at the end of the shoot I didn't want to wash off his beautiful work. However, I consoled myself with the fact that I had some wonderful photographs to remind me of his spectacular work.

Len kept his promise, and the premiere of our promotional video, "Electric Desert," was held at the infamous City bar located in the centre of Mykonos Town. Dressed once again as Marilyn Monroe, Len welcomed the excited guests as they queued on the red carpet outside this glamorous venue.

As champagne corks popped and a sea of white balloons floated down from the ceiling, our video played on huge screens all around the nightclub. It was a very proud moment for everyone at Le Salon. The evening was a great success, and our video was received with rapturous, enthusiastic applause.

One beautiful summer evening, as the sun went down on the whitewashed buildings of Mykonos Town, I realized that the season of fun and sun was once again drawing to a close. I'd had a wonderful time, and I felt that I had grown in many ways—emotionally, through my friendship with the handsome Leon, who I planned to meet in Mykonos the following summer; and creatively, through my artistic contribution to the "Electric Desert" video. I'd played hard, and I had met a lot of interesting people, but now it was time to go home. I decided to make a small diversion on the way back to Leamington Spa to discover a city I had always longed to explore.

As my plane touched down in Paris, I thought of all the exciting things that I wanted to do during my short vacation. I decided to stay in a small, friendly hotel in Saint-Germain, and although I didn't speak French, I was determined to enjoy the delights of this wonderful city. I walked in the elegant Jardin des Tuileries designed by the famous landscape artist Le Nôtre, and I visited most of the usual tourist sites. In a quiet cafe on the Champs-Élysées, I drank delicious French coffee and watched with intrigue as the chic

< 125 >

Parisian people passed by. At night, I took long walks along the Seine, stopping off at small bars for a rest and a cold bottle of beer. I went to a Picasso exhibition at the Louvre and wandered around numerous other museums and galleries. I loved the chic ambience of Paris, with its grand buildings and huge boulevards. I loved its sense of style and culture, the fine wines, and the excellent food.

The most poignant moment of my trip came when I passed by the famous Folies-Bergère theatre, for it was here that the spectacular singer Josephine Baker had triumphantly performed. "La Baker" had taken Paris by storm—the *beau monde* had adored her, and she was made a French citizen in 1937. Josephine was the only American-born woman to receive the French military honours of the Croix de Guerre and the Rosette de la Resistance for assisting the French Resistance in World War II. She was also made a chevalier of the Legion of Honour, which is pretty good for a poverty-stricken girl from Saint Louis, Missouri. Ernest Hemingway once referred to Josephine as "the most sensational girl that anyone ever saw." Passing by the famous venue, I felt a little sad that I was unable to share his experience.

< 126 >

CHAPTER 13

When I finally returned to Leamington spa, a surprising revelation awaited me. As I told Jason and my friends about my recent adventures, I had a sneaking suspicion that something was wrong. My friends seemed happy to see me, but it felt as if they knew something I didn't. My intuition was right. Later that evening, I was informed that Jason had gotten engaged and was shortly due to be married. At first I thought that Chad was joking, but when I looked into his expressionless face, I realized he was telling the truth. As my other friends started to realize that I had been made aware of this recent development, they made their excuses and left. Only Jason, Chad, and I remained.

"I'm the best man, but don't worry, I'm sure you'll be sent an invitation to the wedding," Chad whispered, adding insult to injury.

"Is it true?" I asked Jason. "You're getting married?"

Jason couldn't look me in the eye—he just shook his head and confirmed the shocking truth. I felt like a wounded animal struggling to comprehend what had hit me.

"Is this for real?" I asked. Sadly, the answer was *yes*.

After closing the front door behind them, my tears started to flow. I realized that Jason had gone—gone forever—and that I would never see or hear from him again.

< 127 >

Alone and humiliated, I thought about what might have been, and why Jason had made such a drastic decision. I later found out that his family had threatened to disown him if he continued to see me. They had insisted that he forget about this "phase" he was going through, and they had advised him to find a nice girl and settle down. I felt immense sadness not only for myself but for his bride-to-be; I was absolutely certain that she had no knowledge of my existence. I knew Jason would have no problem playing the husband role to some unsuspecting wife, since he appeared totally heterosexual and followed masculine pursuits. Most women regarded him as a bit of a hunk.

Sometimes I wonder what happened to Jason. I wonder how his life turned out. Did he have a family? Did they live happily ever after?

There are times when we feel that we can't carry on; we cry our tears and feel sorrow, and all our dreams seem to fade. We wake-up in the morning and struggle through another day, numb and broken, and yet something deep inside us carries on. We tell ourselves it will get better, and we learn to live with dejection—the acrid taste of disappointment on our lips that defines the cynic's smile. We fight to survive, to forgive and forget. We're half dead, but oh, so alive.

I spent the next couple of weeks licking my emotional wounds and putting on a brave face—or so I thought. One moment I felt happy, the next moment I felt sad; I felt angry, and I felt bad. I wanted to hurt Jason and luxuriate in revenge, and then next moment, I really couldn't have cared less. I was on an emotional roller coaster, and I couldn't get off. My friends encouraged me to get out and about, and after going through an awful lot of Kleenex tissue, I dried my tears and took their valuable advice. I threw myself into a social frenzy—visiting friends, going to nightclubs, restaurants, and the movies.

Life in Leamington Spa moved at a snail's pace, and everything seemed so predictable and boring. It wasn't long before my taste for adventure resurfaced—or maybe I just felt a need to get away

< 128 >

from the heartache, loneliness, and isolation that I felt in this small town. The year was 1984. I was young—twenty-four years old. I realized that I didn't want to rot in this town for one moment longer than I had to, so I booked a ticket on the Magic Bus. It was time to put my clogs on and go tulip-picking in Amsterdam.

In search of lodgings, I soon found a vacant room in a charming old residence on the Herengracht Canal. The house was tall and narrow and appeared to be squeezed in amongst the plethora of other buildings fighting for space in this central location. The first thing that I noticed about Amsterdam was the hundreds of people riding around on bicycles. This made perfect sense—the city centre was relatively small and easy to navigate, and this mode of transport reduced congestion and pollution and kept parking costs to a minimum. The residents of Amsterdam seemed to use all sorts of alternative transport—a flock of gay rollerblading nuns seemed to appear from nowhere at the oddest times. Speeding by on their rollerblades, they looked heavenly as they sang their songs of praise, although a few of them looked like they needed a good shave—well, I've never encountered a nun with a beard before, have you? I soon made friends in my new Bohemian environment. I found the Dutch people very welcoming, extremely tolerant, and open-minded. Within a few days, I found employment in a trendy hair salon close to where I lived. On my days off, I'd visit all the major museums and art galleries, discovering the works of Van Gogh, Vermeer, Rembrandt, Hals, Van Dyck, Rubens, and a host of other Flemish and Dutch masters. On Sundays, I would picnic with friends in the Vondelpark and wander around the local flea markets. I discovered Indonesian cuisine, art-deco design, and took rides on the tramcars around the city. Once a week, I would buy a bunch of tulips from the local flower stalls; the brightly coloured blooms brightened up my small dark room, which was situated on the fourth floor at the top of the house. Climbing those endless stairs every day certainly kept me fit.

Finding myself lost one day in a myriad of unknown streets, I came across a very interesting wool shop. It was winter and quite

< 129 >

cold, and I suddenly had an idea that I thought might keep me a bit warmer. I entered the shop and left ten minutes later with a bag of thick, brown wool. Later that evening, after a supper of fresh bread, Dutch cheese, and beer, I started to feel creative.

After shaving the sides of my hair off, I decided to glue the waist-length wool to my remaining short hair, matting and mixing the wool to create a "dreadlock" effect. I tied the front part of my new "hair" into a huge knot, and I let the rest fall down my back. An hour later, my face looked like a white porcelain mask, highlighted in gothic shades of antique gold and velvet black. When my midnight-blue nail polish had finally dried, I carefully put on a pair of denim dungarees, a baggy jumper, and some old baseball boots.

When I emerged from my small, dark cocoon out onto the streets of Amsterdam, I felt a little nervous. I wasn't quite sure how people would react to my new look. As I ventured into the night, a man shouted, "You look beautiful! You have a free spirit!" I thanked him for his gracious compliment, breathed a sigh of relief, and carried on walking. As I passed by some ladies of the night, who were advertising their bodies in windows bathed in red light, they smiled, waved, and whistled in my direction. These women were of every age, race, and size, and as I found my confidence, I would return their kind gestures by blowing them kisses and giving them a little bow. They looked forward to seeing me pass by on various nights, and even if my journey didn't entail travelling in their direction, I would do a little detour to brighten up their night and to show them my latest guise.

Like all cities, Amsterdam has its light and dark sides. I learnt quickly about the lives of serious drug users—the methadone vans, dirty needles, desperation, and despair. Young prostitute junkies would come into the hair salon to get their dark roots bleached blonde. Their once-pretty faces were ravished by drugs, and their hands and arms were covered in bruises and sores. As I styled their hair, their heads would fall in all directions as they struggled to compose themselves. Without help or the will to live, it was only a matter of time before they left this world and moved on to the next.

< 130 >

There was nothing glamorous about their sad lives, and there were no exclusive rehabilitation centres for them to check into. Some of them died like neglected animals in the street.

I loved Amsterdam's decadent nightlife and unique cafe culture. I felt a sense freedom and acceptance in this city that I had never experienced before. It was also one of the most cosmopolitan environments that I had ever encountered. It was great to meet up with friends of all nationalities, because although we didn't speak and understand the same languages, we still managed to communicate and have lots of fun.

Since the soft rain fell on a nearly daily basis now, I began to miss the sunshine of Mykonos. I longed to swim once again in its clear blue waters and feel the warmth of the sun on my skin. I felt it was time to go home, so I said goodbye to my friends and caught the Magic Bus back to Leamington Spa.

• • •

In the quiet departure lounge of Nice airport, Aran patiently waited to board the plane bound for London. However, every now and then the peaceful atmosphere was disturbed by a small group of exuberant friends sharing jokes, followed by hysterical fits of laughter.

As Aran sat in his economy seat and looked through his duty-free magazine, his attention was once again drawn to the familiar sound of laughter and a face that he couldn't quite place. Moments later, the face was looking directly at him.

"How's it goin', man?"

"It's all good," Aran replied.

"Those chicks in Monaco are roastin'—hot, hot, hot. Hi, I'm Nelly."

"Like the elephant," Aran joked.

< 131 >

Nelly looked puzzled for a moment.

"I'm Aran, like the jumper."

"I hear the girls in London are hot, hot, hot. Me and ma dogs are goin' out tonight!" Nelly exclaimed excitedly.

"Oh, so you're an animal lover. I love animals, especially dogs. What kind of dogs do you have—hot dogs?" Aran suggested.

Nelly started to laugh.

"No, man. I mean my dogs—ma homeys, ma crew. We're out tonight. Hey, Aran, you're a funny man."

"What do you do?"

"Oh, I'm in the music business. I'm a singa and a rappa."

A few minutes later, a serious-looking lady appeared wearing sensible shoes.

"Hey, Nelly, you comin' up front or what?" she hollered, looking at Aran.

"Well, I'd better be goin'. It's been real nice meetin' you."

Nelly shook Aran's hand and said goodbye.

Upon his arrival in London, Aran rang his nephew.

"Hey, have you heard of someone called Nelly? I think he's an American singer and rapper."

"Are you for real? He's one of the biggest music performers in the world," his young nephew replied, sighing.

• • •

After Amsterdam, Leamington Spa seemed even more boring than when I had left. In my despair, I rang Tamar and Jayne, and I told them that I wanted to move to Mykonos on a permanent basis. They were as delighted by my idea as I was by their response. Within days, I had made arrangements with my housing association to give my flat to one of my friends called "Unicorn Joe." I packed what

< 132 >

clothes and belongings I could carry, and I booked a one-way flight to Mykonos. Although I felt sad when I wished my friends and my home farewell, I also felt happy and relieved, because finally, I was leaving Leamington Spa for good.

< 133 >

CHAPTER 14

U pon my arrival in Mykonos, I moved back into Le Salon. I slept on the floor of the beauty room on a large piece of foam rubber. It wasn't the most comfortable way to sleep, but it certainly gave me the incentive to save my money and find a more salubrious environ in which to lodge. Eventually, I saved the large deposit that I needed and moved into my new home, situated across the road from three windmills that overlooked the deep blue waters of the Mediterranean Sea. It was a sweet little whitewashed place, consisting of a small room that had two single beds, a cooking area, and a tiny bathroom. I bartered hard with my Greek landlady, and I managed to secure my new lodgings for the entire summer at a bargain price. I later enhanced my little *spiti* with a small luxury item—a second-hand fridge that I bought off a friend.

Happy with my new life and lodgings in the sunshine, I felt optimistic about my future. I felt as if I had transformed my life—but that wasn't the only transformation that was to take place that summer.

Ankie and Jan, my two Dutch friends, had also decided to live in Mykonos on a permanent basis. They rented a large house, and with the permission of their landlord, they decided to make the second floor of their accommodations into a gym. Jan, as ingenious and creative as ever, turned his skills to making crude but safe

< 135 >

weight-lifting machines; he ordered any other essential equipment he required from Athens. While Jan was busy setting up his gym, Ankie was busy giving aerobics and yoga classes in a room next door. They had created the first fitness centre in Mykonos, and their establishment became a tremendous success.

One day, the happy "keep fit couple" decided to pass by the salon to say hello. After a brief conversation, Jan playfully suggested that I might consider joining the gym. Horrified by the idea, I made my excuses and changed the subject as fast as I could. Standing five feet eight inches and weighing fifty-four kilos, I had no intention of humiliating myself in front of some muscle-bound hunks. I had never practiced any form of physical exercise, and living within a beach-oriented culture, I had become overly aware of my own physical shortcomings. *I guess he sees me as a real challenge,* I thought.

"Come on—why don't you give it a go? I'll teach you all you need to know," Jan told me.

"I'll think about it," I replied, knowing damn well I had no intention of ever going to his gym.

When I got home that evening, I took off my clothes and confronted my naked reflection in the mirror. Unimpressed, I decided I had made the right decision not to go to Jan's gym. *Hercules or Arnold Schwarzenegger I was not, and never would be,* I told myself. For the next few weeks, I avoided mirrors and the beach, and I suppressed any thoughts of going to the gym, but oddly enough, the more I tried to "blank" any thoughts of physical exercise, the more I became aware of my own and other people's physicality. I had always felt physically inadequate, and I had always disliked myself for not possessing the physical prowess that I thought I should. I now had the opportunity to change the way I felt about myself with someone I could trust—somebody who wouldn't laugh at me for trying. I mustered up my courage, picked up the phone, and arranged to meet Jan at his gym.

Over the next couple of months, we trained together four times a week. Each session lasted for an hour and a half. My body ached

< 136 >

as it got used to its new fitness regime. Jan taught me the names of all the major muscle groups, their functions, and how they worked. I learnt the importance of stretching and warming my muscles up before exercising, and I learnt the benefits of proper nutrition. As my body started to change, I couldn't quite believe it. Feeling encouraged, I continued to eat lots of healthy foods, and I cut down on my alcohol intake and my partying lifestyle. I therefore got more sleep and rest, and my training improved, as did the results of my physical endeavours. As I started to realize that I could control the way that I looked through physical exercise, my life began to evolve around my training sessions at the gym.

For the first time in my life I had found a sport that I enjoyed, and with Jan's help and expertise I trained as hard as I could, pushing myself at each training session to the limit of my physical endurance. Jan always encouraged me and never charged me a fee for the one-to-one training; this generous kindness I will always remember with gratitude. The harder I trained, the more my appetite and muscle mass increased. My friends started commenting on my healthy appearance, which only gave me the incentive to train even harder.

I started to dress in a more traditional manner. I put away my make-up and my outrageous outfits and grew my naturally curly hair into a classical Greek style. People started to admire my physique and they looked in my direction when I occasionally went out to a bar or a club. At first, I thought there must be something wrong with my appearance—maybe I had chewing gum stuck in my hair or a giant spot had decided to emerge on the end of my nose—but after several checks in the toilet mirror, I knew this wasn't the case. I felt nervous and excited by this new attention that my muscular physique provoked. I also experienced another new phenomenon called jealousy. Sometimes I found this emotion to be very cruel, and at others times I found it very amusing.

One day, when I was casually browsing around the shops of Mykonos Town, I bumped into a friend of mine named Brian

< 137 >

Puccini. I hadn't seen this brilliant artist for a while, and he was amazed by my transformation.

"I would hardly have recognized you," he said. "Listen, why don't you pop by my studio? I'd like to show you my new painting."

Several days later, I found myself entering Brian's house. After a brief conversation, he ushered me into his peaceful studio. Amidst this very private domain stood a large easel, which displayed a large painting of the Greek god Adonis. The beautiful oil painting was sublime, and I felt lost for words when Brian asked me what I thought of his latest masterpiece.

"I've painted Adonis, and now I've found my Greek god Apollo. Would you mind if I painted you?"

I could hardly believe my ears. I stood in silence, shocked.

"Of course, I will pay you."

"No, I don't want to be paid, but if you could photograph the painting and sign it for me when it's finished, that would be great."

"OK, it's a deal," he said, smiling and shaking my hand.

At the appointed time, I arrived at Brian's house and nervously knocked on his door. After we greeted each other and began walking towards his studio, Brian explained the composition of the painting that he had in mind. Crouching in the position that he requested, I desperately tried to hold my pose and stay still. This proved to be a lot harder than I had anticipated, but Brian took reference photographs and did lots of beautiful sketches with incredible speed. It was amazing. With Jan's guidance, I had transformed myself from a geek into a Greek god.

Over the next few months, I would pop around to Brian's studio to see the painting, occasionally posing in the same position I had originally taken so that Brian could make slight amendments. When I finally saw the completed oil painting, I was moved by its classical composition. It was odd to see myself portrayed as the famous Greek god Apollo, looking down on the splendid amphitheatre of Delphi. For here, in this ancient city dedicated to Apollo and his muses, Alexander the Great had once consulted its legendary oracle. In one hand, I held a classical mask of Greek tragedy,

< 138 >

whilst a similar mask lay broken at my feet. It was a truly beautiful piece of work, painted in shades of blue, grey, and green. The painting was eventually sold to a rich American for a very large sum. I was sad to see the painting go, but Brain kept his word, and he photographed the painting before he sold it and signed it for me. Many years later I framed the photograph, and it now proudly hangs on my sitting room wall. Of course today, people who see the photograph no longer recognize the Greek god portrayed in the picture, and if they enquire about his identity, I tell them it was a friend I once knew many years ago.

It's funny when you look back—I had rather naively thought that by changing my physical appearance, I could change the way that I felt about myself, and on a very superficial level this was true. However, inside my head, my demons continued to haunt me. No amount of muscle tissue could reduce my deep-rooted insecurities. I was the same person—just wrapped in a different kind of paper.

The summer progressed, as did my renewed friendship with Leon. Although he continued to live with his American friend, we would meet almost every day. One evening as we were walking across Mykonos harbour, Leon suddenly told me that he had grown tired of their relationship, which no longer satisfied him. The next day, he returned all the precious gifts that his rich friend had bestowed upon him and moved in with me. I didn't see any problem with this; after all, I did have two single beds. In our tiny home, and with very little money, we shared some of the happiest times of our lives. I felt that I had found true love and friendship, and I never wanted our happy little existence together to end, but as the summer passed, I knew it was inevitable.

One morning, we got up early and watched the sun rise together. As the new day dawned, I realized the moment I had been dreading had arrived.

"I will never return to this island again," Leon told me. "And when I think of it, I will always think of you."

That winter, Leon started his compulsory national service in the army. He sent me letters and photographs of himself looking

< 139 >

impossibly handsome in his uniform. Eventually, I received the news that I had been expecting. I had always known that Leon loved children and wanted to become a father, and I also knew this was something that his family expected. Although my knowledge of biology was very limited, I knew that giving birth was not going to be on my agenda. And so it came as no surprise when Leon told me he was getting married to a beautiful Swedish girl who was pregnant. Of course, I felt sad to lose my dear friend, but part of me also felt happy, because I knew how much he wanted a family and that he would be a great father. It took ten long years for my broken heart to mend—ten years before I gave my heart to another. Lovers came and went in my life, but nobody really "touched" me.

The cold darkness of fall fell upon me as the season of sun came to its end. All the holidaymakers went home, and the bars and clubs closed down. I felt lonely in my little home, so I decided to move into a bigger place with my friend Diane and her Greek boyfriend, Stavros. Diane was a large, attractive woman who possessed a great sense of humour; her house was always full of laughter. Diane cleaned houses for a living, but this was not her only talent. She could drink like a fish and cook like a dream. Cooking was Diane's passion, and every evening she would spend hours preparing wonderful food. The house was always full of eager people who were happy to help her to eat it. Her cuisine was global, her cookbooks were endless, and her enthusiasm knew no bounds. There was always some new dish she wanted to try, and her friends and family all over the world sent her ingredients that she couldn't buy in Mykonos.

Throughout the winter the salon remained open, catering to the local Mykonians who lived on this now wild and windy isle. Gone was the glitz and glamour of the summer, and a new tranquil existence emerged as the local people went about their daily lives. However, all that changed on Saturday nights, when everyone went to the local Greek taverns. Songs were sung, plates were smashed,

< 140 >

and people danced in a traditional manner. Along the cold, dark streets, a few simple restaurants remained open; their lights comforted and welcomed patrons. Inside, waiters served bowls of steaming hot soup with homemade bread and dishes of fresh fish with vegetables. On candlelit tables sat bottles of wine and beer, their shadows falling tall and dark on the whitewashed walls. Flaming coal fires crackled over hot, orange embers, radiating warmth as the wild winds howled outside.

As the winter months passed, I took long walks in the barren countryside and by the sea. Contemplating my future, I watched ferocious waves crash against the shore on the deserted beaches. I drank strong Greek coffee and Metaxa with the local fishermen, who listened to the weather forecasts as they played cards and smoked hand-rolled cigarettes. Their faces were worn and rugged like the rocks along the Mykonian coastline. I filled my evenings with intensive workouts at John's gym. I read countless books and prayed for the summer to return. I felt as restless as the sea that surrounded the small island, and I realized that I didn't want to spend the rest of my life in Mykonos. This little fish needed a bigger pond to swim in.

• • •

As Hollywood stars shone bright in the night at a celebrity haunt called Spago, Aran ate, danced, stood, and was seated. He got a bit drunk on champagne, but he didn't feel defeated.

Walking towards the terrace to take in some fresh air, he noticed that the rain had stopped. Tiny droplets of water lay on the leaves and the grass outside, and small puddles covered the wet pavement. The moon wasn't asleep; she didn't want to go to bed. She shone like a bright white slice in the sky.

< 141 >

As Aran looked back at the star-studded crowd, he smiled and thought, *Another night, another fabulous party—just business as usual in Hollywood.*

• • •

The arrival of spring yielded the first trickle of tourists through Mykonos Town. As they walked through the labyrinth of white-washed streets, they could smell the fresh paint that had been applied to the pavement and buildings in preparation for the summer's busy season. The Athenians who rented the bars, jewellery shops, restaurants, and clubs slowly started to arrive. Excitement and suspense filled the air as people made ready for the forthcoming season. However, in Tamar's little home, a new kind of smell permeated the air as she changed the nappy of her newborn child, Adara. As Tamar proudly pushed her pram over the cobbled streets of Mykonos Town, friends and local folk who hadn't yet seen the new arrival stopped to admire Adara and congratulate Tamar. It was a wonderful start to the season. The weeks passed by, Adara grew, and summer finally arrived.

Through the open doors of Le Salon, Andreas could be heard laughing and joking with customers on the veranda outside. The methodical, almost mechanical *click, click, click* from the knitting needles in his hands permeated the jolly atmosphere. Andreas made his living from knitting. He was an absolute wizard with his knitting needles—nobody could "knit one, purl one" like him. Andreas appeared to be like some kind of human knitting machine—codes of intricate designs and patterns were logged carefully in his meticulous mind. To Andreas, his knitting needles were a mere tool, but to an uninitiated observer like me, they appeared to be an extension of his limbs. He was affectionately known as "Andreas knitting hands"

< 142 >

(his cousin, Edward, had a similar skill with scissors) by his closest friends, due to the fact that he worked with incredible speed, skill, agility, and determination. His famous, rich, and beautiful clientele clamoured for one of his latest handmade designs; his order book was always full to capacity. Tourists laughed and giggled as they passed by this knitting genius. Old Greek ladies dressed in black with their white hair scraped back into chignons swapped tips and trade secrets on the art of lace-making, bringing their finest pieces of work to be analysed and admired by this mutual craftsman.

Andreas knitted me a gorgeous jumper designed in a multitude of bright colours and textures. In return, I styled and coloured his hair for the entire summer. At night, when the air became chilly, I would pop on my jumper and cruise through the tourists who flocked to the busy town centre. As I strutted my stuff like a peacock, I was constantly stopped in the street by people admiring his wonderful creation. When the summer came to its end, I sold most of my clothes and possessions including my luxury second-hand fridge. I knew it would soon be time to leave Mykonos for good, and I tried to raise as much money as I could for my forthcoming journey across the sea. However, one of the few things that I refused to sell was my lovely jumper; I just couldn't bear to part with it.

Tired of my hedonistic lifestyle, I felt the time had come for me to fly away from this island that had taught me so much. I said goodbye to my friends, new and old, and flew towards my future, frightened and fearful of what lay ahead.

There must be some beautifully dressed angels flying around in heaven who always keep warm in the winter. Sadly, a year after I left Mykonos, I received some bad news. Like so many of my friends at this time, I learnt that Andreas had died from a mysterious virus known as AIDS.

Feeling sad and a little defeated to be back in Leamington Spa, I pressed the doorbell of Flat 4, 10 Parkview Road. My friend Alex greeted me. She now resided in a small blue flat on the second floor. Concerned and worried, I explained to Alex that I had nowhere to

< 143 >

go. Alex told me not to worry—her sisters Cathy and Isabella had moved into a large flat next door. A couple of hours later, Isabelle gave me the keys to her flat and told me I could stay there indefinitely. I couldn't thank her enough for vanquishing my fears of destitution.

As soon as I possibly could, I started looking for work. Within a week, I had found a job in a small barber's shop on the wrong side of town. This temporary position didn't last, and before long I was working at a more reputable establishment in a Rackhams department store situated in Leamington Spa's prestigious Parade area. I became a very popular hairstylist and proved myself to be a worthy employee.

It came to my attention that there were other salons owned by the same hairdressing company that were located in different department stores around the country. The "flagship" salon was centrally located in London, and I decided that this was where I wanted to work next—but how could I get a transfer? I eventually came up with a plan. I told the manager that although I was very busy, I was thinking about leaving in order to pursue a college course that I had applied for. This information had the desired effect, and within two weeks, the company had offered me a position at Dickins & Jones on Regent Street in London.

When I started my new job, I travelled to London every day until I had saved enough money to find somewhere to live. The commuting was exhausting, but I soon got into the swing of things by reading books and taking catnaps as the train soared towards the capital city.

I found the hairdressing department of Dickins & Jones rather old-fashioned. I felt as if I'd stepped back in time when I crossed its antiquated threshold every morning. If you can imagine a hairdressing adaptation of the television sitcom *Are You Being Served?*, then you have a general idea of the environment in which I found myself. The manager reminded me of the character Captain Peacock; he had a strict, abrupt manner and a slightly haughty attitude. The staff was rigidly informed to watch their p's and q's. If they laughed too loud or raised their voices to high, they were

< 144 >

sharply reprimanded. This proved to be a real problem for some of the more flamboyant members of staff, who floated around the salon like the outrageous Mr. Humphries played in the hysterical sitcom by John Inman. In days gone by but not forgotten, our manicurist had performed as a burlesque dancer at the notorious Windmill Theatre in London's Soho area. This decadent establishment had been owned by the infamous Mrs. Henderson and was the only theatre in central London to have stayed open during the entirety of World War II. Although our lovely manicurist was approaching the autumn of her years, there remained a youthful glow in her cheeks and a twinkling clarity in her eyes. With her bright red hair and large heaving bosom, she reminded me of the character called Mrs. Slocombe played by the wonderful Mollie Sugden. I enjoyed working in this eccentric environment with its interesting mix of jolly characters, even if it did mean I had to change my name. When our clients arrived at the reception area, a cheery but bored voice would flow through a large speaker, requesting our presence.

"Would Mr. John come to the reception, please?" the ubiquitous voice would entreat.

Because I shared the same Christian name with another stylist and didn't have a second name to use, I was informed that to avoid any further confusion I would have to change my name. I'd been called a lot of things in my life, so there was no shortage of name suggestions.

Just before I finally left Leamington Spa, Alex and I went for a last cappuccino in our favourite cafe to discuss the matter.

"Alex, what do you think I should call myself? I just can't decide."

"Well, I love the name Aran, like the Irish islands in Galway Bay."

"Yeah, I like that name, too. Well, that's sorted that out. From now on, I'll be known as Aran."

And so, with bags packed and sandwiches made, plus lashings of ginger beer, "Aran" moved to London town to find fame and fortune.

< 145 >

PART 4

CHAPTER 15

U pon my arrival in London town, I moved into a small bedsit situated on the second floor of a shared house in Clapham North. I can't remember the number of the house on Sandmere Road, but I do remember I was so broke and hungry when I arrived at my new abode; I ate a few raw potatoes which were lying around in the shared kitchen. My new haven of domesticity flaunted a built-in wardrobe, a double bed, and a portable television. A large window faced a quiet street. I also shared a shabby bathroom and a payphone that never seemed to work with my other elusive housemates.

Loneliness was the hardest thing to deal with during my first few months in London, because apart from my work colleagues at Dickins & Jones, I didn't know anybody else in this huge city. My fellow housemates were friendly enough when I saw them, but they were more like casual acquaintances that I'd bump into on the landing rather than close friends that I could trust and confide in. During my solitary hours, I'd think about my adoptive parents, whom I hadn't seen or spoken to for years. Sometimes my thoughts would drift to my natural parents, who had bought me into this world—I wondered what they were like and if they ever thought of me. I missed my old friends in Leamington Spa, and I was always on the phone (when it worked) informing them about the latest

< 149 >

scandal at work or a new movie that I had seen. Alone in my room at night, I'd cry myself to sleep, telling myself that things would get better. Slowly but surely, they did.

When I first moved to London, I'd go to the tube station every morning "full of the joys of spring." I'd chat away to the kiosk vendor as I bought my ticket; honestly, I'd chat away to almost anyone. People regarded my behaviour with suspicion, which I found most peculiar. When I first started taking the tube train to and from work, speeding through the tunnels on those huge electronic snakes, I thought it was very odd that so many people would sit by each other in complete silence, avoiding conversation and eye contact. However, I soon learnt the unspoken rules of tube conduct.

My nearest supermarket was about half a mile away, situated on Long Acre Road in Brixton. Luckily, the launderette was closer. Once a week, I'd drag my bag of dirty washing across the road to the launderette and load it into an industrial-size washing machine. As I waited for my washing, all I could hear was the loud, continuous drone of washing machines as they went through their different cycles. Like the character Dot Cotton from the television sitcom *EastEnders*, I found myself shouting loudly above the din as I requested extra washing tokens.

• • •

It was a glorious sunny day. The warm tropical winds of the Caribbean blew gently through the tall swaying palms, and the clear turquoise waters of Tobago swept to and fro along the white sandy shore. It had taken several hours, and a very experienced location driver, to safely navigate the narrow mud roads that led to the remote beach. As the small fashion crew started to prepare for the swimwear shoot, they were informed that the super-talented

< 150 >

photographer Norman Parkinson had once lived nearby. Aran could completely understand why Mr. Parkinson had been so attracted to this beautiful island; it was home to the oldest protected rainforest in the western hemisphere. For thousands of years, giant turtles had returned here to lay their precious eggs. Their giant prehistoric bodies ploughed through the sand as they carried out their precarious mission. Surrounded by nature's gifts, Aran felt happy and alive as he prepared the model's hair and make-up.

As soon as the action started, he observed the model with the scrutiny of a hungry eagle, searching her gorgeous body for any distasteful spots or bruises as she ran up and down the deserted beach. Satisfied with her hair and make-up, he noted the direction of the wind that blew her long blonde hair and the sunshine that seemed to emphasize the golden tones of her long, athletic limbs. As the photographer endeavoured to capture her movements and expressions with his camera, these fleeting moments of her youth—when she was running free as the wind in paradise—were immortalized forever.

• • •

I slowly started to discover London, making new friends, dancing my nights away in numerous nightclubs, and visiting an array of spectacular art galleries and museums. I joined a gym and flexed my intellectual muscles by reading lots of literature. It wasn't long before I discovered the literary works of Colette, Jean Genet, Marcel Proust, Victor Hugo, Honoré de Balzac, John Steinbeck, Harper Lee, Truman Capote, Robert Graves, and many others. Creatively, I felt like I'd come to a crossroads in my life. Although I loved my hairdressing profession, I felt this career was very limited. After careful consideration, I decided the time had come to resume my

< 151 >

musical ambitions. However, I realized that if I wanted to become a singer, I would have to do one important thing—I'd have to learn how to sing.

I scoured through music press in search of a perfect tutor. Eventually, I made my first appointment for a singing lesson. On the debut of my singing tutorial, I promptly turned up outside a large terraced house that was squeezed between two shops on Wandsworth Road. When I rang the doorbell, I felt nervous and apprehensive, but these feelings subsided when I was greeted by the friendly smile of Denise Black. I told Denise about my consuming aspirations to become a singer. We got on well, and I felt happy and confident with my inspiring tutor. Denise told me she was an actress who loved to sing and enjoyed teaching others to do so; little did she know what vocal trials and tribulations lay ahead. Denise dressed in a kind of Bohemian "hippy-chic style"—a mane of dark hair framed her pretty face, and her wise eyes conveyed a sense of warmth, intelligence, and compassion. As we laughed and joked together in her kitchen, I felt very comfortable in the presence of this very talented and creative woman.

Over the next six months, I diligently practiced my vocal exercises every day, much to the annoyance of my flatmates. "Have you heard that dog howling?" they would tease. Every two weeks, I would turn up for my singing lesson with my lyrics in hand; ready to sing my little heart out. Unfortunately, I was tone deaf and sang almost completely out of tune. Courageous, determined, and enthusiastic, I was convinced that given time my vocal abilities would improve. *Practice makes perfect*, I told myself. Denise smiled and encouraged me as I subjected her to the sound of my truly dreadful voice; Pavarotti I was not. Oddly enough, the sound of my awful voice didn't seem to deter me in the least—*onwards and upwards*, I thought. It wasn't until Denise put me in a performance scenario that I finally got cold feet, because the thought of an audience staring at me on a stage truly terrified me. So, I decided it was time to say goodbye to my musical ambitions, but not to my

< 152 >

wonderful singing teacher Denise, who became a good friend and a loyal client.

During this time, one of my flatmates introduced me to a lady who would help me to heal and accept some of the past traumas in my life. Toni was an Italian masseuse. She had beautiful almond-shaped green eyes and a powerful, toned physique. She swam on a regular basis and took classes in yoga and martial arts. One evening, whilst chatting over a glass of wine, we decided it would be fun to barter our mutual skills.

Over the next three years, I visited Toni at her basement flat in Fulham on a monthly basis. Here, in her immaculately clean home, I played with her cats and received all sorts of healing massage. As Toni worked on my mind, body, and spirit, I started to connect with my deeper inner feelings and emotions. Meanwhile, Toni became a kind of chameleon—I constantly changed the colour and style of her lovely hair. With Toni's wise guidance and healing hands, I improved my life in many ways. Eventually, my career took off to such an extent that I was no longer able to keep our arranged appointments, but I am thankful to her for the time, healing, strength, and wisdom that she gave to me.

One of the first steps that I took towards healing my life was to try and let go of the anger and resentment I harboured towards my adoptive father. I realized that if I could forgive him, or at least come to terms with the abuse that he had inflicted on me as a child, I'd be able to dump some of the emotional baggage that I was carrying around and move on with my life. It had been five years since I had spoken with my parents, so I decided it was time to pick up the phone. To my surprise, they were very happy to hear from me, and I arranged to visit them at their mobile home near Grantham in Lincolnshire.

On the appointed day, I bought my return ticket and boarded the train at King's Cross station. As the train drew nearer to Grantham, my anger and bitterness resurfaced.

"I know what I'll do; I'll get off at the stop before Grantham and leave the bastard waiting there," I thought vengefully, a cruel sense of satisfaction comforting me.

< 153 >

After these feelings subsided, I decided that it was better to confront the demons that haunted me rather than run away from them.

When I got off the train at Grantham station, I walked across the platform bridge to the opposite platform. I searched for my father, but he was nowhere to be seen. My heart sank, but part of me also felt relieved, because this meant that I wouldn't have to face a difficult confrontation. As I made my way towards the exit doors, a stranger approached me with a big smile on his face. When he held out his hand in front of me, I realized that it was my father. I hardly recognize him—he had grown into an old man. After our initial greeting, we walked to the car park and got into his car. Just as he was about to start the engine, he stopped and looked at me.

"Listen, I just want to say that I'm sorry for everything I did to you. I never meant to hurt you or Abi. I was just so angry after your mum died that I took it out on you both. I know that wasn't right."

He paused for a moment before continuing.

"Sometimes, I wake up in the night and I can still hear your screams. I'm so sorry."

He started to cry.

"I've always loved you both. I want you to know that," he said, trying to regain his composure.

At that moment, I felt ashamed of all the bad feelings that I had harboured towards him. As we sat side by side, I looked down on his grey hair, his tweed jacket, and his slip-on shoes, and I felt a deep sense of sadness for this once-proud soldier.

"And I have always loved you. I'm so glad you're my father," I replied, giving him a hug.

From that moment of reconciliation our friendship grew, and on the way to my parents' home, we stopped off at a local pub and had a beer—the first we had ever shared together.

• • •

< 154 >

Lady Zara reminded Aran of a character from an Amedeo Modigliani painting or an old aristocratic photograph by Sir Cecil Beaton. When Aran conjured up her wonderful image in his mind, he thought of Sarah Bernhardt, Edith Sitwell, and Nancy Cunard, and one day, he was inspired to record his musings.

> Divine, witty and bright,
> She could cause a dreadful fright,
> Due to her eccentric behaviour.
> Designer clothes she did wear,
> Styling fashion was her flare,
> A weekend country life she pursued.

> With her dogs she roamed
> Lanes long, green, and winding;
> Glorious fields of England, coloured gold,
> She surveyed.
> Her horses she did ride,
> Taking all in her stride,
> Quince jam and cakes she proudly supplied
> To the ladies of the WI.

> At the races it was said,
> By those fashionably read,
> Her fashion forecast was second to none.
> For the leader of "the ton,"
> High stakes could be won,
> Predicting the course of fashion.

> In cashmere she felt at ease,
> Jimmy Choos—they did please,
> She detested polyester and bri-nylon.
> They caused a rash (ended up in the trash),
> Great joy was gained by their disposal.
> Her eyes gentle and blue—cornflower's hue,
> On fashion she drew for inspiration.

< 155 >

As Lady Zara and Aran casually strolled along the Greek harbour, the afternoon sky was as clear and blue as the sparkling waters that brushed softly against the boats and yachts moored close by. The marine craft appeared bright and white with their sleek contours and billowing white sails. Gabriella, the gorgeous blonde bombshell from Brazil, quickly caught up with the gossiping duo.

"Hi, guys. What's happening?"

"Oh hi, darling. We're just talking fashion. What's in, what's out. You know—the usual," Aran replied.

"Shit, I haven't got a clue. Is it big bags or small bags, flats or heels? Come on, guys, surprise me. What's this season's new take on white?"

Lady Zara took a deep breath and sighed.

"OK, you asked for it…Well, Gabriella, darling, personally I don't think you can beat a good kaftan with some fabulous sunglasses. There's no new 'take' on white—white will always be in vogue during the summer. I mean, darling, it's classic, isn't it. Think Bianca Jagger in her white trouser suit; think white Fiorucci jeans; think Halston; think Diane von Furstenberg wrap-over dresses. Imagine Coco in her white jersey trouser suit embellished with strands of ravishing pearls; imagine Erin in Balenciaga and Giselle in Dior. That's my inspiration this season, sweetie. Having said that, I do love what McQueen and Gucci are doing this season, and Roberto Cavalli's collection is simply gorgeous.

"I've had a marvellous trip, apart from the terrible power cuts, the force nine gales, and an awful bout of the runs. It's the first trip I've been on where I've actually managed to lose weight. Great! You never know, when I get home I might finally be able to squeeze into that new Pucci dress that I bought. Oh, don't you think that was a lovely gesture by the hotel staff today?"

"Oh, you mean the rose thing. Yes, wasn't that sweet of them to leave everyone a red rose on their pillow? Even the assistants got one, you know," Aran sighed romantically.

"Well, I didn't," Gabriella confessed.

< 156 >

"What do you mean? You didn't get a rose? Everybody got a rose," Lady Zara stated emphatically.

Gabriella smiled sweetly and cocked her head to the side. The sun highlighted the girlish freckles around her cute little nose.

"I've been a very bad girl. Well, ten days is a long time."

"What are you talking about?" Lady Zara enquired.

For a moment, Gabriella fell silent, biting her bottom lip.

"Well, it wasn't my fault. It was my little friend. You know, my little vibrating friend, if you know what I mean."

"No, I don't know what you mean. Little friend, little vibrating friend—what on earth are you talking about? Oh no! Oh my God—you don't mean...?"

Gabriella nodded her head.

"Yes, I'm afraid so. Anyway, when I got back to my room that's what was waiting for me on my pillow. There was no red rose for me, honey. Oh no, just my lost vibrator!"

"How could you lose your vibrator?" Aran asked.

"If only I knew," Gabriella replied, raising her eyes and shrugging her shoulders.

Within seconds, the astonished trio were dissolving into fits of laughter.

"Hey, I just had to tell you guys—but please don't tell anybody else."

"I just hope your maid washed her hands!" Lady Zara quipped, and more bouts of hysterical laughter ensued.

< 157 >

CHAPTER 16

A lthough I carried on working at Dickins & Jones, I realized that my position there held no further prospects. I didn't become despondent by this realization, because I knew that this quirky salon with its eclectic mix of eccentric characters had served its purpose. It was time to move on; it was time to look for fresh opportunities.

One day, whilst reading a newspaper, I came across an article about a new hairdressing salon called Daniel Field that specialized in organic and mineral hairdressing. The salon used its own environmentally friendly products, which weren't tested on animals. At the time, this concept was very progressive, and the idea immediately appealed to me. The salon was just around the corner from Dickins & Jones, right in the centre of London's Soho area, so during my lunch break, I decided to take a walk and have a closer inspection. As I passed by the small shop, I peered into its old-fashioned window at the clear plastic bottles full of mineral and organic shampoo and conditioner; their soft contrasting colours and tones were reminiscent of pale stained glass. However, I didn't have the courage to enquire within to see if the salon needed any new members of staff. A few weeks later, after reading another article on the salon, I returned. This time, taking courage in both hands, I braved the busy threshold and asked the receptionist if they had a vacancy

< 159 >

for a hairstylist. Seconds later, I left the shop feeling disappointed, wondering what I was going to do next.

The months passed by, and then by sheer coincidence I stumbled across another article about Daniel Field's hair salon. The article said that Daniel intended to give a talk about his products at a nearby "Boots—the chemist's store," as they were now selling his range of natural products. I decided to go. Looking back, I realize that this very important decision completely changed the course of my career, but at the time, I was just curious to know more about his products and how they worked.

By the time I arrived at the store in Piccadilly, quite a crowd of people had gathered to watch Daniel talk about his products. After his enthusiastic oration, he invited his audience to ask questions. I can't remember exactly what I asked, but it appears that I must have made quite an impression, because Daniel asked me to stay back afterwards. He had a few questions of his own that he wanted to ask.

"How would you like to come and work for me?" he enquired.

I could hardly believe my ears. Delighted by his offer, I immediately accepted. I went back to Dickins & Jones the next morning and handed in my notice. A month later, I walked into the Daniel Field hair salon ready for work.

Daniel Field appeared to possess the faculties of a mad professor and the English charm of the actor Hugh Grant. He galvanized his staff with his bright ideas and his vision of organic hairdressing. With a naughty boy grin, cheeky charm, and bright, intelligent eyes peering through dark-framed glasses, he promoted his new concept of hairdressing. Apart from running his business, he frequently gave press and radio interviews and travelled around the country to different outlets of Boots, giving talks and demonstrations.

The small salon had a cosy "cottage industry" feel that conveyed a relaxed, informal atmosphere; however, due to the recent publicity that Daniel's products had received, it was extremely busy. The salon was located on two separate floors connected by a spiral staircase. I worked downstairs in the windowless basement with my

< 160 >

wonderful assistant, Anita. She came from Bradford and spoke with a broad northern accent. Anita was attractive, popular, and dressed with a lot of style. She also possessed an extroverted personality and a great sense of humour. Her skin was the colour of pale porcelain, and her lips were full and sensual. Anita changed the colour of her cropped hair every week and the colour of her nail polish every day, and with a positive attitude and boundless enthusiasm, she worked hard in pursuing her ambition to become a "super-duper" hair colourist. Upstairs, a hairstylist called Emilia never seemed to stop working. Emilia was so busy that we would shout, "It's like a bloody chipolata factory up there! Any more sausages ready for the production line?" Emilia was tall and pretty; she had long blonde hair, blue eyes, and a sexy, curvaceous physique. Like a *charmeuse de serpent*, she was one of those rare women who possessed a wicked sense of humour combined with an almost hypnotic charisma that captivated those around her. She pulled the most amazing facial expressions I had ever seen; sometimes I just couldn't take my eyes off her.

As more and more interviews and articles appeared about Daniel's organic products, the salon became so busy that we could hardly cope. I learnt to work quickly but professionally, and on the rare occasions that I did get a break, I would take a walk along Berwick Street Market, listening to the barrow boys shouting, "Five peaches for a pound!" as I made my way to the nearby coffee shops. It wasn't long before celebrities, fashion and beauty editors, and members of the press wanted to try out Daniel's organic products for themselves.

The first celebrity barnet that I had the pleasure to tint belonged to a singer called Yazz; she'd recently had a number one hit single with a dance track called "The Only Way Is Up." Once a month, I would lighten her short blonde hair using Daniel's hair lightener. Yazz was beautiful, talented, and fun, and occasionally we would go out to the trendy bars and private clubs in Soho.

I began to make quite a name for myself as a hair colourist. I was even voted "Colourist of the Year" in the beauty section of one

< 161 >

leading newspaper. Other beauty editors started to ring me up to enquire about any forthcoming trends in hair colour; they quoted my predictions in their glossy magazines. I felt as if I was beginning to make progress with my career.

Nadine Baggott is a super-talented beauty editor who always has her ear to the ground when it comes to new technology in the hair and make-up industry. Her scientific knowledge baffled me—she was a walking, talking beauty encyclopaedia. Daniel usually coloured Nadine's hair, but one day he became so overwhelmed with his other engagements that he asked me to stand in.

Summer was in full bloom when this wonderful opportunity arose, so I decided to highlight Nadine's naturally blonde hair in shades of cream, light caramel, and warm-honey blonde. When I had finished drying her hair, I nervously waited for her reaction. Luckily for me, she loved her new sun-kissed hair colour. Nadine was gorgeous—she was tall, slender, and super-fit and her flawless, healthy complexion positively glowed. Nadine possessed a warm and friendly personality, and her wonderful sense of humour was infectious. After I had enhanced Nadine's hair colour on several more occasions, she asked if I would like to do a photographic shoot for the beauty section of *Living* magazine with a photographer called David Woolley. I asked Daniel for his permission, and he happily agreed to Nadine's suggestion.

Having never been on a shoot before, I felt terribly nervous when the day arrived. I wasn't quite sure what I was meant to do and how it all worked, although I tried my best to look as if I did know. Nadine and David were very patient, and with their expert guidance everything went smoothly. By the end of the day, everyone was happy and the photographs looked fantastic. That evening, as I sat in my bedsit in Clapham, I thought about my first "break" into the world of beauty photography. I was amazed by the minute attention to detail that had been required and how difficult and time consuming the job had been. I realized that a simple hairstyle that appeared on the page of a magazine could, in reality, be very difficult to achieve.

< 162 >

The next publication that I worked for was called *Clothes Show* magazine; I worked with photographer Ian Philpott. The brief that I was given was quite challenging. I was asked if I could create two contrasting hairstyles on one head of hair. One side of the hairstyle was to be soft and natural, and the other hard and structured, as the article that was to accompany the photograph was about the benefits of organic products as opposed to chemical ones. The hairstyle was a crucial part of the story, and it was important that I got it right. Undaunted, I rose to the challenge, and after many stressful hours I finished my creation—as much to my own surprise as everybody else's. I learnt a lot on this shoot, and slowly I realized that there was much more to "session hairstyling" than I had previously assumed. It was one thing to be able to create a desired "look"; a totally different set of skills was required to cope with the pressure and responsibility of the job.

I started to work with Nadine on a fairly regular basis, and I soon became aware that every shoot presents its own set of challenges. If I wasn't sure how these difficulties could be resolved or how I could achieve a desired effect, I would ask Nadine to make suggestions. With Nadine's expertise and direction, I started to learn the importance of balance, proportion, and product. I also started to acquire a collection of quality make-up items—Dior lipsticks, Yves Saint Laurent eyeshadows, Chanel face powders, Clinique lip pencils, and so forth—all kind presents from Nadine's huge make-up reservoir.

"Take this make-up, Aran; it might come in handy. You never know—you might want to learn how to do hair and make-up one day, and then you'll be able to go on fashion trips," Nadine suggested.

This idea had never occurred to me, but I took her advice and carefully wrapped up these expensive make-up items and stored them away.

One of the biggest things that I learnt at this time is that the human eye doesn't necessarily view things in the same way as the camera. Images that look perfectly OK to the naked eye don't always "work" on film. I started to train myself to see things in

< 163 >

the same way as the camera lens; I started to understand the eye of the camera. My next big test materialized in the form of a photographer called Ursula Steiger. She was the ultimate perfectionist when it came to beauty photography, and her images were simply flawless and beautiful. Dedicated to her art, she would take hours getting her lighting absolutely right, and she expected the same limitless patience and devotion from her chosen team. There was nothing Ursula wouldn't try if she thought it would make an image better, and she always came up with original and exciting ideas. Ursula taught me not to be just content with creative ideas, but to push and explore them to their limits.

As my experience and understanding of beauty photography increased, so did my self-confidence; so, when Nadine asked me to work on the cover of *Living* magazine, I felt absolutely thrilled. It was a challenge that I had been looking forward to. On the big day, we did several "cover tries" until Nadine felt sure that we had captured the perfect picture. As I walked out of the photographic studio I felt ecstatic, and I found myself counting the days and weeks until the magazine was published. It seemed like forever, and then bang, the cover of the magazine was everywhere—in major supermarkets, newsagents, and major retail stores. For the first time in my life, as I gazed with wonder at my first magazine cover, I felt as if I had really achieved something. I remember the immense pleasure and pride that I felt when I went into shops and supermarkets to buy copies, trying to increase the sales of the magazine in my own little way. I rang my mother and told her the good news. She told all of her friends, and they all went on a *Living* magazine shopping frenzy, buying as many copies of the magazine as they possibly could.

Many years later, when I had become more established within the fashion and beauty industry, Nadine and I bumped into each other. We laughed and reminisced about the old times.

"You know, Aran, at the beginning I knew you didn't have a clue what you were doing, but you did make the most wonderful cup of tea," Nadine joked.

< 164 >

I decided to pursue my growing ambition to become a session hairstylist within the fashion industry, and I compiled a small portfolio of all the "tear sheets" (full page, published photographs) that I had acquired. Although I was happy with the results of my photographic labours, I realized there was room for some serious improvement, so on my days off from work at the hair salon, I would work on as many "tests" as I possibly could. Most models, photographers, make-up artists, fashion stylists, and session hairstylists have worked on a test at some point in their careers. A test is composed of a group of the said individuals, who conspire to create a photographic session that is generally not commissioned and is unpaid. However, what the participants hopefully do receive are fantastic photographs that enable them to show their versatility and creativity, making their book (also called a "portfolio") stronger. It was during one of these tests that I was introduced to a make-up artist called Jasmine.

Jasmine was one of those rare, unique individuals who walks into your life and changes everything. She looked like beautiful Egyptian queen: dark, mysterious, and exotic. Having worked as a model for the Gavin Robinson Agency in the 1970s, Jasmine had done very well, but in those pre-supermodel times, the models didn't make the kind of money that they do today. After a very successful career as a model, she had decided to work on the other side of the camera as a make-up artist. Jasmine was always a lot of fun to work with—her sexy, earthy laughter and her naughty sense of humour always bought a smile to my face. Her appeal lay not just in the way she looked, but also in her dynamic personality and her deep understanding of life. As our friendship grew, we spent more time together—which was a little strange at first. It seemed that wherever I went with Jasmine, people would stare in our direction, "walking out" with Jasmine was like going out with a movie star. People would come up to her in the street and ask for her autograph, mistaking her for the stunning supermodel called Iman, David Bowie's wife. I soon found out that her astonishing beauty could also cause some very strange reactions, because

< 165 >

sometimes other women could be very rude or bitchy towards her for no apparent reason. "Don't worry, you'll get used to it," Jasmine assured me—and after a short while, I did. On a few occasions, I tried to persuade Jasmine to go back into modelling, but Jasmine wasn't interested.

"What are you doing working as a make-up artist?" I asked. "If you went back into modelling, you'd make a fortune."

"Oh, Aran, I know what you're saying, but I became so sick and tired of walking up and down catwalks and standing in front of cameras. I'm so much happier working behind them now."

It seems that I wasn't the only person who thought that Jasmine should resume her modelling career. Whilst visiting a friend at a music-recording studio, Jasmine bumped into the gorgeous super-model Kate Moss with the actor Johnny Depp. Kate asked her if she was a model. "Not anymore," Jasmine replied firmly. And so it was that my request for Jasmine to return back to her previous career fell on closed ears. I did, however, manage to persuade her to model for a beauty shot for my book. The photograph is stunning and is one of my favourite pictures—very Yves Saint Laurent.

Jasmine seemed to have a very busy social life. I'd go to her home, listen to music, and watch with fascination as she skilfully applied her make-up whilst getting ready to go out. I would ask her questions: *Why did you do this? Why did you apply that?* I'd sit and watch her apply a foundation that I thought couldn't possibly work, and moments later, once she had applied and blended the right facial powders, her skin looked perfect. Jasmine taught me which "bases" (foundations) work best on darker skin tones, and even more importantly, she taught me which base tones to avoid. She showed me how to shade and highlight a face and how to apply lip liner and lipstick in a softer, more subtle way. Jasmine was my make-up mentor, and she taught me everything that I know about applying make-up on darker skin tones. This knowledge was to prove invaluable later on in my career.

With her wonderful sense of fun, stunning looks, and fabulous personality, it was hardly surprising that Jasmine was a very popular

< 166 >

lady. Before long, she introduced me to her trusted circle of friends: vocalists, musicians, photographers, artists, and writers. One of the first celebrities that Jasmine introduced me to was the singer Mica Paris. We met whilst Jasmine and I were both working on a gospel show at the Brixton Academy. I liked Mica immediately. Talented, pretty, and extremely amusing, she had a very down-to-earth personality. As we chatted away in her dressing room, I felt as if I had known her for years; in actual fact, we had only just met. Jasmine recommended me to another incredibly warm and talented singer, Jocelyn Brown, who was appearing in the same gospel show. When I met Jocelyn, she seemed to be so full of love that all I wanted to do was hug her. It was a real honour and pleasure to work with such a lovely human being. Jasmine also introduced me to the incredibly talented singer called Carleen Anderson. Although all three of us had met privately on several occasions, I had never actually heard Carleen sing live, so one evening Jasmine invited me to go and see her perform at the Jazz Cafe in Camden, London. When Carleen stepped onto the stage and began singing, the hairs on my arms stood on end. Her incredibly powerful and sensitive voice exploded around the venue. It was a truly amazing performance that I will never forget. Carleen's beautiful, haunting album, *True Spirit*, will always be one of my favourites.

One early Saturday evening, I was sitting at home watching my usual round of quiz and chat shows on television when I received a phone call. It was Jasmine.

"Come on, get your butt over here. We're going out."

"Great. Where are we going?"

"Don't you worry about that—it's a surprise."

A few hours later, I arrived at Jasmine's home. Intrigued as to where we were about to go, I watched her closely as she put the finishing touches to her make-up. I could see that she was smiling to herself—happy with her little plan—although she refused to give me any clues to the nature of our nocturnal excursion. We got in a cab and headed towards London's West End. When we arrived at Stringfellows nightclub, masses of photographers were waiting

< 167 >

outside. *What was going on?* The suspense was killing me. Once we had passed through the wall of security guards, we made our way towards what seemed like a private party. We were greeted by the sound of champagne corks popping all around us. Famous faces were everywhere.

"Follow me. I've got somebody I want you to meet," Jasmine commanded.

Seconds later, standing in front of us was a bright, bright smile that I immediately recognized.

"Aran, I'd like to introduce you to Chaka."

"Happy birthday, sweetheart," Jasmine expounded. The pair warmly embraced.

Okay, everything was beginning to make sense. It was Chaka Khan's birthday party, and Jasmine had invited me. I was just a little bit nervous meeting this singing legend for the first time, as you can imagine, but Chaka made me feel welcome at her unforgettable birthday celebration.

Jasmine and I had a great time, and before we left, she introduced me to the very talented singer and musician called Prince. Charming and handsome, Prince had impeccable manners and a wonderful sense of style and taste. He looked like an elegant dandy from the eighteenth century; the word "slave" was emblazoned across his beautiful face.

When the clock struck three, we fled the glamorous "ball" in pursuit of our phantom pumpkins, like two Cinderellas immersed in a state of bliss.

Jasmine and I would often go to Riverside Studios in Hammersmith to watch relatively unknown European films. We both loved films by the Spanish director Pedro Almodóvar, starring Rossy de Palma, Julieta Serrano, Cecilia Roth, Penélope Cruz, Antonio Banderas, and many other actors. We would sit and watch his early films—with their wonderful sense of irony and humour—over and over again. His films made us laugh so much we could barely control ourselves. In fact, on one memorable occasion, I

< 168 >

laughed so much during one of his films that I had to run for the toilet.

It's funny how life works out sometimes. Many years later, I met Antonio Banderas in San Remo, Italy. By this time he had become a famous Hollywood movie star. As I walked away after meeting him, I started to reminisce about the happy times that Jasmine and I had spent at Riverside Studios. It was a time when we both looked at the big screen and watched this relatively unknown actor entertain us—a time when meeting Antonio had just been a dream, for one of his biggest fans.

< 169 >

CHAPTER 17

I continued to work hard at the Daniel Field hair salon. One busy Saturday afternoon, Emilia bravely ventured down into the dark depths of the salon's basement and asked me if I would like to go out for a drink with her "new best friend" called Jake. Apparently, Jake had eyes like shattered blue glass and a body like Arnold Schwarzenegger. It didn't take too much persuasion before I enthusiastically agreed to her request.

Later that evening, we met up at a very smart bar in Chelsea, London. Jake was a handsome fellow with a sociable disposition—his captivating wit and humorous tales stoked the fire of his magnetic charisma. Over the noise of the loud music in the crowded bar, we laughed and joked amongst ourselves as men and women admired Jake's muscular physique.

Every now and then, Jake would drop by the salon to see Emilia, and occasionally, he would venture downstairs for a chat. One memorable day, as we gossiped away in the staff room, he suddenly decided to pull down his trousers so that he could show us his muscular legs. Anita nearly choked on the sandwich she was eating. Jake smiled mischievously. Wide-eyed, Anita looked at me and naughtily suggested that maybe Jake had another big muscle that he wasn't showing us. Jake assured us that "he'd got what it took," and he informed us that he'd rather like to become a porn

< 171 >

star one day. Everybody fell about laughing. Jake did have the most wonderful sense of humour.

Many moons later, I was working in Miami on a fashion shoot. It was a very hot afternoon, and the crew that I was working with decided to take a break. I found myself quietly sitting outside a cafe on Lincoln Road, watching the world and a few dodgy-looking poodles as they passed by. My observations were temporarily interrupted when a man came up to me and gave me a flyer advertising a play. The theatre production was about the porn industry, and when I looked at the flyer, I immediately recognized the leading star. Sprawled across the flyer, wearing very little but a cheeky smile, was a muscular stud called Big Snake, aka Jake. I couldn't quite believe my eyes—here was Jake playing the role of a porn star on stage in Miami—it seemed that his wish had been granted. I couldn't stop laughing. I remembered Anita's face when he had dropped his trousers all those years ago; thank God she hadn't choked on her sandwich.

Another person whose wishes seemed to be coming true was Denise Black. I received an urgent phone call from her at the salon.

"Oh, Aran, I know you're busy working in the salon, but you've got to help me. I've just been given a role in the television drama *Coronation Street*, and they want me to play the role of a hairstylist. I don't suppose you could train me up? You know, show me some basic things, like how to hold a pair of scissors and a comb properly and how to really blow-dry someone's hair. Oh, and could you sort my hair out and come up with a style that would be suitable for my character? I've got a few ideas, but I'll tell you more about them when I see you."

Over the next few months, I thoroughly enjoyed myself while transforming Denise. I tinted her hair dark auburn and added some very blonde highlights, making it a little "brassy" like her character. Always up for a new challenge, I found it very interesting to work with Denise and watch her character evolve. Together, we perfected a versatile hairstyle for her character, and with a little practice, Denise emerged looking like an authentic hairstylist.

< 172 >

During another busy day at the salon, I received an intriguing phone call from a stranger.

"Hi, Aran, my name's Sofia King, I'm a make-up artist at the Randy Oakley Agency. I hope you don't mind me calling, but I've seen some of your work in magazines, and I was wondering if you could possibly show me some basic hairdressing skills. Of course, I'm willing to pay you."

I immediately remembered the conversation I'd had with Nadine, when she'd suggested that it might be a good idea to become a make-up artist. I thought of the exciting possibilities that could potentially arise by expanding my skills. As these thoughts went through my head, I remembered the words that a handsome prince had once told me—"always make the most of the opportunities that life presents to you." As I replied, the idea of going on a fashion trip to some exotic location fuelled my enthusiasm.

"Of course, I'd be more than happy to help you, but I don't want to be paid. I'd rather exchange our skills. Would you be interested in giving me some make-up lessons?"

"That sounds great to me. When can we start?" Sofia replied.

Over the next couple of months, we would meet at the salon for our mutual lessons, using the junior members of staff as our models. I will always remember the first make-up lesson that I received from Sofia.

"Always start at the top of the face and carefully work down; that way, you won't disturb any of the make-up that you've applied. Always brush the eyebrows up and away, and always curl the eyelashes to 'open' the eyes and make them appear more alert and awake."

When Sofia told me the golden rules of preparing a face before applying make-up, it reminded me of an artist preparing a canvas before they apply paint. Of course, hygiene is of paramount importance, and all brushes and implements, including your hands, should be thoroughly cleansed before and after application. It is crucial to keep your brushes clean at all times. You can never clean them too often.

< 173 >

After I had been put through my paces and Sofia was absolutely sure that I knew what I was doing, I was given my first task. Sofia applied eyeshadows in varying shades and tones on one eye, creating a stunning, sexy, smouldering effect. She then asked me to replicate the look on the other naked eye. It took time and patience, but by the time I had finished my first make-up lesson, I realized that I wanted to become a professional make-up artist. Sofia was delighted with my efforts and gave me lots of encouragement. I had always been searching for a new creative medium in which to work, and here, almost by accident, I had discovered it. One piece of good luck followed another.

One of my regular clients who frequented the salon happened to be a make-up artist. When I told Cindy about my about my fledgling aspirations, she asked me if I would like any of her spare make-up, because she was about to return home to Canada. *Is the sun hot and yellow?* I thought, and I accepted her kind offer. Three weeks later, I received an assortment of make-up, moisturizers, and brushes. Slowly, I started to select and buy my own pieces of make-up, and with Nadine's and Cindy's contributions, I built up my own little make-up reservoir. Stocked up, I was eager and raring to go.

When Sofia told me she'd been commissioned to work on a movie, she sounded quite sad. This wonderful opportunity would entail travelling to different locations around the world over a long period of time. I wished her luck on her new venture, and tried hard to conceal my disappointment as we said goodbye. It seemed our amusing lessons together had come to an end; however, a creative passion burned within me, and I decided that nothing was going to stop me from pursing my ambition to become a professional make-up artist.

My first hair and make-up client was the very talented Denise Black. Her successful role in *Coronation Street* seemed to go from strength to strength; her character became hugely popular. Due to this success, I found myself in demand. Denise asked me to do her hair and make-up on countless shoots for magazines and newspapers.

< 174 >

I saw this as an ideal opportunity to practice my make-up skills, and eventually, I recommended a very accomplished hairstylist to Denise called David Wallis, which enabled me to concentrate on perfecting Denise's make-up. David was a genius when it came to dressing hair and applying wigs and hairpieces, and between us, we hatched our creative plans for Denise. With a little help from my stripper friend Rita, I had recently learnt the art of applying false eyelashes—Denise was in for a surprise!

My confidence slowly grew with each shoot that we shared together. We were like a little team. With great patience, Denise would sit for hours as we transformed her into our creative vision. We constantly came up with new ideas so that we could reinvent her "look" on every shoot that we did. David and I would model the clothes and shoes provided by the stylists (What did we look like?), discussing their strong and weak points, until Denise decided what she wanted to wear. Camp, fun, glamorous, and outrageous, life was never dull or boring working with Denise. Like a ray of sunshine, she brightened up our day. These fun-packed shoots were some of the happiest of my career.

After months of hard work, I decided it was time to take a small break from the Daniel Field hair salon, so I booked myself into a bed and breakfast in Scotland for a long weekend away. Well, it wasn't quite a bed and breakfast. The Tibetan Buddhist monastery where I intended to stay was called Kagyu Samye Ling. It was situated in the wild countryside of Eskdalemuir, not far from Langholm, Dumfriesshire.

As my taxi pulled up outside the large country house, I wasn't sure what to expect. Bags in hand, I cautiously made my way towards the reception area. To my relief, the house appeared to be light, bright, crowded, and very friendly. I was warmly greeted and shown to a small simple room with a single bed.

Downstairs in the busy dining area, Tibetan monks and nuns mingled with their guests as they ate their dishes of hot, organic food. I immediately felt comfortable in my new surroundings, and it wasn't long before a monk dressed in robes of dark red gave me

< 175 >

a list of activities that were available during my stay. His head was shaved and his nature seemed kind and tranquil. He offered to show me the Buddhist temple and its grounds.

Walking out of the main entrance of the house into the cold country air, I could see the huge temple with its colourful flags waving in the distance. The building complimented the rugged landscape surrounding it, and for a moment, I felt transported to Tibet. Upon entering the temple, I was greeted by the smell of burning incense and the sounds of a few monks and nuns quietly chanting whilst lost in their prayers and meditation. A huge statue of Buddha sitting in the lotus position dominated the temple; his golden image was imposing yet serene.

Over the next few days, I practiced meditation techniques and learnt the basic principles of Tibetan Buddhism—its central motivating force being compassion. I took long walks in the sprawling countryside, following streams of soft waters whilst ambling amongst the wild poppies, garlic, heather, and foxglove.

I returned to Samye Ling many times over the next six months to practice meditation and discover the inner peace that lies within us all. One day, a nun approached me.

"There is someone who would like to meet you. You are very honoured. Follow me."

As I entered the small room, I was greeted by an elderly Buddhist monk who supervised the monastery. He smiled and wrapped a white scarf around my neck and blessed me.

"Remember—always be mindful, little one," he told me. I felt his wise eyes following me as I walked towards the door, and then closed it behind me.

Later, as I sat alone in my room, my mind was in turmoil. Should I stay here and become a monk, reject materialism, and concentrate on my inner spiritual journey during this lifetime, or follow the path that I felt drawn to in London? What was the purpose of my life during this incarnation? Only I could decide. I meditated over the next few days and finally came to a decision. I caught the train home.

< 176 >

On my return to London, I decided I needed a change of environment. I moved into a high-rise block of council flats in Battersea with a fellow hairstylist named Hannah, who was studying to become an acupuncturist. The only nice thing about the flat was the amazing views of London; I realized pretty quickly that I had made a hasty mistake. What is that old saying? "You don't really know someone until you have lived with them." Well, that seems like a pretty accurate description of what happened. I soon discovered that I disliked Hannah once I really got to know her. Luckily for me, another friend of mine, Leslie, was looking for a flatmate. I packed my bags and moved into a smart apartment block called "The Circle" on Queen Elizabeth Street, not far from Tower Bridge. Leslie was a great flatmate. Between us, we kept the apartment clean and had a lot of fun entertaining guests at our parties; however, we also respected each other's need for a little privacy now and again. I felt relieved after my drama in Battersea. After a year, Leslie and I moved across the river to Wapping, where we shared an apartment near St. Katharine Docks. After six months I decided to visit the Tower of London which lay nearby, I found myself following the endless trail of tourists as they walked around this historical site. During the tour, I learnt of the tower's dark, bloody history, and I watched hungry black ravens fly through the skies and settle on its grey fortifications. The Tower of London must have been a terrifying place, if you were imprisoned within its doomed walls.

Business was booming at Daniel Field's hair salon, and it became obvious that sooner or later, we would have to move to much larger premises. It wasn't long before the salon relocated to nearby Broadwick Street in Soho.

White and spacious, the new high-tech salon had a modern, New Age ambience with its slick chrome hairdressing units and large sparkling mirrors. I felt the new salon lacked the atmosphere and intimacy of the previous salon, but luckily for me, my loyal clientele didn't agree and they continued to make appointments.

< 177 >

I will never forget the first time that I saw Gina. When she entered the salon and walked towards the reception desk, everything seemed to stop for a moment, as if time—like the clients watching her—held its breath. I guess some men would call Gina a "sexy babe"—her statuesque figure was tanned and dynamic, she had a body like Miss Jayne Mansfield. At five feet ten, her long platinum-blonde hair fell past her shoulders and trailed down her slender back, hiding the delicate white strap of the Gucci halter-neck blouse that framed her long graceful neck. Gina's hands were long and smooth; her French manicure was polished to perfection. As she took off her black Chanel sunglasses, diamonds of a substantial size and quality played prettily upon her fingers. A gold Rolex watch lay upon her wrist and a pair of matching Cartier bracelets tinkled softy. The straps of her Jimmy Choo stilettos seemed to wrap themselves around her ankles and trail up her super-long legs. Her firm breasts were like torpedoes that had been kissed by the sun in Saint-Tropez; they swayed gently in time as she walked. Gina belonged to that special group of women who are "once seen, but never forgotten." With curves in all the right places, she had that va-va-voom quality and allure.

When Gina came to see me for the first time, her hair had quite a lot of breakage; it had been very damaged and over processed. Luckily, Gina had very strong hair. Over a period of about a year, I restored her hair to its former blonde glory. A perfectionist by nature, Gina insisted on having her "regrowth" retouched every week. I always used a special tint brush, which I shaped and cut down. This way I could carefully lighten her regrowth whilst avoiding getting any bleach on her fragile hair. Week by week, with a lot of care and the right hair treatments and conditioners, her hair started to recover.

I looked forward to my weekly rendezvous with this glamorous, entertaining woman. We would always have a good laugh and a gossip—although I never heard her say anything derogatory about other people. Gina was kind, sensitive, and generous, and she certainly wasn't a "dumb blonde," as some rather jealous girls

< 178 >

suggested. In fact, Gina was extremely intelligent and ran her own successful business.

I will never forget the day that I heard the devastating news: Gina had been killed in a car accident. When I thought of my dear friend and the happy times we had shared together, my heart overflowed with sorrow. A very special person had left this world, to fly free with the angels in the next.

• • •

The beautiful woman sitting in the back of the yellow cab certainly seemed to have an effect on the driver. Looking into his rear-view mirror, he watched her as she looked into her handbag. Her long dark hair, smooth legs, and full, luscious lips excited him.

Seconds later, she removed her powder compact from her handbag and looked in the mirror. She then proceeded to shave her face with an electric shaver. Aran laughed at the astonished expression on the driver's face when he realized the gorgeous woman was really a man.

"And so if you're looking for a really close shave, use..." The commercial ended.

A couple of weeks later, Aran received a phone call from his booker.

"Hey, Aran, we've got a really interesting job for you. Alde is here from New York."

"Who?"

"You know, the guy from the shaving commercial that everyone is talking about. He's here in London doing some promotion. Are you around on Thursday to do a fashion shoot with him?"

"Yeah, sure. It sounds like fun."

< 179 >

Upon his arrival at the photographic studio, Aran was intro-duced to Alde.

"Hi, you must be Alde. My name's Aran. I'm here to do your hair and make-up. How are you? How long are you in town for?"

"Oh, just a few weeks, but my booker says I might have to stay a bit longer."

"Would you like tea, coffee, or some water?"

"Some water would be great."

Ten minutes later, Aran found himself scrutinizing Alde's extraordinary face. He threw some large rollers in his hair, applied a hairnet, and tried to decide what look he wanted to achieve with his make-up.

Aran didn't apply much base. He didn't have to—Alde's skin was clear and flawless. After he had highlighted Alde's beautifully sculpted face with some natural contour powders, he accentuated the colour of his lovely brown eyes with a shimmering bronze eye-shadow and defined them with black mascara and a few strokes of liquid eyeliner. He then applied a dark claret lip stain and a little lip gloss to his beautifully shaped mouth and removed the rollers from his hair. The pair laughed and joked together until Alde's hair and make-up was finally finished and he was ready to change into his first outfit. Once Alde was dressed in his navy-blue Christian Dior trouser suit and his Christian Louboutin heels, the small crew collected their equipment and walked out of the studio to their first location nearby.

Alde looked stunning. The soft curls of his long dark hair blew softly from under his black beret, his manner was relaxed, and he walked down the street with an aura of Parisian chic. He was greeted by the occasional wolf whistle as men drove past in their cars, and pedestrians looked in astonishment as this truly gorgeous model passed by.

Once the shoot started, Alde became animated. He knew the score in his Christian Dior, and he "worked" his modelling poses like a true professional. After the first shot of the day was com-pleted, the team started to pack their equipment away. It was all

< 180 >

too much for some the workers on the building site nearby; as soon as they realized the fashion crew were leaving the location, they gathered together and gave them a round of applause. "Give us ya phone number, sweetheart!" they cried, waving and smiling happily at Alde. Playfully, Alde winked in the direction of the fashion crew and smiled back at his adoring fans.

If only they knew, Aran thought, packing his Louis Vuitton make-up bag away.

• • •

Life at Daniel Field continued as normal, until one busy day, like Vesuvius, I suddenly erupted. The pressure of constantly being fully booked had finally taken its toll. Disillusioned with "organic" hairdressing, I had come to realize that not everything organic is good for you—deadly nightshade and some varieties of mushrooms can be extremely toxic, even fatal in some cases. So I said goodbye to Daniel, and I told him where to put his organic seaweed conditioner. I behaved in quite an irresponsible manner, but at the time, I didn't care. Later, when I got home, I started to have second thoughts about my irrational decision to leave, but it was too late. What was done was done, and I would just have to live with the consequences of my actions. With no clients and no job, my future didn't look so bright.

In desperation, I quickly bought a copy of the *Hairdresser's Journal* and scouted through its employment pages looking for work. There was only one advert that appealed to me: "Experienced hairstylist required for an established salon in Kensington—hair colouring skills a must. Please contact Annie at the Annie Russell hair salon, One Kensington Church Walk, Kensington, London." I quickly picked up the phone.

< 181 >

PART 5

CHAPTER 18

As I approached Kensington Church walk from the busy high street, I felt like I'd been transported to the English countryside. The noise of the traffic melted away, overthrown by the insistent chatter of excited birds and the soft murmur of summer's busy bees. Golden sunlight played with the languid trees, casting shadows on the worn paving slabs beneath my feet, and buttercups grew cheerfully around the gravestones of the dead near an imposing Victorian church called St. Mary Abbots. The intoxicating scent of roses lingered in the air as I passed by their fragrant garden, and as I followed the pathway, I approached a narrow walk leading upwards. Upon the left-hand side, a row of small shops stretched along the entire length of the walk; on the right, a line of huge trees provided shade for people sitting and chatting on the long wall.

The salon stood in the middle of the walk. Its smart, elegant facade was freshly painted in tones of the palest pastel green. Time had been kind to the handsome building; it still retained its original features. I peered through the large bay windows. The stylish, unpretentious interior evoked a casual country charm, which immediately put me at ease. A slim, elegant lady approached me when I entered the friendly premises. "Hi, I'm Annie. Do take a seat. I'll be with you in a few minutes," she told me. A few minutes

< 185 >

passed, and then I followed Annie up a creaky wooden staircase leading to her office.

Annie was an attractive lady with lovely grey-blue eyes and shoulder-length blonde hair. She spoke "Queen's English" and had a wise, intelligent mind. I had never encountered anyone quite like her. Annie appeared every bit the eccentric Englishwoman, yet she was totally unaware of it. I sat amazed, my mouth slightly open, as she gestured with her hands and asked me questions. Her voice moved, was propelled, from one syllable to the next at varying levels of speed. As I smiled and accepted a cup of tea, I thought, *Gordon Bennett, I'm gonna need a translator to work here.* After our little chat, to my surprise, Annie shook my hand and asked me when I could start work.

I walked towards the tube station feeling a little bemused; I think it was delayed shock. A week later, with a smile on my face and trepidation in my heart, I entered a new salon and a very different kind of world.

Surrounded by hairdressers and clients who seemed to converse in a totally different English language, I wondered if I would ever get used to my new work environment. All sorts of aristocrats sat in the chair before me, and although I felt a little intimidated by the social status of these strange unknown people, I tried my best to converse with them. I peppered my timid dialogue with nods of approval and made small talk about the holidays and the weather. I soon realised that in order to succeed in my new job I would have to overcome my anxious disposition. However, although I felt insecure, I also felt a strange sense of excitement in discovering these fascinating characters. And it wasn't long before I found myself saying *barth* instead of *bath* and *larf* instead of *laff*. It seemed that this new language was contagious.

Despite my inner turmoil, I learnt how to style hair in a completely different manner. I backcombed and teased my clients' hair into huge bouffant helmets, spraying their hairstyles so stiff with hairspray that they could have withstood any test in a wind tunnel. I learnt how "dress" and attach diamond tiaras (family heirlooms)

< 186 >

in a traditional manner, and I attached hairpieces, hats, and feathers for Ascot. In my tiny new flat in the East End of London, their world still seemed a million miles away.

. . .

Sipping the contents of his hot cappuccino, Aran felt relaxed as he sat in the chic lobby of the Four Seasons Hotel—his favourite place to stay in Milan. A proud father, impeccably dressed, walked by with his beautiful daughter, and people clapped and showered compliments on the beautiful bride-to-be.

Standing by the hotel entrance, winter's waiting bride looked composed as she watched the snow gently fall outside. The empire line of her white satin wedding dress and her dark coiffure reminded Aran of a young Audrey Hepburn. Her gown was trimmed with faux white fur around her delicate shoulders; it fitted her perfectly, as did her full-length white gloves. Large cream pearls adorned her long, elegant neck and a simple veil fell down the curve of her back. Having relinquished her bouquet to her father, she carefully adjusted the train of her dress. She carried on adjusting and dusting her beautiful gown until she felt satisfied that any trace of imaginary dust had disappeared. Content with her appearance, she retrieved her exquisite bouquet of white roses and patiently waited with her father for their car to arrive. Every silent second that they shared together seemed like a lifetime.

As Aran finished his coffee, he also watched the snow slowly fall outside. Like the snow, his thoughts drifted as he wondered about the future of the beautiful bride-to-be.

. . .

< 187 >

Flat 2, 5 St. Mark Street, Aldgate East, was the first domicile that I could call my own in London. I revelled in my newfound freedom by walking around my new abode completely naked, enjoying the privacy. Having established that I could do what I wanted when I wanted, I invited friends to stay and left the washing up until I felt like doing it. Although I loved my little home, I did have certain reservations about my bathroom—I wasn't so sure about the 1970s avocado-green bathroom suite and the brown stripy tiles. My shoddy kitchen looked like a domestic relic from the 1960s, and even when I accessorized it with a stylish 1960s retro-lampshade, it didn't seem to give the room the satirical ambience that I had hoped for. However, I wasn't going to let a green bathroom and a tired kitchen get me down. I was blissfully happy and going through my impressionist phase, so I covered my walls with reproduction pictures and postcards of paintings by Pizarro, Degas, Monet, Manet, Gauguin, Van Gogh, Cezanne, and Renoir. I secured my newfound happiness by having a metal security gate put in front of my flimsy entrance door, and I installed a very cheap alarm system and stuck its warning stickers on my windows. I also made friends with some of the residents who lived close by, such as "Pink Annie," who just adored the colour pink.

Pink Annie, who lived downstairs, decided to order her next Saturday Night Fever outfit from a catalogue. Being a plus-sized lady, there were only a few shops and retailers that she could buy from. A few weeks later, Annie excitedly rang me.

"Quick, quick! Come downstairs—my new outfit is here," Annie squealed with delight. I rushed downstairs, and Pink Annie rushed into the bedroom to get changed.

"I'm not telling you what I've bought. You'll just have to wait and see," Annie commented mischievously as she poked her head out from behind the bedroom door.

I waited with bated breath. We were going out this weekend, and Annie had set her heart on wearing her new outfit; it had arrived just in time. I waited and waited; I made a cup of tea, then waited some more.

< 188 >

There must be something wrong, I concluded, softly knocking on the bedroom door.

"*Are you all right in there?*"

"*Don't worry. I'll be out in a minute.*"

Several minutes later, the bedroom door slowly opened and Annie stepped forward.

"*I look like a bag of spuds in this! It didn't look like this in the catalogue!*" *Annie exclaimed, looking at her pink polycotton dress and matching jacket. I tried to soften the blow.*

"*It doesn't look that bad.*"

"*I'm not wearing this pile of doggy doings out; you've got to be joking,*" *Annie declared adamantly.*

"*It's not the most flattering of outfits, and it doesn't look the same as it did in the catalogue, you're right. The shape is different, but then again, you haven't got half a ton of bulldog clips and forty safety pins down your back and sleeves shaping you and holding you in, have you?*"

"*That's true. I never thought of it like that, but what am I going to wear on Saturday?*"

"*Why don't you wear the dress that you wore last week? You looked lovely in that.*"

"*Over my dead body. Come on, we're off. Let's go down to Brenda's Superstore. There might be something in there that I can wear.*"

Annie changed her clothes and put on her coat.

"*Can you imagine if I wore that sack of potatoes to church? I'd be a laughing stock; I'd never be able to show my big fat behind in there again. That's it. I'm going on a diet next week,*" *Annie declared.*

Changing the subject as we left her flat and caught the bus down to Brenda's, it wasn't long before Annie eventually asked, "Do you fancy some jerked chicken with some rice and peas for ya tea? Oh, and I must remember to pick up some of that extra hot pepper sauce. I'm starving," *she confessed.*

Going to work at the Annie Russell hair salon was like going to school. The salon became my classroom, where I learnt to integrate with people from all sorts of different spheres. Whilst talking to one very elegant lady about my ambitions to work within the

< 189 >

fashion industry, Miranda suggested that I go around to her house and pick up some magazines that she thought I might find useful as reference material. Miranda's daughter was a very well-known fashion editor in America, so I figured she knew what she was talking about, and I took her advice.

The next evening, I picked up my treasure trove of reference booty and struggled home under its heavy weight on the tube. As I unpacked the old copies of *Vogue, Harpers & Queen,* and *Tatler,* I started to get excited. Most of the magazines were from the early 1980s, but some were even older, dating back to the early 1970s. My favourite edition of *Vogue* had a beautiful, ethereal cover featuring the iconic fashion director Grace Coddington when she had been a model. David Bailey had taken the photograph, Oliver from Leonard's hair salon had styled the hair, and the master make-up artist Barbara Daily had applied the flawless make-up. I thought the image was extremely daring and experimental—it was way ahead of its time—and I kept the magazine on my bookshelf, where I could view its wonderful cover every day. As I flicked through the other editions of *Vogue,* I felt inspired by the images. There was a stunning black-and-white fashion shoot by David Bailey with the beautiful model Marie Helvin. With her short, dark, glossy bob, the sublime images conveyed an eroticism that was both incredibly beautiful and very alluring. In another edition, the gorgeous supermodel and actress Jerry Hall looked stunning in a sexy swimming costume. Her legs were impossibly long, her lips red and inviting. Looking out across the clear blue ocean, she appeared strong and assured; her eyes seemed almost feline as she scanned the distant horizon. I did my homework and I studied the magazines, memorizing as much as I could about the clothes, the photographers, the models, and their hair and make-up.

• • •

< 190 >

As photographer Barry Lategan walked up the stairs to his studio, Aran followed closely behind him. Aran paused for a minute on the stairs to admire the iconic fashion photographs displayed on the high walls. One of his favourite images was a beauty shot of a very young '60s fashion icon called Twiggy. Aran admired her perfectly finger-waved 1920s bob.

"Did Leonard II of Berkeley Square do the hair for that shoot?" Aran asked.

"Yes, he did. How did you know that?"

"Well, there was only one Leonard, apart from Leonard I. Only he could have done perfect finger waves like that—the man was a genius! He was one of the first celebrity hairdressers of modern times. Mind you, Raymond, the talented Mr. Teasy-Weasy, could do a mean beehive, and nobody cut a bob like Mr. Vidal Sassoon. I could tell Leonard II's work anywhere—it's something about the way he used his comb, the angle that he took. He was incredibly skilful, just like Leonard I—you know, Marie Antoinette's hairdresser at Versailles."

Barry carried on walking up the stairs.

• • •

During my interview with Annie Russell, I'd told her about my ambition to work within the fashion industry. Annie encouraged me and thankfully gave me time off from work when I needed to do tests and shoots. Annie understood my passion and could see my potential. Like a plant, she nurtured my talent and encouraged me to grow. In her youth, Annie had worked within the fashion industry herself, having styled the hair of '60s fashion icon Jean Shrimpton for the English *Vogue*. During the "swinging sixties," she'd had two clients who caused quite a stir, as they were involved

< 191 >

in the scandalous Profumo affair. Annie styled the hair of Christine Keeler and Mandy Rice-Davies on a regular basis, creating all kinds of elaborate hairstyles using hairpieces, backcombing, and lots of hairspray. Apparently, the girls had loved fashion. Mandy even colour coordinated her trendy pink minicar so that it matched with her favourite pink miniskirt. Well, a girl's got to accessorize! Annie also styled the hair of one of the most iconic stars of the twentieth century—her skilful services were requested by the legendary film star Elizabeth Taylor. It seems that Elizabeth was delighted with her hair, because Annie continued to care for her famous tresses for the next twelve years. Elizabeth also introduced Annie to her husband, the illustrious actor Richard Burton, and for many years she shared a close friendship with these two amazing actors, travelling and attending many social occasions with the glamorous couple.

Because of Annie's wise council and infinite patience, I became the happy custodian of self-belief. Slowly, as the dark clouds of my insecurity cleared, my confidence increased and my social skills matured. Annie soon entrusted me with her affluent clientele. She introduced me to actors, artists, writers, and their agents. The first really well-known celebrities that I worked with at Annie's were Susannah York, Joanna Lumley, and Stefanie Powers. It was a wonderful time of personal and professional growth.

. . .

Within the manic confines of a busy modelling agency, a queue of beautiful girls started to form. They waited patiently to see Lemon, a top beauty photographer. Some were silent, and some chatted nervously amongst themselves. Some shielded the vulnerability that hope brings with an air of nonchalant indifference. But within their hearts, they all realized that this

< 192 >

photographer's pictures could change the course of their careers and lead them down the path towards superstardom—or should one say "supermodeldom"?

As Aran and Lemon sat chatting together, patiently going through each of the model's "books," it wasn't long before a sour, distasteful expression found a home upon Lemon's petulant face.

"God, haven't they got any decent girls in London? Maybe we should go to Paris," he suggested.

The hours passed by and the models came and went as the pair searched with vigour for Lemon's new "discovery." But Lemon—oh, Lemon—he wasn't a happy bunny, and he wasn't that funny, either. For although talent, wealth, and fame had entered his domain, charm had never knocked upon his door.

"Her nose is too big, hers is too long, and hers is too wide," Lemon noted.

"Her fingers look like sausages, her ears stick out, and that girl's forehead is really high. Those lips look terrible—they're way out of proportion with the rest of her face—and the shape of that other girl's lipline just doesn't work for me. I'm sorry, but what an awful profile!" Lemon exclaimed, discarding the composite cards in front of him.

"She looks more like a monster than a model. She's too commercial, she's too editorial, and she looks like she needs to lose a few pounds. That other one is far too short—how tall is she again? I don't like that girl's jaw line or the other one's hairline; she looks like a werewolf. That girl's got bad skin. The other one has good legs, but her hips are too wide—she has got lovely eyes, though… but I don't like her teeth. Next."

Just as Lemon was about to completely despair, in walked Blossom. Like the arrival of spring, Blossom smiled and introduced herself, and for a few fleeting seconds, a surge of excitement mixed with hope seemed to animate Lemon's dour form. He turned the plastic leaves of Blossom's book. Had Lemon found his new face? Had he made his new discovery? Everything seemed to be going well, until Lemon saw the last

< 193 >

picture in Blossom's book. Suddenly, any trace of hope faded into disappointment. He gave Blossom her book back and looked away as she left the room.

"She was great. It's just a shame about her nostrils. I almost didn't notice at first, but her right one is definitely bigger than her left. She ought to get a bit of surgery done on that, and then she'd be perfect, just perfect! Oh well, what can you do? Another day wasted. We'll just have to continue looking next week. I'll book our flights to Paris and organize another casting then, shall I? What days are you free?" Lemon asked, as the shadow of his disapproval slowly lifted from his ugly face.

< 194 >

CHAPTER 19

When I walked into the Annie Russell hair salon one busy Friday morning, I didn't realize that a unique surprise lay in store for me. At first, I felt a little intimidated by this larger than life character, but when I realized that our new arrival didn't bite, I started to relax. Val was a very talented hairstylist who possessed a no-nonsense kind of attitude towards her work and life in general; she was the kind of woman that you really didn't want to upset—unless you could run very fast. I loved her down-to-earth demeanour and her witty sense of humour almost as much as she loved to smoke the occasional cigarette and drink the odd gin and tonic. Val was elegant and slim, and she had a pretty face—her features were small and refined, and with her short blonde hair and piercing blue eyes, she was a very attractive lady. Val had a very loyal and royal clientele, and she always made a point of introducing me to these regal ladies and gentlemen of the realm. As I gave them their tea or coffee, we would chat and gossip about the latest outrageous scandals in the news. It was always great fun and very camp, just like Val.

Soon after Val's arrival, I noticed a strange new phenomenon that seemed to sweep through the salon like a rampant tornado. It seemed that some of our client's hairstyles were just getting bigger and bigger as the weeks flew by. At first I thought it was my imagination

< 195 >

playing tricks on me, but after a while it became obvious that my observations were correct. Some bouffant hair creations were definitely growing higher, reaching unknown new heights. *How strange,* I thought to myself. I watched the competitive nature of the hair-stylists manifest before my very eyes. That old saying, "anything you can do, I can do better" seemed very appropriate. Before long, with the help of a lot of hairspray and backcombing, hair creations of all shapes and sizes were floating down Kensington Church Walk. After a while, if it was generally acknowledged that a member of staff had excelled in creating a truly spectacular, bouffant creation, a junior member of staff would discreetly move a rose bowl full of flowers onto the winning stylist's hairdressing section, in secret recognition of their outstanding achievement. I have to admit, to my absolute delight, I did manage to win "the rose bowl award" on a few occasions, and I was extremely proud of that achievement.

Val was Annie's younger sister, and in her colourful past she had worked as a coat-checker at Esmeralda's Barn, a gambling club in Knightsbridge, London, run by the notorious gangsters Ronnie and Reggie Kray. On Sundays, Val would also help Ronnie and Reggie's mother prepare Sunday lunch for "the boys" at their terraced house on Vallance Road in the East End. Ronnie and Reggie and all their "friends" would sit around a large dinner table as Violet and Val ran around serving the food.

"More veg, Reg? More gravy, Ronnie?" they'd ask.

Exhausted by the end of the afternoon, Val would return home with a fifty-pound note in her handbag, which was an awful lot of money in those days.

And so, surrounded by these two wonderful sisters called Annie and Val, this rough diamond was slowly cut and polished, so that one day, when it was ready, it could truly sparkle. We worked together for the next twenty years—it took an awful lot of polish!

• • •

< 196 >

Orchard Manor was the former residence of the delectable actor known as Mrs. Alan Lake, also known as Diana Dors, the iconic 1950s movie star. Tiffany, the curvaceous, glamorous blonde who now resided here, had fallen in love with the place the moment she had laid eyes on it. After passing by some very expensive real estate, Aran's taxi pulled up outside the manor's huge electronic gates. When opened, they revealed a beautiful house set on huge grounds complete with tennis courts, out buildings, and a shed that was occupied by Ollie the owl, who was cared for by Rosy, Tiffany's animal-loving mother.

Upon entering the house, Rosy greeted Aran with a kiss and then ushered him into a large, cosy sitting room. Tiffany was sitting by some open French doors that led onto a stone terrace outside. As Aran approached her, he noticed the soft summer sunlight caressing the ornate plaster cornices encircling the room. Outside, the perfectly manicured lawn stretched out before him like a vast, vibrant green carpet. Hands flat, fingers apart, Tiffany's hands lay motionless upon a small table in front of her. Her manicurist slowly started packing her equipment away.

"Oh, darling, I'll be with you in a moment. Just waiting for my nail polish to dry. What do you think of the colour?" Tiffany asked, carefully lifting up one of her hands to show Aran. "It's Chanel. I do love a good varnish that doesn't chip, don't you? I hate smudging my nails, and Lindy here goes mad, don't you, dear. Well, I guess you would, if it's taken you half an hour to paint them."

Tiffany turned her attention towards Rosy.

"Do you think Aran might like a drink, Mother? Oh, I give up. You know, you just can't get the staff these days, Aran. How are you, darling?"

"I'm fine. How are you? You look fantastic."

"Oh, I'm great. I just wish I could say the same about the damn gardener; he's driving me bananas. I could do the gardening quicker myself. The pool is in a dreadful state—it really does need cleaning—and my hair...where do I begin? It's just—it's just desperate.

< 197 >

What do you think of my new foundation?" Tiffany asked, turning her face towards the window. "I spent hours walking around Harrods, and I'm still not sure that I've got the right skin tone." Tiffany sighed.

As the minutes passed by, Aran started to sense Tiffany's impatience with Rosy.

"I mean, Aran, how long does it take to pour a drink?" Tiffany asked, raising her eyebrows.

Moments later, Rosy re-entered the sitting room holding a glass of white wine. Tiffany turned to Aran and whispered, "I know what the Mother is getting for Christmas this year—one of those electronic cow prodders. A few shocks from that, and I'm sure she'll get the spring back in her step," she wickedly mused.

"Oh, hold your horses! I had to open a new bottle," Rosy exclaimed. Then to Aran she said, "She thinks I can't hear what she's saying. She's such a bad girl. No patience—just like her father." She handed Aran his drink, then proceeded to tell him about the foxes that appeared on a regular basis under the oak trees at the bottom of the garden.

After disclosing her new exciting information, Rosy disappeared, returning once again to the kitchen, where she sat at a breakfast bar next to a pile of *Hello!* magazines. Transfixed, she watched a small television screen and worried about the weather, Ollie the owl, various birds, squirrels, foxes, and all sorts of other creatures.

"Aran, you must come and see what I've done in the pool room," Tiffany suggested, walking towards two massive golden doors that led out from the sitting room.

As Aran walked through the doors, he was amazed by the huge art-deco window that dominated the end of the pool room. Bright sunlight illuminated the beautiful stained-glass panels of red, gold, and blue. Two gigantic black panthers, cast in granite, stood on each side of the small flight of steps, which led into the massive pool. They were poised, as if they were about to jump in. As Aran

< 198 >

took a sip of his drink, he thought about the wonderful Mrs. Lake. He could imagine the parties she must have held here and the fun that her guests must have shared. When Tiffany turned away from Aran, she began scrutinizing the tall green palms that she had placed between the marble pillars running along the side of the pool.

"So, what do you think? Do you like my new organic editions?"

"Yes, I love the palms. The whole ambience reminds me of a set from a Hollywood movie. All you need now is a few starlets splashing around in the pool."

"Come on, Aran, darling, let's go and sort my hair out. I can't wait any longer; it's been driving me mad. I've been simply dying to see you so I can get some new 'swishy' international hair."

Two days later, Tiffany's hair was finally finished, and she was delighted with the results.

"You always get the colour of my tint and highlights right, and I love my new hair extensions. They look fantastic—I feel like a new woman," Tiffany declared, shaking her new mane of swishy tresses.

Statuesque and tanned to perfection, Tiffany crossed Aran's palm with silver and made her next appointment.

"Oh, Aran—after the last time you did my extensions, I was just coming off the escalator in Harrods when this hairdresser commented on my wonderful, thick, gorgeous hair. I told him it was due to genetics from my mother's side of the family, and this wonderful camomile shampoo I had recently discovered. I just couldn't bear to tell him that half of my hair didn't belong to me. Well, I guess in a way it is my hair. After all, it's on my head now! I'm so naughty," Tiffany confessed.

• • •

< 199 >

My life was busy. I worked hard during the week at Annie Russell's hair salon, and I continued to "test" with different photographers to improve my portfolio. Exhausted, I decided to take a vacation.

I had recently read the complete series of *Tales of the City* by the author Armistead Maupin. Inspired by his stories, I decided to go on the trail of Mouse and Mrs. Madrigal, two characters from his books that were based in San Francisco. My adventure started quite disastrously. My flight had to return back to Heathrow after two and a half hours due to "technical difficulties."

A strange silence filled the plane as it approached the runway to land. Even the babies stopped crying, as if they, too, could sense the apprehension and fear in the atmosphere. As I looked out of the window, I saw fire engines, ambulances, and police cars racing down the runway towards us. My stomach felt sick. I crossed my fingers, closed my eyes, and waited with trepidation for the plane to touch down. After the plane had landed safely, the passengers and crew disembarked, and we made our way to a small departure lounge, relieved that our ordeal was over and that we were all still alive. After a three-hour wait and a couple of cups of awful coffee, everybody boarded another plane bound for America.

I arrived in San Francisco feeling tired and hungry. I checked into my "gay" hotel situated on Market Street and decided to have a quick power nap. Later that evening, eager to explore the city's nightlife, I made my way to a cowboy bar called The Rawhide, a venue that had been frequented by Mouse in one of Mr. Maupin's books. Dressed head to toe in cowboy gear, I drank beer and joined in the fun. I line danced, hopefully in time, to the country music. It wasn't long before I met a real cowboy who offered to show me his ranch; however, I decided it was best to decline his kind offer.

I spent my days riding on the tramcars of this liberal city in a state of bewilderment. I saw the Golden Gate Bridge, drank coffee on Castro Street, and took a tour of the infamous Alcatraz prison, where the gangster Al Capone had been incarcerated.

< 200 >

I had spent months training in the gym before I embarked on my American adventure, and I was intrigued to know what it was like to "pump some iron" on the other side of the pond. After a brief training period at The Muscle Factory gym, I bravely joined the world famous Gold's Gym, home to many professional bodybuilders. I had always harboured an ambition to train at this amazing gym, and I wasted no time at all. I poured my body, heart, and soul into some hardcore workouts. Like Narcissus, I admired my muscles from every angle in the gym mirror and satisfied with my reflection, I flew safely home.

I felt inspired by my trip to San Francisco, so I decided to have a night on the town wearing my new cowboy hat. Later that evening, I met Mr. Universe in a nightclub called Heaven. Tall and handsome, this professional American bodybuilder had the kind of physique that didn't move when you touched it—Jeff was solid as a rock. Jeff told me that I had very good muscular development, definition, and symmetry; he gave me his card and we arranged to meet up to do some serious workouts together. It was ironic, really—here was Mr. Universe asking me to meet up for a workout, when I had been bullied and ridiculed for being "Mr. Puniverse" at school. In that moment, I realized that maybe I'd been trying to prove something to myself through my weight training. After my meeting with Jeff, I felt validated in some way, as if I had nothing left to prove. Over the next couple of months, I met up with Jeff on a regular basis. He taught me a lot about diet, supplements, and nutrition. After many intensive workouts, I felt that I had developed my physique as much as I possibly could. I considered taking steroids to develop my muscles even further, but I decided against using these potentially harmful drugs. Instead, I said goodbye to Jeff and decided to concentrate on my hair and make-up career. I realized that the life of a professional bodybuilder required total discipline and dedication, and I knew that very few competitors made it to the top of their profession. Looking back, I'm glad I made that decision, although all of my hard training seemed to pay off, because the stage manager of Heaven nightclub asked me if I would like to become a go-go dancer.

< 201 >

Since I frequented the club on a regular basis, I decided that I might as well dance on the bar or the stage and get paid for it. The following week, I found myself in a cage that was suspended from the ceiling of the nightclub, wearing very little but a smile and a leather thong. I tried to look confident as I struck poses and made my muscular moves in time with the music. I hoped the audience would like me so that I would be asked back the following week; the job paid well and I desperately needed the money. I was also given free drink vouchers and free entry to the club, which was very helpful. The hardest thing that I found about the job was hanging around until four o'clock in the morning waiting to be paid, because sometimes I had to be at work at the hair salon five hours later. However, this occasional dancing job supplemented my real career and enabled me to buy the expensive photographs that I constantly needed to upgrade my ever-changing portfolio. After all, fashion waits for no one. I enjoyed dancing, and as I danced, I dreamt of a better life where I would find love, success, and happiness. Although I knew there were no guarantees of achieving my dream, I was willing to fight for it. I may not have had anyone or anything, but I had my dream, and I believed in it.

• • •

Aran felt excited as he made his way to the Alaska Building in southeast London. The prospect of getting some new pictures for his portfolio brightened the wet, miserable morning. After arriving, he quickly set up his equipment on a large box covered with a plastic tablecloth. Its slippery, shiny surface was copiously printed with scattered images of 1950s "sweater girls." The curvaceous figures of Jayne Mansfield and Bettie Page bought

< 202 >

a smile to his face, and he told himself that it was going to be a good day.

The familiar fashion crew laughed and joked amongst themselves as they enjoyed a brief breakfast of hot coffee and *pain au chocolat*. However, as time passed by, their feelings of anxiety started to gain momentum. Their model had still not arrived. Ten minutes later, the photographer rang the model's agency and was told that Millie was on her way. Maybe she was stuck in traffic, they suggested. Another fifteen minutes had passed, by the time the model agency rang Peter back and informed him that, unfortunately, "Millie wasn't feeling that well," and she was therefore unable to attend the shoot. Had they got any other models available? Peter asked. The disappointed expression on his face told the crew their answer.

Maybe it wasn't going to be such a good day after all, Aran thought. But unbeknown to him, Peter had arranged for some other models to come by during the day so that he could preview their books for a forthcoming assignment. Luck, it seems, was on his side. Peter quickly rang the relevant modelling agencies and asked if any of the models were immediately available for a test. Over the next few hours, models came and went as Peter looked through their books. Eventually, Peter found the gorgeous girl he was looking for. Tamzin was tall and slim—she had a very elegant stature, and her beautiful skin was as smooth and dark as polished ebony.

After a quick chat, a snack, and a drink, Aran sat Tamzin in front of the box covered with the plastic tablecloth and went to work on her lovely face. After he had finished her hair and make-up he carefully scrutinized his work. Nothing seemed odd or out of place, and yet something didn't quite gel—something that he couldn't put his finger on. Aran introduced Tamzin to Katie, the clothes stylist, and hoped with time that he would figure it out. Thirty-five minutes and a lot of clothes later, Katie finally found a look that worked on Tamzin. When Tamzin appeared on set, Aran noticed the huge amount of pins and clips it had taken to fit the

< 203 >

clothes perfectly on Tamzin's lean body. Aran casually looked at Tamzin, and then discreetly turned to Katie.

"You know, Katie, there's something about this girl's hair and make-up that just isn't working for me. I can't put my finger on it. What do you think?"

Katie looked Aran straight in the eyes.

"I'm glad you can't put your finger on it, sweet pea."

"What do you mean?"

"Well, darling, I got quite a shock myself. Tamzin has no hips and absolutely no boobs whatsoever. I think she's a pre-op, darling; who's taking hormones. It must be terribly hard to find oneself in that kind of predicament. I do hope it all works out for her—she's such a sweetie and she's absolutely stunning."

Aran casually turned to face Tamzin, but he could trace no sign of her hidden sexuality. However, Peter also realized that things were not as they had seemed after he started photographing Tamzin and looked at his Polaroids (test shots). After his surprising discovery, Peter continued to photograph the beautiful Tamzin in three more outfits before he finally decided to call it a day. And what a day it had been— the photographs looked fantastic!

After Katie and Aran had packed away their things, they said their goodbyes to everyone and slowly made their way out of the building. Upon reaching the grey pavement that lay outside, Katie turned towards Aran and declared, "Well, darling, that's fashion for you. It's all in a day's work."

"I wonder if Tamzin's agency knows?" Aran asked.

"Who knows, who cares," Katie replied, clutching her Birkin handbag and getting into her taxi, which was piled high with boxes and suitcases.

"Bye, darling. I'll call you later," Katie promised, leaning out of the taxi and kissing Aran on both cheeks. Moments later, the taxi pulled away, and Katie opened the window and shouted,

< 204 >

"You know, darling, you don't know if your model's going to be an Arthur or Martha these days! And who gives a damn as long as they look gorgeous."

< 205 >

CHAPTER 20

Feeling restless and ambitious, I decided that the time had come to test the water, so I endeavoured to make appointments with some affluent hair and make-up agencies. Some agencies wouldn't give me an appointment; others told me to ring back in six months time, but the odd one was kind and helpful and agreed to see me. It was hard at first. I didn't know what to expect when I nervously presented myself and my work to the agency bookers. Most of them searched through my book, scouring it for any flaws that they could find. I tried not to take their criticism personally, but at times it was very hard not to. I also realized pretty quickly that in the world of fashion, people aren't that bothered about hurting your feelings. After all, if your book isn't up to scratch, there's no point in an agency investing their valuable time and energy trying to find you work. I learnt that in order to raise the standard of your work and make your book stronger, you have to learn from your mistakes. These mistakes were not always about the model's hair and make-up (although of course some of them were). They could also relate to the lighting of a photograph or the pose that a model had taken. Of course, I wasn't responsible for those mistakes, but I was responsible for choosing the pictures that went into my book. And although I didn't like the criticism that I received, it taught me what makes a good picture and what does

< 207 >

not. Of course, the opinion of these professional hair and make-up agents was right, but their advice didn't make their rejection any easier, and in my despair, I couldn't see how I could improve my work any further. The fashion industry is a tough business—not only do you have to be extremely talented and determined to succeed within its realm, but you also have to learn how to cope with its mental and emotional demands in order to survive. And so I showed my work to countless agencies throughout London. I got used to their rejection, and with time and perseverance, although no agency took me on, I could tell that my book was slowly improving by the encouraging reactions I started to receive. Eventually, the agency bookers started to see my potential, and occasionally they would recommend me to aspiring photographers who were also testing. I focused totally on my work—all my time, energy, and money was channelled into constantly updating my book. I tested at a relentless pace, striving to improve the standard of my work. It was whilst working on one of these tests that I was introduced to a gorgeous blonde model called Elaine Hughes. We became good friends.

Elaine was beautiful, sexy, and fun to hang out with. Always helpful and enthusiastic, she kindly introduced me to the best photographic printer in town. His name was Roberto, and soon he was printing all my black-and-white pictures. Roberto always encouraged me, and he gave me a huge discount on my printing bills. It was important that my photographic images were of the highest quality, so all of my work was printed by hand, and in Roberto's case, with great care. Soon Roberto invited me to play in his five-a-side football team (crazy man), and when I declined his kind offer (for fear of embarrassing myself) he invited me to play pool instead. I didn't have the heart to tell him that I didn't know how to play pool, either, so Elaine and I would go to his pool-parties anyway. Here, Roberto introduced me to a lot of prominent photographers, hoping that maybe one of them would give me a break.

"You've got balls, Aran. Real balls—do you know that? You'll go far one of these days; you listen to me," Roberto told me.

< 208 >

Whenever I had the time, I would pop by his printing studio to show him my new pictures. I valued his shrewd judgement and honest opinions. We would share a joke and a coffee together, and when a famous photographer appeared to collect their prints, he would introduce me and insist that I show them my book. My work was nowhere near the standards that these "super-duper" photographers demanded, but this didn't stop Roberto from trying to get me a break, and it certainly didn't stop me, either. Actually, to my amazement, one of these photographers did book me for a job. His name was Willy Camden, and I was so proud of his beautiful pictures when I put them in my book that I immediately went round to Roberto's studio to show him my new colourful acquisitions.

"If you don't try, Aran, it's never going happen. You must keep on trying, because one of these days it will. You mark my words. You have something, Aran. I'm Italian—I know about these things," Roberto assured me. His words gave me hope and comfort in my despair.

If only someone would give me a chance, I told myself, but no more chances came. Six months later, Roberto died. I missed this wonderful man so much. I missed his friendship, his encouragement, his wisdom, and his generous spirit and kindness.

• • •

Bleary-eyed and weary, Aran awoke and stumbled into the shower. The long flight to Los Angeles, coupled with the very loud Italian seamstress who occupied the hotel room above him, had taken a toll. It was Grammy Awards time, and Aran was back at work in the City of Angels; the luxurious but discreet hotel where he was staying on Rodeo Drive in Beverly Hills was teaming with people. After a quick a shave, and a subtle sweep of golden bronzer, he

< 209 >

threw on some casual clothes and then made his way to the hotel's small breakfast area. After taking a seat, he browsed through the extensive breakfast menu. He observed the other guests seated around him and immediately recognized the loud, bellowing voices nearby. Stephen, the elderly waiter, came shuffling towards him.

"Hello, Mr. Guest. I haven't seen you for a while. How's London? You look like you could do with a coffee."

"Yes, please. Stephen, do you think you could make that a pot? I had the most awful sleep last night. That Versace seamstress doesn't talk; she screams. I could hear her talking about her dresses all night," Aran commented loudly, so that the premiere Italian seamstress and her assistants sitting nearby could hear him.

Aran's comments were greeted by a look of disdain that could have curdled the freshest milk. Stephen tossed his head, looked towards the heavens, and asked,

"Are you ready to order, sir?"

"I'm sorry, Stephen, but do you think you could give me a few more minutes? I haven't got my knickers in gear this morning."

Five minutes later, Stephen reappeared. As he shuffled towards Aran's table, Aran noticed the synthetic nature of his black toupee when he walked under the bright lights that hung from the low ceiling.

"OK, Mr. Guest. Wada you like this morning?" Stephen asked in a slow, measured voice, leaning with one hand on the side of the table.

"Just a couple of boiled eggs and some toast would be great."

"What kinda toast would you like? Bran, wholemeal, white, or rye?"

"Wholemeal will do just fine. Thanks, Stephen."

"If ya want some more coffee, you just let me know."

As Stephen finished writing down his order, Aran noticed that his eyebrows had been replaced by strokes of thick black eye pencil. Aran decided that they colour-coordinated perfectly with his synthetic hair. Stephen obviously wanted to keep things looking as natural as possible.

< 210 >

"You know, Mr. Guest, things ain't the same in this town, no siree. The youngsters of today ain't got the style or glamour of the Hollywood leading ladies of my day. I can remember when I first met Miss Gloria Swanson down at Harry and Marilyn's Hamburger Hamlet over on Sunset. Now that's what you call a lady—a movie star. She was always so elegant and so well turned out."

Stephen rolled his eyes one more time, took a deep breath, and continued. "Of course, Frances Drake was my absolute favourite."

"God, Stephen, you can't be that old. He was alive in the Elizabethan era," Aran joked.

"Hell no, I don't mean Francis Drake the English sea captain. I mean Frances Drake the movie star. Ya know, I adored her; she was my favourite after 'the talkies' began. And then she went and married that earl's son. What about poor old Zsa Zsa? Can you believe it? She was so fabulous, so on the ball. We all used to go over to her place for lunch. She sure was a lot of fun, and the jewellery! Oh, and Joan Crawford—now there was a lady who knew how to deliver her lines. They don't make 'em like that anymore. It's all fake boobs, teeth, and tan these days. Bette Davis would turn in her grave if she saw how those trollops dress. They've got no style and no sense of real taste—it's all done for 'em. And the language they use! I'd wash their dirty mouths out with soap and water if I had my way."

For a fleeting second, Aran remembered a black-and-white photograph that he had seen in The Beverly Hills Hotel. The image portrayed Jean Harlow and Clark Gable playing tennis on the hotel's magnificent tennis court. Groomed to perfection, the stylish couple laughed and joked together like they didn't have a care in the world. Stephen shuffled back to the kitchen and reappeared a few minutes later carrying Aran's breakfast.

"Would ya like some extra butter with ya toast?"

"No thanks, Stephen. I'm fine."

Stephen winked at Aran and shuffled towards a small bar, where he started to polish some glasses. A few minutes later, he changed the channel on the television above the bar.

"Anyone wanna watch the news?" he hollered.

< 211 >

• • •

I continued to "do the rounds," showing my work to an endless trail of agents. I carried on testing whenever I possibly could, and just when I thought that nobody was ever going to give me a break, I finally got one. Luckily, the agency who offered to represent me happened to be one of the most prestigious hair and make-up agencies in London, representing some of the most successful artists in the fashion industry.

Before I had chance to shake my mascara wand, my new agency had found a major make-up company that agreed to provide me with their products in return for my editorial "credits" in magazines and newspapers, and they also made appointments with a list of respected photographers in the hope of finding me work or better tests to improve my book. This is how I met Mike Owen, whose beautiful photographic studio was in an old church in King's Cross, London.

Mike had worked with so many major celebrities and had done so many campaigns and big advertising jobs that it boggled the mind. He was a brilliant photographer, and he gave me my first break by providing me with regular work as a make-up artist with various hairdressing magazines. Mike also shot the cover for my first card. The beautiful model we decided to use was from Eastern Europe. She was an androgynous-looking girl with striking blue eyes and short brunette hair. The image for my card was inspired by the Hollywood movie star Marlene Dietrich, because I liked the way she could project a strong masculine image whilst still retaining a strong sense of female sensuality and allure. The image was shot in black and white so that it looked like a still from an old Hollywood movie.

Our model wore a black trouser suit by Yves Saint Laurent. I put a side-part in her hair and slicked it back using pomade so that it looked shiny and masculine. After I had defined her eyebrows,

< 212 >

I applied black mascara and added a few false eyelashes here and there. I then accentuated the contours of her cheekbones and shaded her nose, narrowing it slightly. On her lips, I applied lip balm with a light coat of lip gloss, and I decided not to use any form of nail varnish so that her manicured nails would appear to be more masculine.

The photograph was taken on a massive ten by eight camera, and each huge negative was carefully hand printed and sepia-toned giving it an old, authentic feel. I loved the finished image—it was fantastic—and I spent most of that evening looking at it from different angles after I had pinned it to the wall in my sitting room.

It didn't take long before I realized how important it was to socialize and network at the right parties and social functions within the fashion industry. My new agency secured me invitations to these prestigious events so that I might pursue my campaign of self-promotion. I attended the launches for new hair and beauty products, designer clothes, bags, and shoes. I went to photographic exhibitions, film premieres, and I danced my life away in constant array of fashion related parties. I also realized that if I wanted to succeed in a highly visual industry, I would have to play the game and look the part. After all, the fashion industry is about clothes and creating visual imagery. My appearance could influence the way that potential clients perceived me. On a very limited budget, I did my best to enhance my wardrobe. I scoured vintage clothing shops looking for unique bargains, which I then accessorized with discounted designer shoes, belts, and hats.

Over the next six months, my two bookers sent me on countless appointments and "go-sees." They pushed my book like they'd stuck a rocket up its arse. I spent my days walking miles and miles around London, catching buses and tubes to numerous photographic studios. My A to Z street directory became my best friend. Slowly, I established a few regular clients, which enabled me to cut my hours back at Annie Russell's hair salon. This allowed me to concentrate on perfecting my book, and it also meant that I was

< 213 >

able to assist the more established artists at the agency when it came to "show time" during London Fashion Week.

Colin Gold was the first hairstylist that I assisted. He was great fun to work with, and he always came up with original and creative ideas. Colin would show me his reference Polaroids featuring all the supermodels he had recently worked with, and he would explain to me how he had achieved each look. He was super talented and always enthusiastic, and when he eventually moved to New York, I missed him dearly.

My first fashion show was for the designer Vivienne Westwood. I was asked to assist Sam McKnight, who was Princess Diana's hairstylist at the time. I had always admired Sam's skilful work, which I had seen in numerous editions of *Vogue* magazine. He was a bit of a hair hero of mine, and so I felt nervous when I was asked to be part of his team. When I anxiously turned up on the day of the show, the assistants were introduced to their assigned models. As I looked at some of the world's top models sitting in front of me, I was more than a little intimidated, but I tried to appear confident as I was shown how to achieve the look that Sam envisioned. Most of the girls were a good laugh and friendly enough, and I soon found myself weaving and setting their hair onto huge hairpins so that eventually, when their hair came out of the pins, it would be a mass of frizz. When Sam had finished his models, he would then check everyone's work to make sure we had followed his strict instructions. Once he felt satisfied with the results of his team's hard labours, he would dress all the hair and expertly apply any pre-styled hairpieces where necessary, finishing the total look.

They look forward with heads held high—their pace precise and poise evident. Each confident step the youthful models take belies their hours of practice. Their attitude is requested and so desired. Hips sway to the sound of music; beautiful butterflies float by; and the choreographer holds his breath as these birds of paradise are scrutinized by the world's fashion press. After months of preparation, hard work, and imagination, the designer's

< 214 >

collection comes alive. Executed to perfection, every bead and sequin, collar and cuff, accessory and ruff, is captured in this fleeting moment.

Backstage, the guardians of the rail stand by their clothes. Each outfit in order, carefully fitted and selected—creative patterns that time intercepted. Ready to pounce as their prey arrive, the dressers spring into action. With speed and urgency, their fingers search frantically for hooks, buttons, and zips. Each player anticipates the next agile move as they pull down straps and put on shoes.

Ready to go, the goddess called Fashion appears composed, and her followers worship at her feet. In colours of the season she passes by—transient, and oh, so fickle! Favour shifts from one design to the next, and notes and sketches are taken. The show must go on until the collection is spent, upon the dawn to reawaken, next season—spring, summer, winter, and fall.

After the fashion show Vivienne came up to me and thanked me for all my hard work.

"Did you do the show in Paris?" she asked.

"No, I didn't, but I used to go to your shop called Seditionaries to buy my bondage trousers," I replied.

My mind went back to a memorable day when I was walking down Kings Road in Chelsea, London. I had accidently stumbled across a beautiful vision who reminded me of the 1950s rocker Adam Faith. He had spiky bleached-blonde hair and was dressed from head to toe in black leather. With an Elvis sneer and full, pouty lips, this guy had what it took, and he knew it.

"Hey, you look great. What's your name?" I'd asked.

"Billy Idol. I've got a band called Generation X. You should check us out sometime."

As I stood staring at this truly handsome vision in my Seditionaries top that depicted two gay cowboys, I wondered if I would ever see him again. Eventually I did get to see my idol again, when he played a gig at the Mr. George nightclub in Coventry. Needless to say, I was at the front of the stage, "pogoing" like there was no tomorrow.

< 215 >

My thoughts eventually wandered back to reality when Vivienne invited me to share a glass of champagne with her mother. Whilst sipping my fizzy pop, I noticed a strong resemblance between the two women. Vivienne's mother was a very stylish woman; she had a twinkle in her eye and platform shoes on her feet. Her huge "Westwood pearls" looked absolute stunning over her colourful Westwood twinset.

I have always appreciated the unique way in which Vivienne views the world. As we chatted away, she seemed open and philosophical. Her manner was somewhat eccentric, and as we discussed our views on art and literature, I listened with pleasure as her mind wandered from one idea to the next. I was fascinated by her extraordinary character, her intellectual conversation, and her bright orange hair.

My next big fashion show was held at Claridge's hotel in London. The host of this auspicious charity event was the fashion maestro called Oscar de La Renta. This time, I had my own assistant and two supermodels to prepare for the show. Fortunately, the show was a great success, and the next day I received a telephone call from the promoter asking me to go back to Claridge's to do Mrs. de La Renta's hair.

Upon entering a suite of luxurious rooms, I was escorted into a large sitting room. I was offered some light refreshment and casually directed towards a Louis XV chest of drawers and a large gilded mirror. Once I had ascertained a suitable chair for my client to sit on, I took a seat and lent against its soft, padded cushions for a few moments and observed my opulent surroundings, which were decorated with Egyptian motifs. After setting up my equipment, I paced nervously around my little setup as I waited for Mrs. de La Renta.

Eventually, I was introduced to the charming Mrs. de La Renta and her elegant husband, Oscar. With his natural sense of taste and his impeccable manners, I think he could only be described as a gentleman. When I had finished Mrs. de La Renta's hair, she told me she was delighted with the results, and I floated out of

< 216 >

Claridge's to the nearest tube station. As the train whizzed through the long dark tunnels, I missed my stop because my thoughts were still lingering somewhere else.

I did several more shows for London Fashion Week. I would work hard, and then afterwards, I'd run off to the designer's parties, losing myself in their glamorous ambience and vintage champagne. Sadly, however, man cannot exist on champagne and parties alone, and I found it increasingly difficult to survive financially on the paltry amounts that I was paid as an assistant. These remunerations barely covered my expenses after my agency commission had been deducted. I couldn't afford any kind of social life that was not sustained through the social aspects of my work, and my career didn't seem to be progressing as quickly as I had anticipated. As always, Annie Russell was generous and enthusiastic, giving me time off from the hair salon when a decent fashion assignment or an important test materialized. Annie encouraged me relentlessly as I asked myself how much longer could carry on struggling.

I first "wet my toes" in the music industry when I was booked as a make-up assistant for a music video. The video was to feature the Scottish singing sensation called Lulu. I was very excited, because as a young teenager I had regularly watched all of her fabulous television shows. Lulu was kind and compassionate, and she made a point of making everyone feel welcome on the shoot. She was a very enlightened and interesting person, and her cheeky, fun-loving persona brought a smile to my terrified face. To my delight (and apprehension), I was told there were to be some special guest appearances in the video by other celebrities and models. Although I felt very privileged to be working as an assistant to the beautiful, super-talented make-up artist Lee Pycroft, I also felt very nervous. Amidst the turmoil of the busy make-up room, we endeavoured to get everyone ready. Lee suggested that I should do Boy George's make-up when he arrived later in the day; since she would be busy looking after Lulu and the other celebrities "on set" while the video was in progress.

< 217 >

As I went to work on George's face, he suddenly said, "I know you from somewhere."

"No, you don't," I replied.

"Yes, I do. I never forget a face."

"Well, OK, maybe you do. Do you remember…?"

We started talking about old times and the friends that we had known before George had become famous. He was as sharp and as quick-witted as ever. It was good to know that the problems George had endured had not destroyed his wonderful sense of humour. As I looked into his beautiful opalescent eyes once more, I could see that they still held a mischievous twinkle. As we chatted away, I remembered how much he had inspired me when we had first met all those years ago in Birmingham. I'd known then that he was born to be a star.

After the success of Lulu's video, Lee asked me to assist her on several other jobs. Lulu was busily promoting her new single on numerous television shows. Preparing the three gorgeous female backing vocalists was great fun because Lee decided to give them a very 1960s look. By the time I had finished, they looked like they had just stepped out of Tamla Motown—all smoky eyes, false eyelashes, black liquid eyeliner, and pale lips. If I'd had my way, I would have transformed them into the '70s soul divas known as the Three Degrees, but hey, you can't have your own way all the time, and I was quite happy to create my very own interpretation of the 1960s look, which was inspired by the Supremes. I remember one show in particular that was hysterically funny; the guests were Lulu, Ivana Trump, and the drag queen known as Lily Savage (Paul O'Grady). I called the show "the battle of the blondes."

The last time I had seen Lily Savage perform was at the Vauxhall Tavern in Vauxhall, London. It had been an X-rated performance that I found truly entertaining. With Lily's razor-sharp Scouse repartee, it took a very brave—or a very drunk—member of the audience to take the "Birkenhead Bombshell" on. My friends from Liverpool used to call her "the acid-tongued Lily," and they weren't joking.

< 218 >

As they stood chatting, swapping cooking recipes, cocktail tips, and naughty jokes, a more unlikely bunch of characters you couldn't have imagined. Lulu looked fresh and sexy, full of vitality and *la joie de vivre*. Ivana Trump appeared very demure and classy in her little black Chanel dress, with her hair styled to perfection in a kind of sophisticated "walnut-whip" coiffure. Acid-tongued Lily towered high above everybody else due to her huge platinum-blonde wig, complete with its own dark regrowth. She looked as common as muck in her cheap pink-velour trouser suit; her face was plastered with make-up. Everybody laughed when Lily's sharp tongue sprang into action. Lashing out, she bemoaned her daughter called Bunty, her chipped nail varnish, and "the state of the bingo halls these days." The whole scene was a sight, but I can't remember a morning when I have laughed so much and had so much fun.

I learnt an awful lot in a very short period of time with my first agency. Looking back, I think maybe I learnt too much, too soon. I felt as if I'd been thrown into the deep end of the swimming pool, and I don't think I was quite ready or prepared for it. You might say I'd needed a rubber ring, or some water wings and flippers, as I hadn't quite developed my swimming technique. I felt as if I was swimming hard but getting nowhere. My bookers were great, but no matter how hard they tried to find me work, it just didn't seem to be happening. Frustrated and anxious because I wasn't getting the editorial pictures that I needed to further my career, I gave up. *Maybe I just didn't have what it took*, I told myself. I lost my courage and I stopped believing in myself and everything I had achieved. Disillusioned, I thanked my bookers for their support and left the agency. As I walked out of the door, I knew that my dream of having a career within the fashion industry was over, but unbeknown to me at the time, fate had other ideas.

< 219 >

CHAPTER 21

Inside the location house, Aran rummaged through his equipment, searching for his spare box of hairpins. Suddenly, from outside, he heard Annabelle call his name. Her voice sounded urgent. *What on earth could be the matter?*

As Aran walked outside, he pulled down his cap and made sure that his sunglasses were firmly on in an attempt to shield himself from the brilliant sunshine and the ardour of the scorching heat. Approaching the shoot, Aran noticed the astonished expressions of the shocked crew; they stood in their isolated pools of silence. Annabelle sat on the floor, her hands covering her face. It seemed that the intense heat, the bright sunlight, and the endless outfit changes had gradually overwhelmed her. Aran passed Annabelle a tissue and a cold bottle of water, and a few minutes later, he led her into the cool haven of the magnificent location house. The beautiful French model sat on a couch, trying to find her composure.

"I hate this business. I've been out there in that boiling hot sun for ten hours, with a thirty-minute break for lunch!" Annabelle exclaimed, trying to justify her behaviour.

Aran looked at her fragile frame and handed her another tissue.

"Oh, I'm so sorry, darling. I've ruined your lovely make-up."

"Don't worry about that, sweetheart. Are you OK?"

< 221 >

"I've smiled and smiled until I can't smile anymore. What do they want from me? Blood? I don't mind working hard, but this is absolutely ridiculous."

It seems that Annabelle had been pushed one step too far. When asked to change into outfit eighteen after having modelled numerous variations for each shot, her well-trained, disciplined mind had snapped. Annabelle went to the bathroom and washed her face. When she reappeared, she tied her long dark hair back into a ponytail, grabbed her handbag, and then quietly went and sat in the location van that was parked on the secure grounds. Annabelle was ready to go.

As Aran carefully started to pack away his tools, the frustrated client walked into the house and glared at him, as if he was responsible in some way for the dreadful scene that had transpired.

"I don't know what's wrong with her. We're paying her a fortune to do this," the angry client declared.

"I'm not quite sure, either. Annabelle is in the location van if you would like to ask her," Aran pensively responded.

The client looked Aran up and down, shrugged her shoulders, and then strode briskly out of the house towards the rest of the team. Aran picked up his heavy bags full of equipment and went to sit by a very distraught Annabelle in the location van.

"I hope I never work for them again."

"So do I," Aran added, knowing there was little chance of that. "Oh well—another day, another dollar. Don't worry, you'll be flying back to your lovely boyfriend tomorrow," Aran continued, trying to comfort Annabelle.

On the way back to the hotel, nobody spoke to Annabelle or Aran. They were ostracized with a silence that said a thousand words. It seemed that Annabelle had committed the ultimate sin. When pushed to her physical limits, she had dared to say, "No, that's enough. I'm not going to do another shot." Aran had enjoyed the company of the lovely Annabelle, and was therefore seen as complicit in some way. He overheard the client's disgusted comments as she talked to her assistant.

< 222 >

"They should be ashamed of themselves. I'll never book either of them again," she whispered. Then, she opened the pages of the magazine in front of her and started to read:

Life in the fast lane of fashion can be wonderful, exhilarating, and at times very demanding. Sometimes we find ourselves overwhelmed in a world that tells us not to "glide the lily," but at times, can be rather harsh and silly. We look to fashion for direction when we ourselves have none. However, if you possess true taste and style, there is no need to follow fashion, because fashion will follow you.

• • •

The months passed by. Spring slowly turned to summer, and I continued to scrutinize my impetuous decision to leave the agency. *It's too late now*, I told myself. *It's no good crying over spilt milk.* Though I felt terrible remorse, I convinced myself that I had made the right decision to leave the agency. My portfolio sat at the back of my wardrobe gathering dust. I went back to work at Annie Russell's hair salon on a full-time basis, and I filled my spare time by performing strenuous workouts at the gym, wondering what I was going to do next.

One bright summer's afternoon, whilst enjoying a frappé cappuccino outside a cafe on Old Compton Street in Soho, London, a handsome stranger asked me if he could share my table. During our brief conversation, Troy told me that he was a model from New York City, and that he would be staying in London for at least six months while he did the usual rounds of "go-sees," castings, and shoots.

"Would you like to go to a party on Saturday night?" Troy enquired.

< 223 >

"Sure, why not. Thank God I've changed my crochet class to a Wednesday evening," I replied.

Saturday night arrived, and after a few drinks in a local bar, we leisurely made our way to a very smart party in Kensington, London. However, as the night progressed, any of the earlier decorum shown by the guests seemed to fly out of the window. The champagne flowed and the raucous party went into over-drive. Later in the evening, a little bit worse for wear, I found myself sitting on a large, cosy sofa next to a very funny Spanish guy named James.

"What do you do?"

"I'm a make-up artist," James replied.

"Oh, really? I used to do a bit make-up. I love the work of the make-up artist Laurie Starrett, don't you? I think he's great; he's got such a unique sense of style. He always knows how far to take things. He can be so over the top, and yet his work never looks overworked or vulgar."

"I don't believe you said that. I used to assist Laurie."

"You're joking."

I couldn't believe it. Seized by excitement, I went on to describe some of my favourite shoots that Laurie had done with the amazing photographer Ellen von Unwerth for *Vogue Italia*.

James and I talked late into the night about our passion for fashion. We talked about make-up, photographers, and our favou-rite models. I told him about my brief flirtation with the fashion industry, and he suggested that I go and see his booker, Justine, at his agency. When we said goodnight, James wished me luck and gave me her telephone number.

For weeks I looked at the telephone number. My indecision drove me and my friends mad. Should I give the agency a call? Should I give the fashion industry one last try? I just couldn't decide, but one thing was for sure—I had to make a decision fast. Amidst my career crisis, I decided there was only one thing for it—I picked up the phone and rang my best drag-queen friend called Barry. If anyone could help me, he could. After a brief

< 224 >

synopsis of my dilemma, we decided to meet at a small club in Falconberg Court, Soho.

Barry wore 'is best wig and 'is longest lashes.
'Is white lines a joke—
A large vodka wiv coke.
'E 'ad a big jam tart,
'Is designer clobber from
A rag-and-bone cart.
'E was done up like a right old kipper,
That girl-boy thing
Stank of good times and promises.
In 'er shiny black PVC catsuit and boots,
She was Diana Rigg wiv a platinum wig,
And 'er best friends called 'er Treacle.

"Do you believe in fate, Treacle? You know—that everything's predestined?"

"Well, I think we 'ave many fates in store for us in our lives. I think it's up to us what fates we encounter by the choices we make. Now come on, dolly, let's not get deep and meaningful, for gaud's sake."

Holding onto the bar with one hand whilst clutching his drink in the other, Treacle looked at me and continued.

"Now, you listen to me, sweet 'eart. You might nevah get another blow of the whistle again, if ya know what I mean. None of us are getting any younger, and if ya don't go for it now, you could end up an old tart like me. Now, do you think you could walk in these `eels? No, I don't think so. Now, you get your knickers in gear and get your skinny little arse over to that agency as fast as those terrible trainers you're wearing can take ya. Remember, mummy knows best, and make sure you call me when you've done the dirty deed. Now, shut the fuck up! You asked for my opinion and you've got it. Anyway, do you fancy one of those funny sambuca drinks that light up? I've always wanted to try one of those.

< 225 >

Hey, if it don't work out, who gives a shit? At least you've given it your best shot. Speaking of which, do you fancy another vodka chaser to go with that?"

Two days later, after I had recovered from my hangover, I rang the agency that James had recommended and asked to speak to Justine.

PART 6

CHAPTER 22

Amidst the frantic hustle and bustle of the busy agency, I bravely entered the large offices situated off Eagle Wharf Road near Old Street, London. When I was introduced to Justine, a rare and strange thing happened to me—for a few seconds, I found myself rendered almost speechless as I looked upon her incredible beauty. There seemed to be something so balanced and perfect about her refined facial features and her dark, beautifully shaped eyes. Justine's hair was short and dark, her lips full and defined, and her flawless skin was as smooth and pale as the finest alabaster. Looking at her face was like looking at an exquisite piece of art. Justine was one of the most beautiful women that I had ever encountered. When she stood up to lead me to a quieter location where we could talk in private, she towered high above me. As I followed in her footsteps, I felt in awe of this extraordinary woman who possessed such a powerful physical presence.

It's strange, those odd, occasional times in your life when you meet a total stranger who you feel you have known forever; you find yourself conversing as though they're an old friend that you haven't seen for a while. It's almost like an invisible magical chemistry immediately connects you to them, and like a magnet you are drawn together. This is how I felt as I talked to Justine and answered her questions about my book. I felt as if I had finally

< 229 >

found the right person to represent me. It seems that the beautiful Justine felt the same way, because after our little chat she showed my book to her boss and then came over to me, shook my hand, and offered me a place at the agency. As I walked out of the office and down the metal staircase towards the pavement below, I could feel my excited heart pounding. I realized that I was in the right place, with the right person, at the right time. I immediately rang Treacle and gave him the good news.

Before Justine became a booker representing hairstylists, make-up artists, and fashion stylists, she had worked within the fashion industry as a model. This unique insight into the world of fashion proved to be an invaluable source of education for me, because Justine taught me to see images in a different way. I stopped viewing images from just a hair and make-up perspective and began to see the bigger picture. I started to see the importance of a picture working as a whole in order to create its strongest impression. With my newfound awareness, we decided it would be a good idea to change the images in my book. It was hard to let go of pictures I had worked so hard for—pictures that I loved and was so proud of—but in order for my book to become stronger, adjustments had to be made. I learnt that sometimes it's better to have just a few really strong images in your book rather than to mix them with mediocrity. I learnt to be very strict and ruthless when it came to editing my work.

Justine's career as a top model had really become established after she was introduced to David Bailey at a party in Milan. Mr. Bailey decided to use her for a beauty shoot for *Vogue Italia*, and the next day, by chance, she bumped into Barry Lategan, who also asked her to do a shoot for the prestigious magazine. After these shoots her career really took off, and her beautiful face appeared on the covers of *Vogue Italia*, French *Elle*, *Amica*, *Grazia*, and many other publications, so I felt that I was in more than capable hands as she directed my career.

Justine was a lot more than a booker, she was an inspiration, and like a muse she rekindled the flames of my dead imagination

< 230 >

and creativity. My strength and determination returned with a renewed vigour when I realized that somebody believed in me and my abilities.

The first major questions that came to mind when I joined my new agency were what did I want to achieve within the fashion industry, and how should my abilities be channelled within its tumultuous realms? After having established that I wanted to be both a hair and make-up artist and follow a more commercial path within the fashion industry, I then had to decide how I should market myself. Was I predominately a hairdresser who did make-up or a make-up artist that did hair? If I had a penny for every time a client asked me, "Which particular aspect of your work is your strongest?" I would be a rich man. The truth is, I felt equally talented in both areas of my work and enjoyed them both. It was confusing and very frustrating at times to have to make big decisions that were going to affect the rest of my career. Up until this point, my book had been tailored towards the high end of the fashion industry—it was highly creative, extreme, and very experimental, and it contained just the sort of images that would terrify any commercial clients away. On occasion, some commercial clients had even laughed at some of the images in my book, ridiculing them because their avant-garde nature. Well, I decided the time had come to change their opinion of my work. I decided that I'd run around London for long enough with my highly creative book, which had got me noticed and respected but didn't seem to be able to get me any paid work. I was tired of my frugal existence of living on fried-egg sandwiches and toast, and I felt that it was time for my book to move in a different direction.

Justine worked hard. With my new "commercial" book in hand, I once again walked the A to Z of London's streets in pursuit of endless castings and photographers' appointments. I got used to rejection, and I learnt not to take disappointment personally. I soon realized that rejection is part and parcel of the fashion business; the quicker you got used to it, the better. However, it seems that I must have made a good impression on some the clients and photographers

< 231 >

that I saw, because I received some good news from Justine: my first "catalogue" booking had been confirmed. Although I was happy to do the job and earn more money in two weeks than I'd seen in my entire life, I still had reservations about doing this kind of work, as I regarded "catalogue work" as creatively "selling out." However, regardless of my personal artist feelings, I thought, *I'm going away into the sun and getting paid for it. Who gives a monkey's?* The flights were booked, I said farewell to Justine, and then I found myself lost, frightened, and on my way to Portugal to work with a photographer called Bill Ling.

This trip would prove to be one of the most important of my career. I soon realized that catalogue work was not as easy as it appeared, and that there was a whole host of new skills that needed to be mastered in order for the hair and make-up to work within this fashion genre. With a lot of help from the models, I started to understand the essential skills needed to style and dress "catalogue hair" and maintain the hairstyles in all kinds of weather conditions. This was an art in itself, especially when it was very windy or humid. I also discovered that our two models were like "supermodels" of the catalogue world. Although they didn't work for French *Vogue* or do any of the major fashion shows, they worked constantly, made an awful lot of money, and had a great lifestyle. After these new realizations, my perception of the catalogue world rapidly changed. I also learnt that it's a good idea to get on with the models your working with, because if they like you, they will usually tell you if their hair can be difficult and how you can avoid any foreseeable hair disasters. After all, nobody knows their hair and make-up better than they do, and you can learn an awful lot of tips and tricks from their valuable experience. Most models appreciate it if you work quickly and efficiently, especially when most "call times" are at five thirty or six in the morning—sometimes even earlier if a particular location is far away. Catching the right light at the right time is the name of the game in this particular field of fashion.

< 232 >

One of the models working on the catalogue shoot was a stunning Brazilian girl called Jacqueline. She looked like Cindy Crawford's twin. Beautiful Jacqueline was from a humble background, and the money that she had made from the fashion industry had allowed her to financially support her entire family. She was a lovely girl, and we got on immediately. I loved her warmth, her generosity, and her natural sensuality.

One very hot afternoon, we were told that we could have a break, so Jacqueline and I decided to go to the beach for a swim. As we walked over the hot sand, I began to notice people staring in our direction. *That's odd*, I thought. I looked behind me. No, nothing strange happening there. I asked Jacqueline if I had anything on my face. No, that was OK. I looked fine, she said—but the staring continued. When the penny finally dropt, I felt embarrassed and a little stupid, because I realized that our audience were staring at my beautiful companion.

That day, as we walked along the beach, I started to understand what it might be like to be absolutely drop-dead gorgeous. The reaction Jacqueline caused as we casually walked down the beach was something that I will never forget. On that bright and sunny day, I learnt a little about the power of true beauty.

I returned back from my trip looking like a lobster, but feeling a lot wiser. I think one of the hardest things for me to except when I first started travelling and working within the fashion industry was its transitory nature. You could work, socialize, and become quite close with some people on trips, and then when it was all over, they were gone out of your life forever. It felt very odd, although it was very interesting meeting so many different characters. Every trip employed its own photographer (along with their assistants), production team, creative director (representing the client), fashion stylist (or editor), hairstylist, and make-up artist, and the models were usually flown in from all over the world. On some jobs I was booked as a hair and make-up artist, and on others I was booked as a make-up artist or hairstylist. Of course, after working for so many

< 233 >

years on countless trips, you do stay friends with some people, but by and large, that's the way the transient fashion cookie crumbles.

My next foray into the world of commercial hair and make-up came in the form of a major tabloid newspaper, working on stills for their very successful game called Pronto Bingo.

Busy set designers and builders joked amongst themselves as they put the finishing touches to their handiwork; they had transformed part of the photographic studio into "Santa's little grotto." As I sat and patiently waited to make my final hair and make-up checks, my lovely models were pouring themselves into their skin-tight costumes. I felt excited on this shoot, as I had never worked with glamour models before, and I hoped that they liked their sexy hair and make-up. I had decided to give them a sultry look—dark damson-stained eyes, defined eyebrows, and false eyelashes with lots and lots of black mascara. I painted their lips nude and applied lashings of shiny lip gloss. After moisturizing their sun-kissed skin, I applied lots of shimmering body bronzer, and I painted their beautifully manicured nails in soft, natural tones. I wanted their long blonde hair to look sexy and a little dishevelled, so I tonged their hair with large curling irons, creating a soft "tussled" effect. I then added a little backcombing to their sexy coiffures and dressed their hair out. The whole look was inspired by the gorgeous French actress Brigitte Bardot.

As Melinda Messenger and Emma Noble changed into their costumes behind the curtain, I could hear the muffled sounds of giggling and laughter. Ten minutes later, the mischievous pair appeared.

"So, wada ya think?" Melinda asked, as the dynamic duo stood before me in their matching Santa outfits. What could I say? I just loved their very short, red-satin skirts and figure-hugging tops, which were trimmed with white ostrich feathers. Yes, they seemed fine, but I wasn't so sure that Santa's little helpers would have worn bobby socks and trainers in the Arctic. Their jolly costumes were accessorized with large red-and-white Santa hats, from which hung

< 234 >

small golden bells that occasionally tinkled. Of course, every time we heard "a little tinkle," we would all burst into fits of laughter.

All day, I listened to the photographer shout, "Bright, sunny smiles, please, girls!" as the fake white snow fell and the girls held their large bingo cards towards the camera.

The next glamour model that I had the pleasure to work with was the wonderful Jilly Johnson; the original "page three" girl. Jilly was sexy, intelligent, and very sophisticated. It was a real treat to watch her, because she "worked" the camera like a true professional. She knew exactly what she was doing, and she knew exactly what the photographer wanted. Of course, the fact that she was gorgeous and had the most incredible body did help.

I stumbled across one of the world's most iconic glamour models by mistake, as I waited in a corridor while backstage at a television show.

As Jordan came out of her dressing room, her "money-makers" came first, as Pamela Anderson would say. Her beautiful face followed shortly afterwards. A fire burned within her feline eyes, which were outlined in the blackest kohl and a shadow of peacock blue. An invisible wisdom seemed to lie upon her smooth brow, as she stood in cut-off shorts, cut high and coloured white. I heard her earthy laugh as she passed by—my motorbike jacket she liked—and I watched as she climbed the steep stage steps with expert ease. She was there to talk of love and her new book.

Things slowly started to take shape for me at my new agency, and for the next few years I worked really hard, constantly upgrading my book, travelling, and getting used to my new lifestyle.

At times it could be intimidating, such as when I was invited to sophisticated restaurants. I'd never eaten in such establishments before, and on many occasions I'd sit and read a menu without understanding what was actually on it, let alone how to use the array of cutlery in front of me. Lobster, crab, and oysters I avoided like the plague, as I had absolutely no idea how to eat them correctly. On one particular trip, whilst working for *Cosmopolitan*

< 235 >

magazine, the crew decided to go for dinner at beautiful fish restaurant. I didn't know how to eat oysters, but in spite of my frustration (or because of it), I decided to order them anyway. When my lovely oysters arrived, I casually carried on talking until the other diners started to eat their wonderful seafood. That way, I could see how they opened their oysters and observe which sauces and dressings they applied. I thought it all looked simple enough; however, as I swallowed my first oyster, I realized I had forgotten to do one crucial thing, and that was to cut the little blighter from its shell. Suddenly, I found myself choking and turning very red as I struggled to detach my little friend. Everyone was in fits of laughter, including me—I guess we all have to learn somehow. In many ways, the fashion industry opened up a new world to me: it was exciting, fun, and very hard work. I soon got use to my new world, but one thing that I never got used to were certain individuals who seemed to moan about nothing. I would sit and listen to them waffle on about rubbish—their pillows weren't stuffed with goose feathers, or their fruit wasn't cut properly, or the water pressure in their shower wasn't quite strong enough. *They should try the water pressure in the council flats in Wood End*, I thought. Yes, there were a few spoilt individuals floating around certain hotel swimming pools, but there were also a lot of fantastic folks, too, and those were the people that I chose to hang out with.

With my new agency, I felt that I was definitely making progress with my career, and just as I was beginning to feel comfortable and settled within my new life, Cupid put another arrow in his bow and fired it in my direction.

< 236 >

CHAPTER 23

O ne fateful evening, having finished a strenuous workout
at a gym I had joined in Soho, I made my way towards
the tube station to go home. Suddenly, a little thought
popped into my head, suggesting that I go and have a nice cold
beer. *Because you're worth it*, the thought assured me. I decided to
take the thought's advice and soon found myself ordering a beer
in a local bar. Amidst the loud, pumping music, I took a seat at
the bar and tried to look relaxed and cool as I opened a magazine
and pretended to read it. The bar was quiet, the night was young,
and I felt conspicuously alone. My attention was drawn to a small
group of friends laughing and joking together. Amongst the jolly
crew was a short, dark, handsome stranger—I couldn't stop myself
from staring. Embarrassed, I tried to pretend that I was looking for
a friend who was about to arrive. There seemed to be something
different, something special, about this person that I couldn't quite
fathom. I felt intrigued as I watched him, although he paid no
attention to me. I was disappointed and unimpressed when one of
his friends came over and asked me out. I declined his kind offer
and finished my drink.

It's *always the bloody same*, I thought to myself as I left the
bar—always the bridesmaid and never the bride. At the age of
thirty-four, I had become a little disillusioned with the gay scene,

< 237 >

accepting that I was never going to find my Mr. Right. Feeling dejected, I decided it was too early to go home, so I went on a little tour of Soho instead. Several beers and a few bars later, I made my way towards the tube station to go home. As I walked past the first bar that I had visited earlier in the evening, I wondered if my "special friend" might still be there, so I plucked up some Dutch courage and decided to go back in for another drink. Unbeknown to me, this decision would be one of the most important of my life.

The bar was very busy now. I sucked in and squeezed through the masses of people, looking for my "friend," but alas, he was nowhere to be seen. He must have gone home, I concluded, holding my drink securely and searching the faces in the crowd. However, just as I acknowledged that I had lost my friend for good, I turned around and there he was, standing next to me at the bar.

A few hours after I had met "Shaky," I told him that we would be together for the rest of our lives. He told me I was mad, and that he already had a boyfriend. I told him that I didn't care, and that I would wait for him for as long as it took, because I knew that he was the one for me. Well, it seems I wasn't so mad after all, because two weeks later Shaky moved in with me, and for seventeen years we have shared our lives together.

My next lucky break came when Justine sent me on a casting to one of the largest plus-size retail companies in the UK. It seemed that their new art director, Regan Sin, was looking for hair and make-up artists who could bring fresh ideas and breathe new life into the dated looks of the current models who appeared in their catalogue. Regan wanted a more "real" feel for the hair and make-up that would complement not only the clothes, but also the location and dynamics of her new images. Regan didn't want to see her models fully made up with lots of foundation, powder, and lipstick when they were meant to be casually relaxing on the beach modelling swimwear. Regan showed me some pictures from the current catalogue and asked me what I would do to improve the models' hair and make-up, having been given my recent "brief."

< 238 >

Well, Regan must have been happy with my response, because three weeks later I found myself in a huge silver location van, bound for a small town in the middle of the Arizona desert, near Phoenix.

Looking out of the dusty windows, the dry, desolate desert seemed to stretch forever in every direction. Cacti of every age, size, colour, and variety grew from every crevice of the "cowboy and Indian" landscape. As our location van rolled into the little desert town, a small group of locals gathered to see the new arrivals. When our weary crew made its way out of the location van and stepped onto the dusty terrain, we were greeted with a variety of curious, puzzled looks. "Who were these strange people and what were they wearing?" the locals appeared to be thinking, as they stared at Regan Sin. Dressed in Prada, Gucci, and six-inch Christian Louboutin spikes, her choice of clothing may not have been the most appropriate, given the rural surroundings. For a moment, as I stepped off the location van, I felt a little bit like Calamity Jane getting off her stagecoach, and judging from the looks I received from some of the local cowboys, it seems they thought the same. Maybe it hadn't been such a good idea to change into my Jean Paul Gaultier shorts after all. I decided to take a little stroll around town while Regan and the photographer decided what to do next.

You could get lynched in a town like this, I told myself, as I swung open the saloon bar doors in search of a cold beer and some shelter from the searing heat. As I sat in the old western-style saloon bar and ordered a drink, I almost expected Jesse James to appear "full guns blazing"; for here, in this small town, many a Wild West outlaw had lived and died.

Our first location was a short distance away from the small town. When we approached a huge oasis of gigantic rocks and trees amidst the endless desert, I felt surprised and excited. Climbing over the huge rocks and boulders was a tricky business; the crew had to be very careful to keep their balance as we carried a huge array of clothes and equipment, but it was all worthwhile when we reached our goal—the view was truly amazing. Looking down on the enormous prehistoric lakes from the huge rocks surrounding

< 239 >

them was a wondrous thing. A silence—a stillness—emanated from this deserted, forgotten, timeless place. As I surveyed the deep blue waters of the ancient lakes, I felt almost like an intruder.

After hours of travelling and painstaking preparation, the crew made their final checks just before the shoot was about to start. The photographer's assistant took his final light reading and the models took their positions standing on the rocks, contrasted against the incredible panoramic scenery. Suddenly, out of nowhere, we heard loud voices followed by raucous laughter. As the whole crew turned its attention towards the lake below, two naked cowboys accompanied by their dogs sprinted to the edge of the lake, shouting and wildly splashing each other as they jumped into the water. However, the noise soon died down, and their attention was swiftly drawn to us when they noticed our crew and our two beautiful models.

"Don't suppose you fine young ladies fancy goin' skinny dippin'?" They hollered. "The water's mighty fine, although folks do say a few real big water snakes have been found around these parts," the cowboys joked, proceeding to wash themselves and their dogs in the lake.

"Thanks for the offer, but we have to work now," one of our models bravely replied.

Immersed in the cool, refreshing waters of the lake, the two naked cowboys and their dogs watched with fascination as the shoot began. They clapped and whistled and cheered with approval as the models changed their outfits in the mobile changing room amongst the rocks, saving precious time and light by not going back to the location van. Upon leaving the lake, the cowboys wore very cheeky smiles and nothing else. They covered up their "bits and pieces" with their hands and told us "what a mighty fine time" they'd had.

As the sun went down on the cooling plains of the Arizona desert, our location van drove swiftly on. Through the descending dusty night we travelled; eventually, we arrived back in Phoenix.

< 240 >

That evening, I dreamt I was a little boy again, playing with my fort, my plastic pistol, and my cowboys and Indians.

Regan Sin was a pretty, pale heiress from an affluent and wealthy family in Australia. She could have been a socialite, a top lawyer, or a rich man's "trouble and strife," but Regan had more sauce than that, and she had decided to follow a financially independent and creative life. Regan loved to drink vintage champagne, but she hated to sit out in the sun. I wouldn't say she was a slave to fashion, but her passion for designer labels sometimes got out of control. Her hair was short, sharp, dark, and chic. Regan had excellent taste—her addiction to shopping at Prada was her only expensive disgrace. Regan didn't really care, though. She figured what the hell—her grandmother also wore designer clothes. She just preferred to shop at Chanel.

Regan Sin changed my life and gave me hope as she revolutionized the plus-size fashion industry. Sales soared with the success of her first catalogue, and I found myself working with her on a regular basis, frequently travelling to Miami, New York City, and Cape Town. For the first time in my life, I started to make some real money.

Unlike some of my contemporises, I didn't spend my hard-earned cash on fast cars, designer clothes, expensive restaurants, or drugs. Instead, I was boring and sensible and I saved my cash, in the hope that maybe one day, Shaky and I might be able to buy our own home.

The first time that I went to South Africa was shortly after apartheid had ended. A few years earlier, I had attended a premiere for a film called *Cry Freedom*, directed by Sir Richard Attenborough. The film told the story of the escape of some political activists from South Africa, so I had some idea of the struggles, victimization, and injustices that had actually taken place in this country. However, I had no first-hand experience of the incredible, excruciating poverty in which black South Africans lived.

< 241 >

Nelson Mandela was free, and I sensed a feeling of hope and excitement in the air as I walked out of the airport and into the African sunshine. Sitting in the front of a transit van bound for Geneva Drive in Cape Town, I welcomed the cool air-conditioning. As our van sped down the motorway, the first thing that I noticed was the other vehicles on the road. Overloaded to the maximum, every inch of space in the vehicles was utilized. Crammed vehicles full of black South Africans made their way into Cape Town. The next thing that I noticed as we drove down the motorway was the huge sprawling townships on both sides of the road. I felt deeply moved and shocked when I saw the inhumane conditions in which these people fought to survive; I had never seen anything like it. For the first time in my life, I felt ashamed and embarrassed of my white skin. Thousands upon thousands of people were living in abject poverty; their homes were like cattle sheds made from cardboard, broken wood, loose bricks, and anything else they could find. However, as I arrived at Geneva Drive, I saw a different world—a "white world" full of luxury houses with swimming pools, expensive cars, and servants. I didn't see anyone going hungry in this domain. These two opposing worlds couldn't have been more extreme, but the white folks living here didn't seem too concerned. Their only real concern was for their own safety, so they made sure they hired top-notch private security firms to enforce it.

The first photographer that I worked with in South Africa lived in London, but he had been born and bred in Cape Town, so he knew all the best clubs, bars, and restaurants, and he showed us Cape Town's vibrant nightlife.

One evening he took us to a very exclusive restaurant, where we all laughed and had fun enjoying the five different courses of excellent food served with champagne and the finest South African wines. It was one of the most superb meals I had ever eaten, and we all felt in good spirits as we left the restaurant under the star-spangled skies of the warm African night. Outside, I paused for a

< 242 >

moment to light a cigarette when I felt a little "tug" on my trousers. When I looked down to see what it was, a little boy who couldn't have been more than four and a half years old looked up at me. "Please, please, sir—could you give me some change for some food?" he asked. I couldn't quite believe what I was seeing; it was late at night, and the little boy seemed alone. As I looked at his cute little face, I started to search for some change, but I soon realized that I didn't have any. A colleague who I had been talking with turned to me and said, "Don't give him anything, darling. His parents will only spend it on drugs. If you give it to one of them, you'll have to give it to them all," she assured me.

"What's wrong with that?" I asked. I turned to the production manager and asked him if he would go back into the restaurant to change my money.

When I gave the little boy some change, his little face lit up. "Thank you, thank you sir!" he joyfully exclaimed. Then he ran away. Within seconds, more children appeared, as if from nowhere. I quickly divided my money amongst the children and made my way towards the transit van, where an impatient crew were waiting to go home. Just as I was about to get in, I noticed one little boy that I must have forgotten. He was very distressed, and as he started to cry, he looked down and said, "But you—you didn't give me anything. Please, sir, please," he pleaded. I asked one of the crew to lend me some money to give to the little lad. When I gave him the money, he looked up at me. His tears were still wet on his face, and he clenched the precious note in his hand. "Thank you, thank you, sir," he cried in disbelief, as I said goodbye and closed the van door. Just as I was about to put on my seat belt, one of the members of our crew remarked, "You'll never get rid of them like that." I had to bite my lip and ignore her ignorant comment, as I knew I couldn't afford to upset anyone and risk losing my biggest client. As the van pulled away, the smiling children ran after it, waving and cheering madly until we were out of sight.

< 243 >

As they disappeared into the night, I thought about their young lives. I thought about their future, and how hard, cruel, and unjust this life can be.

The first production team that I worked with in South Africa had their work cut out for them when our photographer requested a location van. They had a big problem trying to find a vehicle that had the right facilities, since professional location vans didn't exist in South Africa at that time. However, our photographer was adamant about his request, and he told them to do their best, as he wanted to shoot some pictures on location in a desert outside of Cape Town.

And so, one bright South African morning, I was greeted by a small caravan with no air conditioning. *Just what you need*, I thought to myself, anticipating the scorching heat of the arid desert. Upon entering the antiquated caravan, I was greeted by my lovely models as they got stuck into their hearty breakfasts, followed by numerous packets of crisps, potato chips, and chocolate bars of every description. The production team certainly knew how to keep their plus-size models happy.

"Well, girls, it's nice to see some models enjoying their food, and not just pushing a lettuce leaf around their plate," I quipped, putting down my bag.

"In this business, a girl's got to look after her figure," Angel informed me, as she stuck out her bosom and winked.

It was hard work preparing my three models in the confined space of the hot caravan, and even harder to acclimatize them to their new hair and make-up. Gone were their heavy bases of foundation, concealer, and powder. Their false eyelashes, lipstick, and lip liner "bit the dust" as I implemented my new style of maquillage. However, like magic, every now and again after a visit to the caravan's toilet, that tired old lip pencil or heavy lipstick would reappear on one of the models lovely mouths. Did they seriously think I wouldn't notice? Anyway, after much wrist slapping and debate, I eventually found myself making my final hair and make-up checks in the hot, windy desert of South Africa.

< 244 >

Like beautiful maidens from a sultan's harem, the girls looked gorgeous in their colourful, romantic evening dresses; their hair and the chiffon from their dresses blew softly in the hot desert winds. However, that was not all that was blowing in the wind. Just as the photographer was about to shoot, a very loud and prolonged fart was heard coming from the direction of the models, projecting itself with a vengeance through the warm desert airwaves like some kind of supersonic stink bomb. The photographic crew covered their noses and looked with suspicion at the models. Seconds later, the very gorgeous but guilty-looking Angel declared,

"I guess folks are right to call Cape Town 'the windy city.'"

"Well, it sure smells and sounds windy out here, girlfriend!" Keisha confirmed, turning towards Angel.

"Damn, it must have been all that cereal I ate at breakfast," Angel surmised, while Keisha, one of our other gorgeous models, held her nose and ran for it.

"Sorry, guys. I couldn't help it—it just popped out," Angel innocently announced to the crew, who were by now convulsing in laugher. I could feel the tears of laughter running down my own face, as I looked at the bewildered face of Regan Sin who was so shocked by the recent events that she speechless.

Over the years I have worked in Cape Town many times, and I am amazed at remarkable changes this vibrant city has undergone. Investments in the infrastructure are reshaping the landscape and skylines of this lively community; it seems more tolerant and prosperous, and more racially integrated and cosmopolitan. However, some things don't seem to change at all.

As the location van drove swiftly down the N2 motorway, Radio Good Hope played "Lovely Day" by the soul legend Bill Withers. I looked out the window at the torrid township that bled into the distance for as far as I could see, and I wondered if its inhabitants felt the same way. Slowly, the van dropt speed as we came to a sign that apologized for the road work in progress. The sign stood on the edge of the motorway, right in front of the township. It read, Sorry for the Inconvenience.

< 245 >

CHAPTER 24

Having established some regular commercial clients, I felt that I could now concentrate on the more creative, editorial fashion scene. After a lot of careful consideration, Justine and I decided that it might be better to have two separate portfolios that could specifically target each of these particular areas. More rounds of appointments followed, as I hit the tangled streets of London in search of fashion editors and exciting new photographers that I could work and test with. All my hard work and perseverance was rewarded when Justine started to get some positive feedback.

A couple of weeks later, I did an amazing 1950s-inspired test with a stunning blue-eyed blonde called Joanna Rhodes and a beautiful brunette called Saffron Burrows, who later went on to become a very successful actress. I also did another wonderful test with two other beautiful models—Lisa Uphill, who looked like a young Vivien Leigh, and Charlotte Weston, who was a sultry brunette with beautiful green eyes. I was told that Charlotte had once been the muse of the wonderful photographer Bob Carlos Clarke. All of these girls were top models, and although at times I found my nerves getting the better of me, I felt inspired working with them and I learnt an awful lot.

I was not the only seed slowly learning and steadily growing within the agency, and so it came as no surprise when I was told

< 247 >

that our very busy organization was expanding and moving to bigger premises in Westbourne Park, London.

After the agency had moved, it was suggested that everyone should make a fresh composite card in a quest for a new creative beginning. I started negotiations with Justine as we searched London for talented photographers who were working with great fashion stylists and art directors. I was commissioned to do some amazing beauty shoots with the super-talented Australian photographer Bronwyn Kid, and I quickly did an amazing test with a wonderful Danish photographer called Rene Dupont. I also received a commission from the brilliant Swedish photographer Anders Petersen. As I slowly gathered my new images together for my new card, I had a lot of creative meetings with a photographer I had previously worked with named Jack Zalowski, and he introduced me to a new stylist who had just joined my agency. This amazing "style guru" had great ideas, great enthusiasm, and a beautiful girlfriend called Tess Daly. Tess was a very successful model who had recently had her long blonde hair cut off into a short style that looked soft and sexy. Tess was gorgeous, and her new look totally flattered her beautiful face. With her down-to-earth, fun-loving, up-for-it personality, this stunner from Manchester could be "one of the lads" one minute, and look like the most gorgeous goddess the next. We had a lot of laughs working together, and the pictures that came out of our collaboration were fantastic. I used some of the best shots for the cover of my new card. In fact, I used another picture of Tess that Jack had taken for the *London Evening Standard* for the entire cover of my next.

I'm not quite sure how my career started to take off. To me it seemed to take forever, but in reality, I was a bit like a ball rolling down a hill, slowly gaining momentum until suddenly, everything happened at once. I guess things really started to change when my creative dreams were answered by a photographer called Nick Clements. I met him whilst grooming some gorgeous male models on a menswear shoot for Debenhams. I'd heard rumours about this photographer, and I'm happy to report that they are all

< 248 >

true. Nick is very funny, intelligent, and creative, and he is also an exceptionally gifted photographer. I loved working with Nick. I loved to watch him as he photographed and questioned the world around him—the way that he captured life through his camera lens fascinated me. His mind, like his camera lens, was always open, always looking, always exploring. I worked with Nick on some major advertising assignments for Ellesse, Pierre Balmain, and No. 7 Cosmetics. Nick's photography is unique and truly astounding. I will always be grateful to Nick, because the creative opportunities that he gave me in his amazing books of photography totally changed my editorial book.

I had also worked on a regular basis for the smaller editorial sections of *Cosmopolitan* magazine with a fashion stylist called Mary Eustace. Of course, I kept my fingers, toes, and everything else crossed, in the hope of working on the magazines main fashion pages. It was a long wait, but eventually I got my chance when I was booked for an eight-page "story" for their supplement.

I felt very excited when I turned up outside the photographic studio of the famous fashion and celebrity photographer Tony McGee. I had enjoyed working with him on several previous occasions, so I was familiar with the way that he liked to work. I appreciated his down-to-earth sense of humour, as he always "told it like it was" in a very funny way. Like his beautiful, strong, black-and-white portraiture, Tony was powerful and direct.

I respected the way that Tony valued the importance of a moment—that fraction of second when everything comes together, which can be so easily overlooked and lost forever. When Tony worked, he became totally absorbed with his subject matter. He lost himself, and nothing else existed or mattered until he'd captured that fleeting moment he had been searching for with his camera. He worked with complete focus, passion, and professionalism.

Our gorgeous model was called Sophie Anderton, and she was "the talk of the town" due to her sensational advertising campaign for Gossard lingerie. The first thing that struck me about Sophie's classical good looks was her wonderful skin. I didn't have

< 249 >

to use any base, just a little concealer and a touch of powder. Excited by the shoot, I decided to "go for it" and so I emphasized her lovely brown eyes in tones of chocolate, metallic gold, and dark charcoal. I finished off my handiwork with a little kohl and lots of my favourite black mascara. I highlighted her cheekbones and temples using a natural blusher, and I painted her lips using a dark shade of plum lipstick by Christian Dior. Sophie looked stunning, and Mary, our lovely fashion editor, was very pleased. I set Sophie's long brunette hair on large rollers, and afterwards I sprayed it very lightly with a fine mist of water, so that it looked relaxed and natural whilst still retaining its body and movement. The shoot was all about colourful coats, jackets, sexy boots, and fun, so Tony tried to capture this mood by using a wind machine to create a sense of drama and movement. Sophie worked hard by running, walking, skipping, and jumping around the studio for hours. She knew the mood and feel that Tony and Mary wanted, and she did her very best to achieve it. When the pictures were published, I loved them—they reminded me of the New York fashion scene in the early 1970s. I worked with Sophie on several other occasions after this shoot, and I always found her to be a lot of fun and a great model.

My next big break came along when I was introduced to the legendary photographer called Clive Arrowsmith. As soon as I met this larger than life character, I knew that we would get on. During our conversation, I told Clive about my previous visits to the Buddhist monastery known as Samye Ling, and he showed me a remarkable portrait that he had taken of His Holiness Tenzin Gyatso, the fourteenth Dalai Lama of Tibet. I felt that he had truly captured the grace, gentleness, humility, and compassion of this man in his astonishing portrait. Another iconic picture that I greatly admired by Clive was a black-and-white portrait of the beautiful actress Charlotte Rampling. This captivating image had graced the beauty pages of *Vogue*, and I wasn't surprised. For me, the photo captured a sense of mystery and French eroticism. The first time that I saw this picture, its brilliance moved me, like all

< 250 >

great art should. Clive is an amazing photographer, and during his career he has photographed some of the biggest models and celebrities of our time. His work has appeared in numerous editions of *Vogue* magazine, and he is the only photographer to have shot the famous Pirelli Calendar twice. I couldn't believe it when Justine told me he had booked me for a job. I felt very honoured to be working with such a "master of the light."

Working with Clive was never dull. He always had a lot of funny, interesting tales to tell, and his skill and effervescent personality captivated and charmed those around him. He was a master of his art and a true perfectionist. With infinite patience, Clive showed me a variety of ways that I could improve my skills, and he showed me the results through his camera lens so that I could understand the benefits of his instruction. I worked with him on numerous "bling" jobs for clients such as Asprey, Cartier, and Boodles; his photographic style was perfectly suited to these upmarket jewellery brands. I was also delighted because I got to try on the odd huge rock (or three) when the armed security guards who were escorting the jewellery weren't looking. Clive also introduced me to another gorgeous gem in the form of a stunning model called Lili Maltese, during a shoot at Leighton House in Kensington, London.

Another memorable shoot that I did with Clive was in and around the grounds of a very large Victorian castle in Scotland. The cashmere company that we were working for wanted their brochure to have a rural but classical feel. We had a great time, and the pictures were wonderful, but staying in a place so vast can have its drawbacks. My room was in one of the turrets of the castle, so if I forgot anything important, it could take me a good twenty minutes to go and retrieve it, depending on where I was in the house or grounds. Of course, whilst getting ready for dinner, one had to also account for the time it would take to walk to the extensive dining room in order not to be late, as we had been warned that Her Ladyship liked her guests to be punctual. Upon entering the large wooden-panelled dining room, we

< 251 >

were greeted by Her Ladyship, who took her seat for the evening meal at the end of an extremely long table. His Lordship sat at the opposite end. This totally eccentric lady insisted that I sit next to her during every evening meal, and here, surrounded by old portraits of her husband's ancestors, she informed me of her passion for polo and told me that she was reputed to be "the scarlet woman of the borders." I didn't really converse with Her Ladyship; rather, I sat happily listening to her, since she talked at a rate of knots without drawing breath long enough for me to make any contribution to her witty repartee. Occasionally, I did manage to squeeze in the odd comment like "yes" and "no." Her Ladyship was a very knowledgeable historian, and she showed me some Elizabethan artefacts that had been in her husband's family for centuries. One document was a handwritten letter from Queen Elizabeth I, which stated her refusal to send any further monetary assistance to her troops. The letter looked like a wonderful piece of art, as her majesty's handwriting was executed with a quill and ink and was incredibly beautiful.

I must have had some kind of "bling radar" at this time in my career, because I also found myself working for another famous jewellery brand with the super-talented photographer Terry O'Neill at Blenheim Palace, home to the Duke of Marlborough. It took me hours to prepare my bevy of lovely models. I decided to give them a classical look, so I dressed their hair in simple French chignons and kept their make-up fresh and natural, so that they complimented the stunning, natural jewels that they were wearing. I vaguely remember drinking a few cocktails too many, and I asked the security guards if I could try on a large diamond tiara with a pair of matching diamond earrings. They didn't seem too keen on the idea; they just smiled at me politely. Oh well, you can't say I didn't try!

• • •

< 252 >

Aran met the legendary supermodel Lauren Hutton in an elevator in Miami. As he stood next to the fashion icon, he found himself saying the words that he swore he would never speak:

"I'm sorry to bother you, but I just have to say, I think you're wonderful!"

The handsome Lauren was as elegant and charming as she looked in her photographs. She was "totally awesome," you might say, and she smiled at Aran in her special, unique kind of way.

• • •

Although my career was going well, and I had found a partner that I could love and trust, every now and again the ghosts of my past would come back to haunt me. Who were my real parents, and why had I been adopted? I decided it was time to trace my past in an attempt to find some sort of peace and closure on these personal issues. I contacted the Family Records Centre and arranged to go for an interview. A few weeks later, I arrived at the centre and was introduced to a very caring lady in her mid-fifties. She tried to prepare me for any unforeseen scenarios, and she explained to me that if I did manage to contact my natural parents, they might not want to make any further contact with me. Did I want to continue my search for my parents? She asked. The answer was yes.

About a month later, I found myself back at the centre listening to the information that my adviser had gathered. It was a very emotional meeting because my ghosts became real people with names, histories, and feelings. However, I felt that I had got a clearer picture of my history, and it felt good to know who my parents were and where they had originated. As I left the centre, I was told about another agency that specialized in finding natural relatives. I rang their number and gave them all the information

< 253 >

I had. In a state of nervous expectation, I waited for more news. It felt strange. After all the years of speculation, I felt as if I was about to find the answers I'd been searching for—but sadly, this wasn't to be. When I finally received the telephone call that I had been waiting for, I was informed that they had traced my mother's whereabouts to Birmingham; however, they didn't know if she still resided at that address. The agency couldn't trace any further records, and I was told she could have passed away. I immediately sent off a letter to her last known address and waited patiently for a reply. Sadly, I received a letter from the current tenant informing me that they knew nothing about the previous tenant's whereabouts, as they had not left a forwarding address. There were no further leads to the whereabouts of my father, and so my search had come to a disappointing end. However, a different kind of search proved to be more successful.

After a lot of very hard work and relentless saving, "Shaky" and I finally scraped enough money together for a deposit to buy our own home. After viewing some very dodgy, overpriced properties in the East End of London, a friend of mine who was a very successful architect suggested that we start looking in Bermondsey, on the south side of the river. I went to check the area out and unfortunately got off the bus at the wrong stop, having arrived in Rotherhithe Street SE16 instead. However, as I looked around at the old converted warehouses that lined the street and overlooked the river Thames, I knew this was where I wanted to live, and I felt sure that Shaky would feel the same way. I immediately looked up some properties that were for sale in the area and made some appointments to go and view them. The first house that I saw in this area was set back across the road from the river and had numerous little parks nearby. As soon as I walked in, I knew I had found our little home, and excited by my find, I quickly rang Shaky and told him the good news. Shaky hadn't even seen the house when he agreed to buy it, but he trusted my judgement, and we moved into our little house a couple of months later. It was one of the happiest days of my life.

< 254 >

I remember many years earlier, when I had just moved to London and was living in a bedsit in a shared house, the tenants said, we would never own a property. Ten years later, on February 14, Valentine's Day, Shaky and I opened the door of our new home. That night I thanked my lucky stars as I lay in bed and looked out of the skylight window as they shone in the dark sky above.

Moving home wasn't the only transition I decided to make at this time. After seven long years with my current agency, I decided it was time for a change. Within a month, I had moved to a new agency near Gloucester Road, London SW5. My new booker, David, otherwise known as "Cashmere Connie," had a contagious enthusiasm and an instinctive ability to be able to put a book together with panache and creativity. This Welsh "super-booker" spent weeks perfecting my book, and he soon found me new exciting photographers to work with, such as John Swannell, Fabrizio Gianni, Wolfgang Mustain, and Sheila Rock. In order to improve the editorial look of my book further, David suggested that it might also be a good idea to join an agency in Paris. I soon found myself on the Eurostar train, bound for the City of Love. Nervously, I waited my turn to be seen by a top Parisian agency.

I had worked very hard for this opportunity, and I realized that it could open up a whole new world for me by enabling me to meet some of the world's most talented photographers and fashion designers. But would my book be strong enough? Several hours past my given appointment time, I was called into their office. As I sat before the bookers and gave the agency representatives my book, I got the distinct impression that no matter what I showed them, they wouldn't be impressed. *Oh well*, I told myself, *it was worth a go.*

"We're not really mad about English make-up artists. Their style doesn't typically suit the French market," the bookers told me, but as they started to look through my book, their attitudes seemed to change.

"You have something, definitely. Your work is beautiful and unique," they commented, turning the pages.

< 255 >

Over the next couple of hours, the bookers stripped my book and reassembled it using their favourite images.

"Do you speak French?" the bookers inquired.

I smiled politely and told them that I spoke a little; however, I promised to take a crash course (crash being the operative word) if they were willing to represent me.

"You're almost there, but not quite. You need a few more strong images to really give your book that 'wow' factor, but what you have achieved is really very beautiful and not at all what we were expecting. If you can learn to speak a little more French and deliver some more creative images, we would be happy to represent you. You would do very well here in Paris. Come back and see us when you feel your book is ready."

In a state of shock, I said goodbye and promised to return with more images. I walked out of the offices and floated down the grand French boulevards towards the train station. In a haze of euphoria, I misread the train timetable, confusing the arrival times with the departures, and I nearly missed my train home.

Upon arriving back in London, my mood swiftly changed when I received some devastating news. My stepmother, Doris, had been diagnosed with colon cancer. I immediately caught the train to visit her in Long Bennington, just outside of Grantham in Lincolnshire. Now in her early seventies, my mother had naturally grown a little frail, and everyone was very concerned how she would react to the surgery that she had been prescribed. It was a very worrying and traumatic time, but although my mother was ill and physically weak, her spirit was strong; she had a will of steel. I put any immediate plans to return to Paris on hold so I could be around to support her, and I prayed that my mother would make a full recovery. After her surgery, the doctor advised her to go to a convalescent home for three weeks to recuperate. I visited her regularly, and in an odd way we became closer. She opened up to me emotionally in a way that she had never done before. I guess when you face your own mortality, the way you see the world changes. Doris was born in 1916, and she had been bought up in a world where you didn't

< 256 >

show your emotions or talk about the way that you felt, and if you were a lady, you certainly didn't smoke in the street or use bad language. In the forty years that I knew her, I only ever heard her swear once, when she said "bloody hell," and it shocked us all. Of course we all laughed, but my mother was terribly embarrassed about her little outburst and apologized profusely. I'm happy to say my mother made a full recovery and went on to live for another seventeen years. Those girls from Nottingham are made of strong stuff.

Meanwhile, my career was going from strength to strength. I worked with the lovely actress and model Anita Pallenberg, who had the most unique accent and a wonderful sense of style and humour, and I worked with the gorgeous model Lisa Snowdon on a lingerie shoot for Debenhams. David was a fantastic booker, and boy did he push me. I didn't stop working, but I wasn't complaining. I realized that in the competitive world of fashion, you have to take the work while you can.

< 257 >

CHAPTER 25

I don't know why I decided to visit a clairvoyant. Maybe it was the unstable nature of my work (after all, in the world of fashion you can be flavour of the month one minute and be forgotten the next), or maybe I was just curious, but it wasn't long before I found myself at Waterloo station, boarding a train bound for the outskirts of London. As I walked up a hill towards my appointment, I wasn't sure that I had made the right decision. However, all my reservations were forgotten when I was greeted by the wonderful Sally Morgan. Today, Sally is a well-known psychic, author, and celebrity who's had her own very successful television series, but when we met, fame and fortune had not yet smiled so brightly upon her. As I took a seat in the comfortable surroundings of Sally's home, I felt a deep sense of relaxation. During my appointment, I was absolutely amazed when Sally told me that my natural mother was still alive.

"Yes, I'm definitely being asked to tell you that your mother is still alive, and by this I mean your natural mother. Does that make any sense to you?" Sally gently asked me.

I noted that Sally didn't say the same about my natural father. After an hour of more amazing revelations, I felt excited as I walked back down the hill towards the train station. I had decided to

< 259 >

resume my search for my natural parents, something I would never have done without Sally's spiritual guidance.

I decided to hire a private detective to help me with my quest. Sure enough, about a month later, he rang and told me that although he had been unable to trace my father, he had definitely located my mother.

"Are you sure you have the right person?"

"Definitely. There is no question about it," the detective assured me.

As I wrote down the relevant information and put down the phone, I felt a mixture of emotions. I struggled to comprehend the enormity of the situation. I immediately rang my sister Abi and told her the news, and I compiled a letter with some photographs and posted it to my mother. I waited with apprehension for her reply.

A couple of days later, whilst immersed in my spring cleaning, the phone rang. Drowning in soapsuds and smelling of furniture polish, I managed to remove my marigold gloves and answer the phone. It was my mother. It was strange chatting away to this total stranger who had given birth to me. I could feel my heart pounding as we talked, and I could tell from the sound of my mother's voice that she was obviously still in a state of shock, although she was friendly, welcoming, and very happy to speak to me. Oddly enough, although I felt nervous and excited, I didn't become emotional, which surprised me. However, I did feel curious to know more about my family.

Sadly, I discovered that my father had recently passed away (two years previously), and I was told that his father had been a giant, standing six feet seven inches. Apparently, my grandfather only had one leg and was quite a linguist. He could speak fluent Hindi due to the fact that he had been stationed in India during World War II. I found out that I had several other siblings—a half brother and an older sister, who also had a very handsome son. A couple of hours later, I spoke to my auntie for the first time, and she introduced me to her children. My family seemed to expand overnight. I also

< 260 >

learnt that my mother's father had led a very challenging life during the 1930s, travelling the world as a professional boxer. It was interesting to learn about my family's colourful history, and over the next few weeks the phone didn't stop ringing, as I spoke to my new relatives and heard about their lives. Eventually, my newly acquired sister suggested that we should all meet up, so we made arrangements and I counted the days. Finally, after all these years, I was going to meet my "natural" family.

As the taxi pulled up on the quiet residential street, I looked out of the window at the row of terraced houses. I felt a nervous, almost sick feeling in the pit my stomach as I took out my wallet and paid the driver. Abi looked at me and held my hand for a few seconds.

"Well, it looks like we're here. There's no turning back now," she said resolutely, getting out of the cab.

Searching for the door number and our courage, it wasn't long before we were walking down the short garden path towards the looming parameter of the front door. I could feel my heart pounding when we paused for a moment on the doorstep. Abi brushed some specks of dust from the shoulder of my jacket as we tried to compose ourselves.

My sister's boyfriend answered the door, and with his friendly smile came relief. I crossed the threshold and walked towards the kitchen, where my mother and sister where anxiously waiting to meet us. As we hugged and kissed each other, it really did feel like a family reunion or like meeting some dear friends that you haven't seen for a long time. When my sister and I conversed, our dialogue seemed to flow effortlessly, and as I observed her pretty face, some of my own genetic traits seemed to greet me. I recognized her mouth, her startling blue eyes, and other familiar facial characteristics. A mane of long blonde curls framed her fair face. Her skin was smooth and clear, and her graceful hands were long and slender. I noticed Abi's striking resemblance to our mother. They had the same nose, bone structure, and physique. It was strange to observe the shared genetic fingerprints that nature had sprinkled within

< 261 >

our family, and it made me feel connected with these strangers in a way that I hadn't expected.

After a few hours and several glasses of white wine, other members of my family started to arrive. I lost myself in conversation and tried in vain to remember all their names and how we were related. The whole evening was quite overwhelming and totally fantastic—it was certainly one of those special occasions that I will always remember. As I drifted off to sleep that night, I felt as if I had found the missing pieces of a jigsaw that I had lost as a child.

• • •

Aran breathed a sigh of relief when he arrived on time at the photographic studio. Clutching his bags, he quickly made his way over to the hair and make-up area, grabbed a coffee, and thought about his instructions from the art director. He knew the brief, so there shouldn't be problems. Unpacking his hair and make-up equipment in front of the large mirror surrounded by bright lights, Aran caught a glimpse of his tired reflection. "Oh, *Hammer House of Horror*!" he exclaimed, taking a sip of his coffee. Seconds later, Dusty, the superhot beauty model, breezed into the studio.

"Come on, darling. Make me beautiful," Dusty joked, taking a seat on the tall stool in front of Aran.

Sitting perfectly still with her eyes closed and her head slightly tilted back, Aran had a chance to survey the beautiful structure of the flawless face before him. A few minutes later, his attention was studiously immersed in his lotions and potions, and the small mounds of face powders that he mixed to achieve his desired shading and contouring effects. Slowly, Dusty's face started to take shape; things were looking good. However, as Aran applied a stroke of black liquid eyeliner to define her famous almond-shaped eyes,

< 262 >

disaster struck. In the blink of an eye, Aran wiped off the eyeliner with a wet cotton wool bud, avoiding a complete catastrophe.

"I must be allergic to the eyeliner. Thank God you took it off in time. I've got some wonderful news!" Dusty exclaimed, hugging Aran in relief.

"I'm 'on option' for the Max Factor campaign. They've got it down to two girls, and I'm one of them. Can you believe it?" Dusty excitedly exclaimed, squeezing Aran's arm. "I hope I get it," she sighed wistfully.

"So do I, sweetheart. If anyone deserves it, it's you," Aran replied.

Dusty, "the nearly new face of Max Factor," had worked for almost all the major beauty companies, and now it seemed that her big break had arrived. Her chance to shine was almost within her grasp. All the hours she had worked and all the miles she had walked felt like they had been worthwhile now.

"I know. Let's use a Max Factor eyeliner. You're obviously not allergic to their make-up," Aran suggested, gently wiping his canvas clean and preparing it again.

A few months later, bored at home with a beer in hand, Aran casually flicked through the television channels. By chance, he stumbled upon a gorgeous-looking Dusty starring in the new Max Factor campaign. Spilling his beer he jumped up and down, and ran around the room like a mad man. It seemed the lovely Dusty had gotten what she had worked so hard for and what she'd truly deserved. Aran felt delighted as he cracked another beer open.

"This one's for you, babe," he said, raising his glass.

Many moons later, Aran went to see Mr. Factor's exhibition at the Hollywood Entertainment Museum in Los Angeles. Walking around the exhibition, Aran thought about the beauty shoot he had shared with Dusty. He looked at the tiny lipsticks that Mr. Factor had created for Clara Bow and Jean Harlow when they had been the leading ladies of Hollywood in the 1920s and 30s during Hollywood's "golden age." Aran marvelled at the beautifully crafted silver compacts and the handmade false eyelashes on

< 263 >

display, and he studied "the master" at work in some old black-and-white photographs. Max Factor's beauty parlour near Hollywood Boulevard had been a haven of glamour for Joan Crawford, Mary Pickford, Jean Harlow, Gloria Swanson, Claudette Colbert, Pola Negri, Bette Davis, Norma Shearer, Judy Garland, and a host of other celebrity superstars.

Born in Poland in 1872, Max Factor began assisting a pharmacist at the age of eight, and he soon developed an interest in developing and producing cosmetics. After living in Russia for a time he moved to America, where his revolutionary cosmetics became an instant hit with the movie stars of the day. Mr. Factor created the first eyebrow pencils, wand mascaras, false eyelashes, coloured eyeshadows, and lip glosses. He even coined the term *make-up*. Before that, the word *cosmetics* had always been used. Walking out of the insightful exhibition, Aran started to hum the classic song "Hooray for Hollywood," and as he remembered the lyrics "But if you think that you can be an actor / See Mr. Factor / He'd make a monkey look good," he smiled to himself and wondered what Mr. Factor would have thought about the make-up industry today.

< 264 >

CHAPTER 26

As the wounds from my past started to heal, my confidence grew and my career went into overdrive. The tide of celebrity culture had well and truly arrived, and I was immersed in its waters. I was promptly booked to work with Jamie Cullum, Lauren Bush, Emilia Fox, Samantha Womack, Tamara Beckwith, Tamzin Outhwaite, Rachel Weisz, and a host of other bright stars.

David certainly kept me busy. I didn't know whether I was coming or going, and I felt like I was never off a plane. One minute I'd be in the Caribbean, and the next, I'd be in Portugal, Egypt, Tunisia, Morocco, Canada, France, Switzerland, Austria, Australia, Japan, Greece, Germany, Spain, Italy, South Africa, or America. I just didn't seem to stop. However, I wasn't complaining, because I realized how lucky I was to be working in an industry that allowed me to travel and discover the world. It was whilst on one of these trips to South Africa that I met a super-talented photographer called Thomas Reuter.

From the moment that I met Thomas, something clicked (and it wasn't his camera). I have to say that out of the hundreds of photographers I have worked with, Thomas is one of the most talented and intelligent. When it comes to his work, he is a perfectionist like myself (after all, I am a Virgo), so I respect the meticulous attention

< 265 >

to detail that he bestows on every aspect of his breathtaking photography. Thomas is always professional and he has the patience of a saint—after all, he has put up with me on numerous commissions. He is also great fun to work with, and there have been times, when I have just had to look at his mischievous face, to dissolve into fits of laughter. Thomas always takes time and great care to ensure that his models look incredibly beautiful. His lighting is always superb, and he gives one hundred and ten percent to each carefully crafted picture that he takes. It is always a pleasure to work with Thomas and his wonderful assistant called "Mouse," because this creative duo always see their work as a challenge. Come hail, wind, rain, or sunshine, they can always foresee a way around an obstacle and get the job done, even if it entails working in force nine gales or occasionally looking like a drowned rat. However, I never really cared, because when you're working with extraordinarily talented people, it's surprising how your tolerance levels increase.

David also confirmed bookings with Perry Ogden, Julian Broad, and Grant Sainsbury. They all inspired me greatly. Grant Sainsbury is one of those photographers who are passionate about their profession. He constantly pushes himself to his limits in order to capture the perfect image with his camera. His energy and enthusiasm are limitless. Mr. Sainsbury can do things with his camera that could make your hair curl. In his book, only the "golden shot" matters, and how you get it is up to you. If somebody told him that he could get a better angle for a picture by climbing Mount Everest, he would brave its harsh, snowy peaks and climb its deadly icy terrain in order to get it. Eccentric, humble, and ultra-talented, this supersonic photo phenomenon is never content with mediocrity, and he is never boring.

I met the beautiful actress and model known as Camilla Rutherford whilst working with Grant at Annabel's nightclub in Mayfair, London. This luxurious celebrity haunt had its own exclusive magazine to promote it, and when I arrived on the doorstep of its newly refurbished art-deco precincts, I started imagining Elizabeth Ponsonby, Brenda Dean Paul, Sir Cecil Beaton, and the

< 266 >

divine Stephen Tennant having a whale of a time within its sumptuous interior. And it was with these influences in mind that I started to get a clear idea of the look that I wanted to create for Camilla and the magazine. The walls were adorned with huge mirrors and posters from this decadent era of "the bright young people" during the 1920s, and chrome tables and stylish lamps were scattered amongst plush sofas and chairs of dark red velvet. Their elegant linear designs still appeared to be modern and sleek. I decided to try and capture some of the glamour of the Roaring Twenties, so I dressed Camilla's hair in a style reminiscent of this period by tonging her sandy-blonde tresses into loose curls and finger waves. I arched her eyebrows, defined her eyes, and painted her lips in a soft rose tone, adding lots of highly polished lip gloss. By the time I had finished, Camilla looked like a very glamorous 1920s movie star, and I felt sure that the wonderful Mr. Tennant would have been proud of my "bright" retrospective endeavours.

Imbued by the helpful guidance of my booker, David, I discovered a new sphere within the hair and make-up industry that I hadn't explored—that celluloid realm known as the television commercial. Once I passed into this unknown territory, I found the medium to be great fun and a real eye-opener. I think after you have worked on your first television commercial, you never quite see them in the same way again. Instead of just watching the commercials as you would normally, you start to dissect them, to see how they have been put together. You see them in a more technical, manufactured way. A few weeks after I had worked on my first commercial, I found myself sitting at home, transfixed to the front of the television screen analysing hair-removal creams and boxes of breakfast cereal. I asked myself questions, such as, "I wonder how many 'takes' that took?" or making statements like, "I think that part of the commercial was added in post-production." It's amazing what these technical geniuses can achieve. The first commercial that I worked on advertised a very well-known washing powder and was commissioned by the media company Saatchi & Saatchi. The poor model smiled brightly and opened and closed that washing

< 267 >

machine door a million and one times. She "worked" those soap-suds, believe me. Making a commercial is a bit like shooting a short film or cooking a superb meal—you need all the right ingredients, and everything has to be timed to perfection. I remember one of the crew asking me how long it would take to prepare our lovely model. When I replied, he took out a stopwatch and started to time me. I guess the budgets involved in producing a commercial can be enormous, so time and soapsuds can be very valuable. The finished commercial looked great, and I proudly received an enthusiastic phone call from my mother, Doris, informing me she had seen it on the television. For the rest of her life, my mother never used any other soap powder. She swore by it, and she managed to persuade half of her neighbourhood to use it. Like my mother used to say: "Nothing will get your whites whiter."

Working within the fashion industry as a hair and make-up artist, you never quite know what you're going to be working on next or where that path might lead you. As my car drove towards "Tinseltown," I remembered the enormous thrill that I'd felt when I first saw the famous Hollywood sign advertised in huge letters across the sprawling Hollywood Hills. Yes, I had arrived in the town that I had dreamt of so many years ago when I was a young boy. I just wanted to get out of my car and jump up and down because I was so excited; I could hardly control myself.

It's an unpredictable vocation that the hair and make-up artist follows. One minute you could be working backstage at the Academy Awards, and the next, you could be pushing your shopping trolley around a Tesco's superstore.

On the most glamorous night in Hollywood, huge crowds gathered outside the Kodak Theatre in the hope of seeing their favourite movie stars as they arrived at the Academy Awards ceremony. A multitude of camera flashes greeted Hollywood's most famous celebrities, who talked about their latest films and posed for the television crews and photographers on the red carpet. Meanwhile, millions of people across the globe watched the ceremony unfold by satellite.

< 268 >

Groomed to perfection, Hollywood's leading ladies looked gorgeous in their couture gowns of every conceivable design and colour. Their jewels sparkled; their smiles were wide and bright. Yes, this was the night they had all been waiting for. Handsome heros and reluctant rebels of both stage and screen looked smart in their suits of black; their hair was either gelled for texture or slicked back. As the nominees for the most prestigious awards in the world slowly made their way into the theatre, desire, hope, and excitement lay within their hungry hearts. The seating cards that had been placed on the vacant red velvet seats were now replaced with some of the most talented people in the film industry—actors, directors, producers, composers, singers, and cinematographers. Everywhere that you looked, there seemed to be a recognizable face.

Backstage, I watched the show slowly unfold on a monitor in the pristine dressing room. As the music started and the ceremony began, I could feel my heart pounding. *Stay calm*, I strictly told myself, as a sense of fear and dread flooded my confidence for a few seconds. *Just do it*. I picked up my make-up brush, took a deep breath, and started to go to work on the beautiful face in front of me. Everything in my career seemed to have led to this moment— all the years of struggle and heartache, all the years of castings and go-sees. Here in Hollywood, victory was mine tonight. In those few moments as the ceremony began, I realized that I had fulfilled my dream.

After I had made my final checks, I put the last finishing touches to my client's hair and make-up and watched as they slowly turned around and walked up the small flight of steps onto the most famous stage in the world.

Watching the monitor backstage, I noticed Barbara Streisand and Robert Redford happily chatting to each other close by; scenes from their iconic films flashed through my mind, as I tried not to stare in their direction. I thought of my mother Eva, whom I had lost so many years ago, and I hoped that somewhere in heaven she was proudly looking down on this special moment. I thought about my family back home, who were watching the Oscars on

< 269 >

television—my mother Doris, who was now in her mid-eighties, and my father Glen, who had worked so hard for so long on that filthy factory floor. I thought of Shaky and Abi, and of my newly found sister, who was holding a little party to celebrate this special occasion. I felt proud and enormously privileged to have been given the opportunity to contribute my talents on such a wonderful occasion. That night, the stars shone brightly in Hollywood.

After the awards ceremony, I went to a party that was held by the "Queen of England." I watched and listened with amazement as he had a good tinkle on the old ivories. Nobody plays the piano like Sir Elton John.

Two days later, I found myself searching for a shopping trolley outside Surrey Quays Shopping Centre in Rotherhithe, London. As I walked towards the entrance of Tesco's supermarket, I repeated my new mantra—"washing powder, washing-up liquid, and dustbin liners"—over and over again in my mind, in a vain attempt not to forget what I was shopping for.

Gliding towards aisle twenty-four, which was marked "household cleaning items," I paused by a special offer. "Buy one, get one free," the offer promised; however, not being a big fan of hula hoops in tomato sauce, I decided to decline the store's kind offer. As I found the dustbin liners on the second shelf of aisle twenty-three, it all seemed a bit surreal now. Had I really gone to the Oscars? Did I really get in a lift with Jennifer Lopez, or accidently bump into Glenn Close? It all seemed like a dream now. *Well, I guess it was my dream*, I concluded. I picked up my dustbin liners and washing-up liquid, and walked towards the checkout, forgetting my washing powder.

I feel very fortunate that I've had the opportunity to travel and explore our fragile planet. I've had the pleasure of working with some of most beautiful women in the world and some of the most talented photographers, fashion designers, video directors, and celebrities. I've rubbed shoulders with Hollywood's A-list stars, and I've lived a life I could never have imagined all those years ago

< 270 >

in Coventry. I believe that if you truly believe in your dream, you can make it happen, as long as you are prepared to work hard, stay focused, and have faith, determination, and perseverance.

Sometimes people ask me if I ever worked with some one that I haven't liked. Haven't we all? As that old saying goes, "there's always one"—or in my case, two—but hey, that isn't so bad in a career that has spanned more than twenty-three years. In that time, I have seen many positive changes within the fashion industry.

The lifespan of a model's career is, on the whole, much longer, with magazines and make-up companies using older models and actresses to promote their products. Of course, women of all ages can be beautiful. You only have to look at actors like Audrey Hepburn and Katharine Hepburn to see that—they just seemed to get more beautiful with each passing year. I recently worked with a lovely American model called Kathy, and she told me that she was working more as an older model than she had as a younger one.

The plus-size industry has really taken off, and fashionable, affordable clothes are now available to women of all shapes and sizes. Today, clothes don't have to cost a fortune to look great, with high-street stores providing designer-inspired clothes to suit every pocket.

It's also nice to see people of every race and colour being used for magazine covers and advertising campaigns, and thankfully, there is a much wider range of fashionable make-up available for all skin tones. Fashion and photography are still fun, creative, and exciting, with new designers reinventing the way that we look, and ultimately, the way that we feel about ourselves.

As I come to the end of this journey, I sit like an eagle in its eyrie, looking out of the window at the top of the Park Hyatt Hotel in Tokyo, Japan. A multitude of red lights greet me as I look out into the night; they twinkle like giant rubies in the nightscape of this strange, wonderful place, where ancient culture meets twenty-first-century technology. I catch the reflection of a man in the window who is worn but still a little handsome, and for a few fleeting seconds I feel my emotions rise when I think of how lucky and

< 271 >

blessed I have been in this lifetime. I have no more illusions and no more dreams to follow.

At some point in our lives, we are all touched by ignorance, heartbreak, and sorrow, but if we can take courage and inspiration from even our darkest moments, we can cross the most unsurpassable mountains and brave the most dangerous seas, ultimately finding a sense of peace and happiness and realizing our hopes and dreams.

< 272 >

CPSIA information can be obtained at www.ICGtesting.com
Printed in the USA
LVOW131535030513

332228LV00002B/291/P